Motto — HLM

In

/526-2?

Start w/ HLM + humor
Book
end with Woke as substitute religion
    not humanistic / as righteous
        apocalyptic

THE CHURCH OF
SAINT THOMAS PAINE

The Church of
Saint Thomas Paine

A RELIGIOUS HISTORY
OF AMERICAN SECULARISM

LEIGH ERIC SCHMIDT

PRINCETON UNIVERSITY PRESS

PRINCETON & OXFORD

Published by Princeton University Press
41 William Street, Princeton, New Jersey 08540
6 Oxford Street, Woodstock, Oxfordshire OX20 1TR

press.princeton.edu

All Rights Reserved

Library of Congress Cataloging-in-Publication Data

Names: Schmidt, Leigh Eric, author.
Title: The church of Saint Thomas Paine : a religious history
    of American secularism / Leigh Eric Schmidt.
Description: Princeton : Princeton University Press, 2021. |
    Includes bibliographical references and index.
Identifiers: LCCN 2021022302 | ISBN 9780691217253 (hardback) |
    ISBN 9780691217260 (ebook)
Subjects: LCSH: Secularism—United States—History. |
    United States—Religion—History. | Paine, Thomas, 1737–1809—
    Religion. | BISAC: HISTORY / United States / Revolutionary Period
    (1775–1800) | BIOGRAPHY & AUTOBIOGRAPHY / Historical
Classification: LCC BL2760 .S36 2021 | DDC 211/.60973—dc23
LC record available at https://lccn.loc.gov/2021022302

British Library Cataloging-in-Publication Data is available

Editorial: Fred Appel and James Collier
Production Editorial: Debbie Tegarden
Text and Jacket Design: Karl Spurzem
Production: Erin Suydam
Publicity: Maria Whelan and Kathryn Stevens
Copyeditor: Gail K. Schmitt

Jacket image: Portrait of Thomas Paine by William Sharp, engraver, and
George Romney / Romney pinxt.; W. Sharp sculpt. United States, 1793.
London: Published by W. Sharp, No. 8 Charles Street Middx. Hospt.
Courtesy of the Library of Congress.

This book has been composed in Arno

Printed on acid-free paper. ∞

Printed in the United States of America

10 9 8 7 6 5 4 3 2 1

CONTENTS

ILLUSTRATIONS

PREFACE

America's most famous infidel orator, Robert Ingersoll, was a paradoxically religious man. The son of a Presbyterian minister, he skewered his natal faith with a sharp wit and a silvery tongue on lecture tours all across the United States during the last three decades of the nineteenth century. But even as he tore down orthodox Christianity, he offered a new religion to take its place. "Secularism is the Religion of Humanity," he told one admirer in 1887. "It is the only religion now. All other is superstition." He was the sonorous bearer of "the religion of the future," in which this world—not some celestial realm beyond it—would be the sole focus of human endeavor, purpose, and meaning. "Whoever imagines that he can do anything for God is mistaken," Ingersoll elaborated. "Whoever imagines that he can add to his happiness in the next world by being useless in this, is also mistaken. And whoever thinks that any God cares how he cuts his hair or his clothes, or what he eats, or whether he fasts, or rings a bell, or puts holy water on his breast, or counts beads, or shuts his eyes and says words to the clouds, is laboring under a great mistake." Ingersoll's secularism was built, both rhetorically and corporeally, on a long series of such negations—all the theological assumptions, bodily habits, ecclesial rituals, and devotional objects that had to be jettisoned in order to stride into an emancipated future. Yet the freethinking secularism that Ingersoll broadcast was not simply destructive;

it was also productive; it carried a religious gravity of its own, a surrogacy that was also a supersession. The religion of secularism would have its own saints, martyrs, and relics; it would cultivate its own liturgical projects and material practices; it would build its own churches of humanity to replace churches of God; it would reembody religion even as it disembodied it. "We are laying the foundations of the grand temple of the future—not the temple of all the gods, but of all the people," so Ingersoll prophesied in 1872, "wherein, with appropriate rites, will be celebrated the religion of Humanity."[1]

That grand temple did not carry the future in the way that Ingersoll and his many collaborators imagined. They dreamed of Christianity receding in the American landscape as their own religion of humanity advanced; more than that, their vision was both cosmopolitan and imperial—an assurance that their universalistic faith in an age of reason would sweep the globe and leave old religious authorities in ruins everywhere. Despite the alarm of secularism's critics—from the nineteenth century forward—nothing like that church-usurping dominion came to pass. Christianity's role in American statecraft has hardly been curtailed through a program of political secularism; the exercise of Protestant and Catholic power has remained evident, time and again, from the local to federal level. Nor has American public life been denuded of religious symbols, rituals, and utterances—indeed, far from it. Instead, secularism in the United States has operated, more often than not, as a movement for minority rights; that is, a congeries of groups and individuals who sought equal liberties for nontheists under the American constitutional order, whether in public schools, courtrooms, and state offices or in relation to conscientious objection, tax exemption, and freedom of expression. When functioning as a humanistic religion—say, in the form of a positivist Church of Humanity—secularism has been little more than a series of sects: marginal in numbers, divisively protective of their own distinctions, and possessed of millenarian fantasies of imminent triumph. In both public life and before the law, freethinking petitioners have looked a lot more like the Jehovah's Witnesses than the hegemon of moral decline over which culture warriors despair. Secularists have been embattled sectarians, struggling to build up usually fleeting organizations, to honor their maligned heroes, to ritualize their lives and memorialize their dead, and to create solidarity among themselves in their alienation from Christianity and the prevailing religious order.

To write a religious history of American secularism is to compose only a portion of secularism's history—one frequently contested by atheists, freethinkers, and humanists themselves, many of whom never bought into the project of organizing themselves on religious terms. A significant bloc repeatedly insisted that all mention of religion in connection to their secularist worldview was anathema; they had no interest in preserving churchgoing as a habit, even if in service of ethical ideals that they would otherwise have endorsed. When avowed freethinkers found themselves trading on a religious lexicon—showing their devotion to Thomas Paine as a secular saint, cultivating their own sacraments in imitation of Auguste Comte, or building a Church of This World for Sunday fellowship—they often hesitated over their own doubts or stumbled over the objections of their peers. Such misgivings often turned adamant. That was as true among secular humanists in the late twentieth century who disclaimed any religious dimension to their philosophy as it was among nineteenth-century purists who rejected the espousal of any religion at all, no matter how it was framed. Religion was a bad word, and so were its many derivatives—from relics *evangelists, not HLM* [handwritten margin note]

and spirits to angels and fetishes. Purgation was the mark of clarified rationality; the erasure of religion, not its reclamation, was the essence of secular enlightenment. Nonetheless, religious language and religious practice proved inescapably tempting for an array of secularist projects. As one proponent of the new humanistic faith declared in 1873, religion "is too good a word to lose; it is quite worth saving. It has a spell in it which is not yet broken." Any number of positivists, freethinking liberals, humanists, and agnostics agreed—they were uninterested in an enforced purity; instead, they were intent on salvaging religion through redefinition, ritual through reinvention, and church through recalibration.[2]

This book offers a history of those liberal secularists who courted religion, often with forthright ardor and hopeful anticipation, frequently with poetic license and unresolved ambivalence. "Beloved brethren! Among all your gettings, get religion!—this real, true up-to-date religion of Ingersoll," so exhorted the *Torch of Reason* in 1903, a freethought newspaper then operating out of Kansas City. The paper's editor knew that many of his colleagues thought it impossible to have a "religion without superstition"—it was about as likely as having "whisky without alcohol," one critic quipped. Still, the publisher of the *Torch of Reason* had seen the light and urged others to join him at the altar of "the new 'Religion' of Secularism." The scare quotes around the word religion—paired with its capitalization— bespoke the equivocation at the heart of secularist enthusiasms: somehow to witness to the humanistic religion of the future while simultaneously dismissing religion as a superannuated relic of the past. This book provides an account of those who got that "Emancipated Religion"—that "real Religion of Humanity"—and who promoted it in the face of their own doubts, the admonitions of colleagues, and the rebukes of

the book [handwritten margin note]

believers

Christian critics. It is about <u>those who worked to materialize</u> <u>"the real religion of Thomas Paine"</u> despite their announced aversion to all fetishistic entanglements. It is about those who <u>found religion in and through their own irreligion.</u> It is about those who cultivated secularism's distinctly precarious and circumscribed enchantments.[3]

To acknowledge that liberal secularists often claimed a religious mantle for themselves is not to vindicate conservative critics who have been decrying "the religion of secularism" over the last half century and more. Especially since the Supreme Court decisions of the early 1960s forbidding state-mandated prayer and Bible reading in the public schools, the religion of secularism has often been invoked as a nefarious, all-determining force bent on supplanting the Christian mores of a nation under God. It is atmospheric and inescapable, a doctrinaire regime disguised in the garb of neutrality. The story told here shows instead <u>the fragility and sectarian peculiarity of</u> <u>secularist designs to build</u> up a religion of humanity or a religion of this world. Perhaps the most consistent ritual among freethinkers—the celebration of Thomas Paine's birthday— never came close to being a red-letter day in the nation's civic calendar or in the public schools. It was a minority rite among a faction of dissenters, a distinct sect of "Paineites," who set themselves against the religious majority with contrarian persistence. If anything, close attention to the practices of committed secularists exposes the spectral fears and rhetorical excesses of their Christian critics. Humanism was often cast as a religion—with just enough presence to serve as a convenient scapegoat of right-wing Protestants and conservative Catholics but never with sufficient clout or appeal to rival the nation's dominant faith, let alone displace it as the established religion. The religion of secularism, in the twentieth century as much as

holy
day

Today's believers
Covid , race
Climate race

in the nineteenth century, was always far more provisional than preponderant in actual expression: a small Church of Humanity in Oakland, California; an undersized Fellowship of Religious Humanists being run by a retired Unitarian minister in the Missouri Ozarks; or a twelve-year experiment with a Society of Evangelical Agnostics in the Sierra Nevada mountains. A religious history in an ethnographic register renders secularism less familiar, less ascendant and age-encompassing—finite, fractional, and strange for all the triumphal assurance of so many of its prophets.

————

I am grateful for all the support I have received over the years to help advance this project and bring it to completion. The John C. Danforth Center on Religion and Politics at Washington University in St. Louis has afforded me an outstanding academic community in which to pursue my research. It is a collegial, engaging group of faculty, postdoctoral fellows, and staff, and my work has benefited much from that intellectual company. I give a special word of thanks to my fellow colloquium members at the center, where we have vetted our works-in-progress from one year to the next. I count your critical acumen and good cheer as gifts.

I have been fortunate as well to have fellowship support from the National Endowment for the Humanities; that funding made all the difference in giving me the opportunity to work on this project in a sustained way over the course of 2019–2020. Also, I offer my thanks to the Bentley Historical Library, at the University of Michigan, for a short-term research fellowship that allowed me to explore its rich collections in greater depth than would have been the case otherwise. Even as more and more of our historical research gets moved online through digitization, my work continues to be sustained by brick-and-mortar archives and the people who staff them with such knowledge and care. In addition to the Bentley Historical Library, my research has been enriched by access to the holdings at the Chicago History Museum, the Institute for Thomas Paine Studies at Iona College, the Wisconsin Historical Society, the Rare Book and Manuscript Library at Columbia University, the Bishopsgate Institute in London, the New York Public Library, the New-York Historical Society, the Library of Congress, the American Philosophical Society, the Harvard University Archives, the Shelby County Historical Society, and the Special Collections Research Center at Southern Illinois University in Carbondale. I had the opportunity to try out some of the themes in this book in a short piece entitled "Monuments to Unbelief," which was published in *Aeon* in 2017 through the editorial guidance of the historian Sam Haselby. His encouragement early on about the possibilities he saw in the project proved an important impetus in my pursuing it further. I owe thanks as well to Grace Goudiss, who obtained photographs of Humanist Hall for me after the pandemic grounded my travels, and also to Ronit Stahl for connecting us. Finally, I am grateful for my long-standing collaboration with Princeton University Press, which now reaches back three decades. This particular project has benefited greatly from the expert editorial engagement of Fred Appel, James Collier, Gail K. Schmitt, and Debbie Tegarden.

As always, I feel keen appreciation for my family's part in my work—not for easing it along really, but for sharing in its ethos. Learning, I see now more than ever, is a family affair: my eldest son, a PhD candidate at the same place I went to graduate school, though in a vastly different field; my daughter, a blooming poet whose capacity for sequestering herself to write greatly exceeds my own; my younger son, an inquisitive student who takes his education with a seriousness that, no doubt, a middle-schooler should be spared; my spouse, a scholar who carries on her own research and writing with a dedication that keeps the rest of us on our toes. I am grateful for the mutuality we find in our discrete curiosities.

Learning was also a family affair for me growing up—all the books of poetry, history, and philosophy, not to mention mystery novels, that my parents crammed into one room or another. It is a fine library to which my mother still attends with a bibliophile's affection. Acts of memorialization loom large in the pages that follow, and here is a small one of my own at the outset: I offer this book in memoriam to my father Roger L. Schmidt, also a scholar of religion. One of the last pieces he wrote up before he died was a short record of his own religious journey, a story that moved from his relatively unchurched youth through his evangelical conversion while serving in Japan during the Korean War to his engagement with ecumenical Protestantism from the mid-1950s on. The religious narrative ended several decades later in atheism, but his lost faith did not keep him from continuing to teach an adult class at the First United Methodist Church or from years of close collaboration with Buddhist monastics at the University of the West. It is a story not too far removed from many of those in the pages that follow—those who continued to invest themselves in religion after the loss of religion. "My orientation has shifted to humanism and the natural world and especially to the earth which is our center of the cosmos," my dad wrote. "As Robert Frost observed in his poem 'Birches,' 'Earth's the right place for love: I don't know where it's likely to go better.'" He would have read this book and shared his reflections with me. It is a discussion I will especially miss having.

THE CHURCH OF
SAINT THOMAS PAINE

The Religion of Secularism

why !

In 1892, Henry Shipley, a self-proclaimed liberal in Van Buren, *1892* Arkansas, wrote a letter to the editor of the Manhattan-based *Truth Seeker*, the leading journal of its day for freethinkers and secularists. His first order of business was to salute the Smithsonian Institution in Washington, DC, as a crucial ally, as "a model of just what we need: library, museum, reading-room, with a free platform." But that was not the only institutional paradigm he had in mind for the advancement of liberal secularist principles. "There is another thing that I have thought of *joiners* much and regretted, and that is to me the fastidiousness of many of our friends in regard to the use of the words 'religion' and 'church.' What we want above all things is the religion of humanity and a church of humanity." Among Shipley's reasons for embracing religious nomenclature was that it would help nonbelievers claim their "civil rights" in a country where the Protestant majority routinely linked good citizenship to churchgoing. Surely, having a congregational home would offer freethinkers some relief from the "unnecessary odium" accorded atheists and infidels. But even more, liberal secularism needed the affective solidarity that came with religion as an "organized body": "The essential idea of religion is devotion. We want good and true men and women devoted to humanity." Shipley clinched his argument with a motto attributed to the revolutionary hero Thomas Paine—one that was so recognizable in these circles that it amounted to a scriptural verity from the founding father of American freethought: "The world is my country, to do good my religion." If "the immortal Paine" so obviously embraced the notion of religion in this cosmopolitan and deistic formula, then surely his faithful heirs should as well. Stop the "quibbling about the etymology of words," Shipley entreated, and get on with building Paine's temple of reason, a new church of humanity, a new religion for forward-looking liberals and secularists.[1]

Five years later, in 1897, Channing Severance, a sharp-elbowed carpenter in Los Angeles who hammered Christianity every chance he got, wrote a piece for the *Truth Seeker* that made apparent why Shipley's church-affirming approach was not going to stop the quibbling. "As religion is a system of worship based on a belief in some kind of a God," Severance explained, "all talk about the religion of humanity is a misuse of the word; and when I see a Freethinker trying to define his 'religion,' the inclination rises to call him down; for a man with a head afflicted with 'plenary' baldness would not be more ridiculous talking about his hair." A thoroughgoing atheist, Severance could not abide any religion at all, however rationalistically, humanistically, philanthropically, or naturalistically it was rendered. He also turned to Paine to underline how serious he was about the totality of this purge, offering "an up-to-date change" of Paine's ubiquitous saying: "The world is my country; to do good my desire; but I have no religion, and see no use for any." Between Christianity and atheism, between religion and irreligion, there was no gray area, no defensible middle ground. The distinction between the religious and the secular could not be fudged; it required unbroken monitoring to preserve reason's translucence from piety's pollution. Those mealy-mouthed folks like Shipley who wanted to pursue the practical interconnections between religious and secular liberalism looked nonsensical, even abominable, to purists like Severance. Every last shackle upon the human mind needed to be broken; every religion—"without exception"—needed to be expunged.[2]

Shipley and Severance were but two local American voices in a multifaceted debate that had arisen repeatedly across Europe and North America since the Enlightenment and still resonates in the contemporary religious landscape. For those who disengaged themselves from Christianity and Judaism, for those who could no longer identify with the scriptural traditions they had inherited, what was left of religion? Were they to be defined by the wholesale negation of religious belief and practice, by the rejection of religious affiliation and obligation, by unremitting antagonism toward the Bible and the clergy? Were they to settle instead into a shoulder-shrugging indifference and have no care for something called religion at all? Or were the disenthralled to build a new religion on the ruins of the old? Were they to throw themselves into reconstructing religious community— with new material forms, ritual practices, hallowed texts, and associative opportunities—after they left church and synagogue? More basically, what did the word *religion* even mean once it became an object of reflection distinct from specific traditions and cultures? Was it necessarily connected to reverence for a Supreme Being, as Severance assumed, or could it be nontheistic? Was it grounded instead in the sociality of collective devotion, as Shipley suggested, a functional consecration of group solidarity? Was there a universal essence to religion— ontological, psychological, or anthropological—that would stabilize its definition? By the late nineteenth century, there were no straightforward, agreed-upon answers to any of these

questions, only multifarious responses. The learned abstraction
of religion as a category for analysis and comparison had not
fixed its significance but instead multiplied its indeterminacy.
That definitional manipulability made it possible for secularists,
by turns, to claim the term for themselves or to deny entirely its
pertinence and applicability.

This book takes historical stock of what religion looked like
for those who shared Shipley's hope of finding a space between
Christianity and no religion, between being a Christian com-
municant and an unchurched freethinker. Those searching for
a religion within secularism were intent on creating mediating
terms and designations—on defining religion in such a way as
to deemphasize the supernatural and to accentuate moral responsibility, intellectual freedom, cosmopolitan universality,
and this-worldly progress. Hence they floated any number of
alternatives for identifying themselves: they might be agnostic
moralists, free religionists, ethical culturists, religious positivists, moral philanthropists, or simply nontheists; they might
espouse the religion of humanity, the religion of this world, the
religion of Thomas Paine, the religion of deeds, the religion of
life, or the religion of the future. *Secularism* was itself a coinage
of the mid-nineteenth century originally designed to break
down the prevailing dichotomies between Christianity and infidelity, revealed religion and freethinking unbelief. Its chief
initial expositor, the British freethinker George Jacob Holyoake, minimized the importance of metaphysical or theological
differences and concentrated instead on shared affirmative
commitments, a "simple creed of deed and duty." Secularism,
Holyoake liked to say, was "the only religion that gives heaven
no trouble"; its energies were entirely focused on "immediate
service to humanity—a religiousness to which the idea of
God is not essential, nor the denial of the idea necessary." By

Holyoake's lights, secularism did not stand in stark opposition to Christianity; instead, it was a broker of common moral ground; it offered an irenic space that would bridge the antagonistic divide between believers and nonbelievers. To emphasize the religiousness of secularism was a pragmatic effort on Holyoake's part to bind theists and nontheists together through an enlightened, universalistic humanitarianism.[3]

The declaration that "secularism is a religion"—as Robert Ingersoll claimed in 1887, following one of Holyoake's conflations—left a lot to be elucidated. For all his stature among freethinkers and agnostics, Ingersoll was not particularly adept at sharpening such an assertion. "Secularism is the religion of humanity; it embraces the affairs of this world," he elaborated, stressing a this-worldly focus as a secularist first principle. But how much did it help clarify matters to equate the religion of secularism with the religion of humanity? As the freethinker Moncure D. Conway remarked in 1880, "The phrase Religion of Humanity has been much and vaguely used; and best phrases so used are liable to degenerate into cant." Conway recognized that the expression had a distinct lineage through the French philosopher Auguste Comte who, by 1855, had developed an ornate sacramental system to consecrate positivist science as the evolutionary fruition of all previous religions, the universal religion of the supremely enlightened. But Conway rightly indicated that the religion of humanity had largely broken free of that specific pedigree in the parlance of post-Christian liberals and freethinking secularists. "It would include the idea of human progress," Conway suggested, "also the sentiment of charity, of sympathy with mankind, and a spirit of benevolent reform." It had as its telos "the promise of a perfectly developed Humanity implying a perfect world"—one freed of violence, superstition, poverty, pain, injustice, and disease. On this side of human perfectibility, however, the religion of humanity—or, in another of Holyoake's formulations, the "religion of daily life"— had more mundane, utterly familiar projects of self-improvement, self-culture, and self-control: hard work, cleanliness, sincerity, cheerfulness, thrift, familial constancy, sobriety, and a cultivated taste for the arts. Even in the hands of its most illustrious proponents, the religion of humanity was often little more than pleasant bromides, refined in tone and short on detail. "Adorn your life with the gems called good deeds; illumine your path with the sunlight called friendship and love," so went one of Ingersoll's embellishments of the new religion's imperatives.[4]

The religion of secularism was frequently left vague and unspecified for good reason. Beyond its claim to be the religion of this world, it also made intellectual independence and the displacement of all religious authorities foundational to its platform. As Thomas Paine had famously announced in *The Age of Reason*, "I do not believe in the creed professed by the Jewish church, by the Roman church, by the Greek church, by the Turkish church, by the Protestant church, nor by any church that I know of. My own mind is my own church." Every secularist, Ingersoll explained, constituted "his own church, his own priest, his own clergyman and his own pope. He decides for himself; in other words, he is a free man." With so much emphasis placed on individual autonomy and the overthrow of all forms of ecclesiastical tyranny, whatever garb the new religion assumed would almost certainly be worn lightly. Any effort to build a church of humanity would have to overcome this bedrock suspicion that churches as institutions were at cross-purposes with the mental liberty that liberal secularists presupposed. When the freethinker G. L. Henderson suggested building a "Liberal Church," as a local branch of the "Religion of Humanity,"

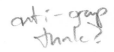

in New York City in the 1870s, he immediately had to answer
that skepticism. Since "the existing churches" were all "despotic
and unprogressive," would "it not be better to avoid the formation of churches altogether?" It was always a lot clearer what
secularism forbade its devotees—"no mysteries, no mummeries,
no priests, no ceremonies, no falsehoods, no miracles," to cite
one of Ingersoll's lists—than what it allowed. Liberal, humanistic forms of religion were seemingly designed to be nebulous
and disaggregated, at odds with organizational elaboration and
ritualized embodiment.[5]

It was not even clear, as Channing Severance's complaint
suggested, that freethinking secularists wanted to allow themselves the space to have something called a religion at all. The
contortions were frequent and readily apparent. "Liberalism is
not a system of religion," the ex-Methodist preacher J. D. Shaw
explained from Waco, Texas, where he had built an independent congregation of freethinkers after the Civil War. "It is a
creedless, unecclesiastical, non-political, anti-theological system of ethical culture." In many ways, to be an advocate of the
religion of humanity demanded ambivalence about being an
advocate of the religion of humanity. "If you choose to call it a
religion of any kind," Shaw continued, "I would say it is the religion of humanity, and not of God—of this world, and not of
another." The conditional *if* was critical, an apology for the awk-
wardness of the embrace that followed. "If we must have a religion," another freethinker opined, "let us discard the religion of
Christ and try the Religion of Humanity." Those who wanted
to build a new religion for those who had left religion confronted a challenge internal to their own freethinking liberalism: the very notion that "religion" was a desideratum—that it
was a valued feature of social life, that it was worth salvaging in
one enlightened form or another—had been rendered highly

problematic. "That which shall take the place of religion and serve to inspire our conduct shall not even be called religion," one freethought lecturer maintained in the early 1880s, "for this word has become so thoroughly identified with the worship of God that it can never be made to express the emotions that are in perfect harmony with reason and nature." (That this renunciation appeared in a lecture called "What Is Religion?" in a volume entitled *The Infidel Pulpit* suggested the persistent engagement with religion even in its denial.) Were committed secularists only supposed to negate, neutralize, and regulate religion, or were they permitted to express it? And, if there was room for the latter, what varieties of religion would freethinking liberals allow themselves?[6]

What is religion? That was a thorny definitional question that by the late nineteenth century had been deprived of any catechetic simplicity: "What is religion? Thinking about God and doing his will.—What do you think you ought to do? Pray to him, praise him, keep his word," so went a typically pious answer in 1839. Instead the question was a philological and comparative puzzle, made especially intricate through the emergent scientific study of religion. Francis Ellingwood Abbot, a primary architect of nineteenth-century secularist demands for strict church-state separation, knew how much "modern scholarship" had complicated his task of claiming "religion" for freethinking liberals. In *A Study of Religion: The Name and the Thing* (1873), Abbot reflected on the derivation of the word *religion* from the Latin word *religare*, signifying "*to bind back*" or "*to bind fast.*" If that etymology proved correct, then religion suggested "the idea of bondage," which would be very much at odds with the "free religion" he advocated and which would suggest that he needed "to abandon the word religion altogether"—just as he had already abandoned the word *Christian* to identify himself.

Abbot insisted, though, that the best scholarly authorities derived religion from *relegere*, meaning to go over or read through a text again. If that "root-meaning" were true, then religion could be understood as "*the application of the intellectual faculties under direction of conscience.*" To reach that tendentious conclusion, Abbot performed a lot of laborious research, and he knew he was likely to bore "a popular audience" with the gleanings from his notebooks. Still, if he were going to rescue the word *religion* for liberal secularists, he felt he had little choice but to begin at the beginning—with historical philology. After two or three years of such investigations, Abbot was happy to conclude that the word "most certainly belongs to us," those freethinking mutineers who had left Christianity behind and embraced a cosmopolitan intellectualism. Moreover, he concluded that a definition limiting religion to a belief in God or gods was utterly provincial: the possibility of nontheistic religions had to be acknowledged. Studies of Buddhism made this point, Abbot suggested, but so did Comte's religious version of positivism. "Atheistic religions" should not be excluded from "the family of recognized religions."[7]

It took a lot of work for Abbot to satisfy himself that religion as a construct was salvageable as a live possibility for humanistic liberals, agnostics, and even atheists, but he hardly tired of such labors. His philological efforts were emblematic of a vast number of nineteenth-century projects to engage religion on secularist terms despite the recurrent challenges of doing so. This book explores such experiments through three case studies. Each dives beneath the altruistic and cosmopolitan generalities surrounding the religion of humanity (and parallel formulations) into more localized and materialized forms of actual practice. The first chapter focuses on the devotion to Thomas Paine, whose sanctified memory was central to the development of a ceremonial life for freethinkers—one that centered on his birthday (January 29) and on his violated grave in New Rochelle, New York. The fact that Paine's remains had been snatched from his tomb a decade after his death gave rise to a relic-seeking quest that lasted the better part of a century. Through examining the quite tangible piety surrounding the "Secular Saint Thomas"—as one versifier dubbed him in a poem commemorating his birthday in 1901—a more densely particular version of the religion of humanity comes into view. It was a visible fellowship that cared as much about enshrining a saint and honoring a prophet as it did about globalizing enlightened rationality or privatizing religious belief. While unmistakably opposed to the Christian materiality of relics, to the sacramental aura of "sacred things," Paine's American devotees nonetheless gave perceptible expression to the seriousness of their discipleship through the pursuit of their saint's lost bones. Secularism had a body—or, rather, a missing body that was repeatedly mythologized in its absence as a token of Paine's universal spirit. Paine was the rock upon which the American church of humanity was built.[8]

Next, the book examines the life-cycle rituals, particularly the funeral practices, which humanistic freethinkers developed to counter the liturgical conventions of the churches. In his capstone work, *The Origin and Nature of Secularism* (1896), George Jacob Holyoake considered it axiomatic that nontheists needed to invent their own "secularist ceremonies." Ritual, after all, was a universal ethnological phenomenon from which the enlightened were hardly exempt: "Certain ceremonies are common to all human society, and should be consistent with the opinions of those in whose name the ceremonies take place." Looking askance especially at the marriage and burial services that the church offered, Holyoake suggested that secularists had to find a way to replace them with more appropriate rites. It was an experimental project that many freethinkers and agnostics pursued, including the British secularist Austin Holyoake (George's brother) and the American positivist Courtlandt Palmer. Two groups, in particular, serve to demonstrate these humanistic efforts at ritualization. First, a small band of religious positivists, active on both sides of the Atlantic, built on Auguste Comte's elaborate calendar of saints and festivals in hopes of creating a new sacramental order for the enlightened. These positivist endeavors failed to win a multitude of converts, but the failure itself could be spectacular, as was the case with such passionate ritualists as David Goodman Croly and Malcolm Quin. Second, another pocket-sized assemblage, the Society of Moralists, based in Hannibal, Missouri, proved adept at inventing liturgies for secularists. The group's leader, a physician named A. R. Ayres, produced his own manual, *A Secular Funeral and Marriage Hand-Book* (1886)—a guide that ended up providing ceremonial refuge from the clergy for freethinkers across the country. The ability to conduct memorial services without clerical supervision became a badge of secularist triumph in death; secular funerals offered performative proof that freethinkers had died as they had lived, emancipated from Christianity. At a dirt-and-dust level, the advancement of secularism was measured not through the political success of liberal demands for total church-state separation but through the local availability of properly performed funerals and burials.[9]

Thereafter the book examines the churches that humanistic liberals and secularists built. When organizing themselves, American freethinkers often mimicked Protestant churches and Sunday schools. Katie Kehm Smith's First Secular Church in Portland, Oregon, in the 1890s was exemplary in that regard, but so were the churches organized by post-Christian Unitarians

around the principle of "free religion." Octavius Brooks Frothingham's Independent Liberal Church in New York City was a
prime example of that impulse, as was the People's Church in
Kalamazoo, Michigan, led by Caroline Bartlett—a congregation that both Robert Ingersoll and George Holyoake enthusi-
astically endorsed in 1896 as an embodiment of their own secular religion. Flowing in the same currents of "free religion" were
the Ethical Societies, organized by Felix Adler and his disciples,
first in New York City, and then in Philadelphia, Chicago, and
St. Louis. While Frothingham and Adler carried lingering affec-
tions for the traditions they had left, others reveled in the oppositional distinctiveness of the freethinking communities they
were trying to build. M. M. Mangasarian's Independent Religious Society (Rationalist) in Chicago and John Emerson Roberts's Church of This World in Kansas City were two exemplars
of that more sharply contrastive approach. Still, both were ex-
Protestant ministers with a refined, gentlemanly air; both assembled their new congregations in fashionable urban theaters.
For grassroots combat with Christianity, the schoolteacher
Katie Kehm Smith was battletested on the ground in her promotion of secular churches in Oregon; so was W. H. Kerr, a
farmer in Great Bend, Kansas, who founded the unambigu-
ously atheistic Church of Humanity in 1903.

Such experiments with institutionalizing churches for secularists continued apace through the middle decades of the
twentieth century, especially under the ascendant rubric of religious humanism. It was a pair of tax-exemption cases in the
1950s—one surrounding a Fellowship of Humanity in Oakland,
California, and the other involving an Ethical Society in Washington, DC—that initially allowed such nontheistic groups to
be counted (in American jurisprudence) as having religious
standing in their own right. A subsequent Maryland case

involving an atheist named Roy Torcaso, who was denied certification as a notary public for being unwilling to avow God's existence as the state required, became a critical moment in ratifying the equal rights of nonbelievers. Handing down its decision in 1961, the Supreme Court vindicated Torcaso's right to hold an office of public trust irrespective of his nontheistic beliefs. Inadvertently, by way of a footnote, the unanimous opinion also provided a stimulus for the notion that "secular humanism" was in itself a distinct religion; if so, Christian conservatives argued, then that religion also had to be monitored for its own violations of the Establishment Clause. Even as the threat of secular humanism kept getting bigger as a phantasmal menace in the evangelical imagination, organized groups of religious humanists remained small, hardly living up to their culture-war billing as the puppet masters of American moral decay. Their fellowships were islets of humanistic community in a sea of evangelical megachurches, television ministries, and lobbying groups; they constituted a fringe more than a powerhouse. These legal, political, and cultural developments are addressed in the closing section of this book.

Having humanistic groups count as a "religion" or a "church" in legal terms wound up being a mixed blessing. The downside became quite evident in the wake of two Supreme Court cases, *Engel v. Vitale* (1962) and *Abington v. Schempp* (1963), in which the Protestant-derived religious exercises of prayer and Bible reading in the public schools were found to violate the First Amendment's Establishment Clause. No longer could any state legislature or local school board require students to pray or read the Bible in America's public-school classrooms. The uproar over both decisions was sustained and intense. For many American Christians, the Supreme Court was not defending a neutral religious environment in the schools but instead creating one that was overtly hostile to pious expression and practice. They found fuel for their fight in the lone dissenter in *Abington v. Schempp*, Justice Potter Stewart, who argued that in barring school-sanctioned prayer and Bible reading his fellow justices had failed at "the realization of state neutrality" and had instead effectively endorsed "the establishment of a religion of secularism." Stewart's colleague, Justice Tom Clark, directly rebutted that claim in his majority opinion. In no way was "a 'religion of secularism'" gaining preferential treatment; the court had no intention of favoring nonbelievers over believers; the schools were free to have pupils study the Bible "for its literary and historic qualities"; what they could not do is mandate particular religious exercises and devotional practices. Clark's rejoinder failed to soothe the court's critics; Stewart's dissent proved all too resonant going forward.[10]

Stewart's dissenting opinion gave a new judicial authority and a sharpened critical edge to the construct "a religion of secularism." After 1963 it became an increasingly recognizable idiom among religious conservatives, ready for deployment in a long series of debates about religion's place in American public life. Ronald Reagan would decry the "religion of secularism" in his efforts to restore prayer to the public schools in the 1980s, and Mitt Romney would dwell on its dangers in his attempt to generate solidarity, as a Mormon, with evangelicals. "In recent years, the notion of the separation of church and state has been taken by some well beyond its original meaning. They seek to remove from the public domain any acknowledgment of God," Romney explained on the campaign trail in 2007. "It is as if they are intent on establishing a new religion in America—the religion of secularism. They are wrong." Amid the long-simmering heat of the culture wars, few have had in mind Ingersoll or Holyoake, Paine or Comte when invoking the religion of secularism, but instead Potter Stewart and the fire of conservative Christian critique that his dissent helped stoke.[11]

The demons of secularism, secular humanism, and the religion of secularism—all became interchangeable fiends for arguing that evangelical Protestants were being unfairly disadvantaged in American social and political life, both within and well beyond the public schools. From this conservative Christian vantage point, liberal secularism had set itself up as a neutral arbiter but was actually operating as an established orthodoxy that excluded other forms of religious expression from the public square. As a critique, this evangelical reading of secularism's regulatory force lines up with an array of critical theorists who have indicted secularism's discursive authority in which the requirements of liberal statecraft set the terms for what counts as acceptable religion: the private and interior, the immaterial and disembodied, the tolerant and nonsectarian. Secularists may have led with notions of religious liberty, equal rights, and freedom of conscience, but that rhetoric recurrently masked more proscriptive policies and objectives. The "Dream of Emancipated Religion," as one nineteenth-century apologist dubbed his secularist faith, was always as much a negative as a positive vision—liberation for "enlightened" forms of religion combined with protection from "unenlightened" varieties. Secularism's advocates often had expansive disciplinary ambitions: they hoped at least to tame, if not eventually supplant, all types of religion that they considered inimical to liberal democracy, scientific rationality, and didactic supervision—from "primitive fetishism" to camp-meeting Methodism to priest-ridden Catholicism. The secularist aspiration for an emancipated, enlightened, and ethical religion was scarcely neutral or disinterested. It was always an adjudication of what religion should become and what it should cease to be.[12]

For the political stakes of secularism's regulatory aims, one need look no farther than Ingersoll himself, whose expositions were often especially revealing because they were especially unsubtle:

> Secularism is a religion that is to be used everywhere and at all times—that is to be taught everywhere and practiced at all times. It is not a religion that is so dangerous that it must be kept out of the schools; it is not a religion that is so dangerous that it must be kept out of politics. It belongs in the schools; it belongs at the polls. It is the business of Secularism to teach every child; to teach every voter. . . . Orthodox religion is a firebrand; it must be kept out of the schools; it must be kept out of politics.

Religion that subscribed to liberal secularist principles was safe; it was good for the nation; it was good for democratic citizenship; it was good for the world as a whole; hence the freedoms it enjoyed were clear and expansive. By contrast, both Protestantism and Roman Catholicism, in Ingersoll's view, posed disruptive sectarian dangers that needed to be cordoned off, as much as possible, from the public sphere. Secularism was, transparently enough, presented as the gauge of benign and permissible religion—the instrument used to manage religious differences rather than safeguard them. All too clearly Ingersoll's exhortation displayed the kind of underlying logic that contemporary evangelicals have highlighted in order to expose secularist professions of neutrality. All too clearly as well, his reasoning evinced the sort of disciplinary regime that critical theorists of secularist discourse have repeatedly unmasked, though here in Ingersoll's paean it wore no mask at all.[13]

Ingersoll was hardly alone in his offhanded exposure of secularism's ruling suppositions. Along with his philological efforts to rescue *religion* as a useable word for freethinkers, Francis Ellingwood Abbot codified a nine-point platform for strict church-state separation, labeled the "Demands of Liberalism," that he began to agitate for in 1872. Government-funded chaplaincies, Bible devotions in the public schools, and Sabbath laws—all the state-sanctioned preferences accorded Protestant Christianity—needed to be eliminated. Abbot thereafter took the lead in organizing the National Liberal League in 1876 to pursue those secularist demands and to counter evangelical activists who had proposed amending the Constitution to make the United States an officially Christian nation. A former Unitarian minister turned proponent of "scientific theism," Abbot made plain how integral his vision of an emancipated religion was to his secularist projects: "Free religion, on its political side, is absolute secularism—the absolute restriction of government to the transaction of all public affairs by the simple rules of intelligence, justice, liberty, and equal rights, and the absolute exclusion of all rules introducing revelations or supernaturalisms or ecclesiasticisms of any sort. *This is the common religion of mankind,*" Abbot explained with his own italicized emphasis in his founding report on the National Liberal League. American Christians failed to live up to the ideals of this "purely natural and secular religion" because they were party to a particularistic, exclusive religion—one that was all too prone to using the apparatus of the state to extend its authority and influence. Abbot's "free religion," his "secular religion," was emancipated from particularity; it had "no special religious beliefs and practices"; its principles were pure and universal; it was the "common religion" of the republic—indeed, of all humanity. Political secularism was, for Abbot, the impartial guarantor of religious freedom and equal rights, but it nonetheless clearly had a preferred religion—a "free religion" that would protect

Americans from the evangelical "treason" of Christianizing the Constitution. This open endorsement of a post-Christian liberal religion as the nation's baseline faith raised serious doubts about the capacity of Abbot's secularism to be a vessel of even-handed neutrality.[14]

Ingersoll's oratorical bluster and Abbot's liberal organizing indicate that secularism's critics make indispensably important points about its governing ambitions and discursive contradictions, but those trenchant appraisals also need to be set alongside the reverse dimension of secularism's politics. As was evident in Shipley's argument, postulating that secularists themselves had a religion was not a bid for majoritarian power—at least, not a realistic one—but instead a way of claiming civil rights for a widely ostracized minority. That liberal secularism, especially in the nineteenth-century United States, was going to act as a hegemon was largely a fantasy of its most excited enthusiasts and its most zealous adversaries. Holyoake himself spent six months in a British jail for blasphemy in 1842—no wonder that he was interested in finding a way to include avowed secularists under religion's protective umbrella. One of Holyoake's American counterparts, D. M. Bennett, the editor of the *Truth Seeker*, was sentenced to thirteen months in a New York penitentiary in 1879 for his blasphemous and obscene infidelity—no wonder that he wanted to see religious freedom expanded to include irreligious freedom. When equal rights and liberties were accorded atheists and freethinkers, it was often done with profound reluctance—as if the social, moral, and political order could not bear the open presence of such misfits and shirkers. As one Protestant writer in Boston aphorized in 1837 (the year before the ex-Universalist minister Abner Kneeland was sent to jail in the same city as a pestilent infidel), "A nation of Atheists is a nation of fiends." Secularists, including Ingersoll and Abbot, had good reason for wanting to whittle away at Christianity's own governing exclusions and suppressive dispositions.[15]

The demand for minority rights, for the full inclusion of nonbelievers in civil society, was front and center for the British freethinker John Sholto Douglas when he gave the address *The Religion of Secularism* in 1881. It was absolutely crucial, Douglas argued, that the British Secular Union "be acknowledged and recognized as *a religious body*. We who have, in obedience to the dictates of our reason, repudiated the orthodox faith, have constantly to hear brought against us that we are an irreligious body, having no religion at all." In point of fact, Douglas averred, "the real meaning and definition of the word 'religion'" had to do with that which "binds or unites mankind into one homogenous whole"; it was of sociological, not supernatural significance. And, by that definition, "we Secularists . . . do justly claim to possess a great and ennobling Religion." Liberated from "any dogmas respecting a personal Deity," freethinkers cultivated instead "our common Religion of Humanity," again crystallized in Paine's one-line motto: "The world is my country, and to do good is my religion." In Douglas's view, once secularists were seen as having a religion of their own, there would no longer be any reason to withhold civil recognition from them alongside other dissenting minorities—Quakers, Jews, and Roman Catholics. Douglas had lost his own seat in Parliament as a result of his heterodoxy and was still waiting to see if his duly elected colleague, the atheist Charles Bradlaugh, would ever be recognized as an MP (it would take another five years). For Douglas, concretizing "the religion of secularism" was a critical step forward in claiming full enfranchisement and equal rights for a much maligned religious minority.[16]

By the second half of the twentieth century, religious conservatives were eager to confer religious status upon secularism, to claim that the religion of secular humanism—thanks to a way-ward Supreme Court—had become the nation's established religion, dominating the public schools and controlling American public life. In the nineteenth century, as Douglas suggested, orthodox Protestants were hardly interested in dignifying the religion of humanity as a religion, no matter what its apologists claimed. The *Northern Christian Advocate*, a Methodist news-paper, scoffed in 1888 at the notion that an agnostic like Inger-soll or a positivist like Comte could have an actual religion: a religion of humanity, a religion of deeds, a religion of hope and help—all such infidel constructions were disingenuous dodges; they were gross misuses of religious language; they were empty shells of unreality. "This religion is no religion," the paper con-cluded with complete assurance. Better to "deny that man has any need of religion" at all than to pretend that subscribing to Ingersoll's creed or reiterating Paine's motto counted as a reli-gious profession. Likewise, in 1889, when a Congregational minister saw the idea of a secular religion being bandied about by some religious liberals, he dismissed it with a summary defi-nition: "'Secular Religion'—no religion at all!" The essence of religion, he insisted, depended on belief in the living God and in the hereafter; commitment to a this-worldly ethic of "social regeneration" was not enough to qualify. That default Protes-tant perspective—that an individual's relationship to God was the sine qua non of religion—long excluded humanistic forms of religion from the kind of legal standing and social recogni-tion that proponents asserted was rightly theirs. The twists and turns in that debate over defining religion, the switchbacks of evangelicals and secularists alike on the question of whether humanistic beliefs and practices counted as religion or not, have been important markers on the American religious and political terrain across two centuries.[17]

The three case studies that follow—of relics, rites, and churches—shift attention back to the nineteenth-century roots of the religion of secularism as a tiny and often disregarded sect. Bringing the local, fractional, and particularistic dimensions of this religion into view provides an alternative vantage to the culture-war representation of it that has come to prevail over the last half century and more. The religion of secularism was a splinter—or, rather, a series of them. Consigned to the nonbelieving margins of a covenanted nation, the devotees of its various strands struggled to gain equal footing in American civic life. Whatever their dreams for secular statecraft and rational enlightenment, they were hardly in a position to keep their Christian adversaries out of the public square or to put their demystified imprint on the culture as a whole. The rubrics of the religion of secularism—its devotion to Thomas Paine, its calendar of rites and ceremonies, its fellowship meetings— were ultimately more parochial in expression than insidious in reach. The religion of humanity, the religion of this world, the religion of ethical culture—such nineteenth-century constructs signified an assortment of undersized fellowships, affective rituals, and visible memorials that supporters cultivated against the odds of Christian dominance. They pointed to embattled local associations trying to create space for humanistic communities, for secularist lives and deaths, apart from the cultural authority and political power of a Protestant majority. To be sure, the religion of secularism had wildly imperial pretenses—it would be the universal religion of the future—but time and again, it had to settle instead for being the sanctuary of a sectarian minority. When Francis Ellingwood Abbot sent a gift copy of his founding report on the National Liberal League to the library at the University of California in 1880, the Berkeley cataloguer performed a suitably deflating gesture. Inside the front cover, the librarian assigned this congress of Paine-venerating liberals to the category of "non-Christian sects." The cosmopolitan sweep of Abbot's "secular religion"—his "common religion" of all humanity—was pigeonholed as a sectarian project of a freethinking clique. It was the kind of reality check that proponents of the religion of secularism got accustomed to facing as a minority within a nation under God.[18]

CHAPTER 1

Relics of the Secular Saint Thomas

[handwritten: Why Paine]

In 1885, the agnostic orator Robert Ingersoll, with his usual "bewitching eloquence," offered up a new lecture entitled "Which Way?" for rapt audiences across the country. Drawing a forceful contrast between an inherited Christianity and a forward-looking secularism, Ingersoll insisted that the animating concern for most Americans was no longer other- *[handwritten: Public Health]* worldly salvation but material improvement. Engineers, not preachers; science, not sacred books—these were the preferred guides. "At last we know how religions are made," Ingersoll proclaimed, jubilant over the dispelling of the pious illusions that had so long beguiled humanity. "We know how miracles are manufactured. We know the history of relics, and bones, and pieces of the true cross." It was a point to which Ingersoll frequently returned—"this belief in the efficacy of bones or rags and holy hair" as the crowning emblem of outmoded superstition; "no intelligent person believes that holy bones, or rags, sacred hairs or pieces of wood" could possibly have any particular power or sanctity. "We now know that all the sacred relics are religious rubbish; . . . and that those who rely on them are almost idiotic," Ingersoll concluded with his usual flair for dramatizing the superiority of the enlightened rationalist over the reverent votary. The material advancement of civilization depended on the methodical displacement of religious materiality, on the thorough demystification of "sacred things."[1]

If Ingersoll was the leading voice of freethinking secularism in the late nineteenth century, the Missourian Watson Heston was its primary artist. Relics provided a predictably fruitful source for his cartoonist's repertoire. In "A Few of the Fraudulent Relics Exhibited to the Faithful," Heston lampooned the exuberant multiplicity and redundancy of Roman Catholic artifacts, the all too numerous fragments of the true cross or the surplus supply of breast milk from the Virgin Mary (fig. 1.1). Among the relics that Heston specifically derided was a coffin filled with "the bones of a malefactor palmed off on the ignorant as the bones of a saint." The accompanying commentary drew from the works of both John William Draper and Andrew Dickson White, a pair of Victorian intellectuals who sweepingly redefined the relationship between science and religion as one of interminable warfare. That epic conflict, so selections from Draper and White demonstrated, was crystallized "in the matter of relics"—in the "impostures" surrounding bones, blood, milk, and miraculous images. Much of this, of course, was little more than a familiar Protestant polemic against Catholic materiality refitted for secularist purposes, but Heston made plain that it was more than that as well. In "A Worshiper of Moldy Relics—Why the Christian Cannot See the Truth," Heston suggested that Protestants had their own fetishes in the Bible and the cross (fig. 1.2). As long as they bowed down before those relics, the light of reason and critical inquiry would never penetrate their musty devotions. "Relics of barbarism" was a cliché of the era—handy for the aspersion of everything from Mormon polygamy to papal authority, from ghostly séances to indigenous rituals. Seemingly across the board, the enlightened staked their

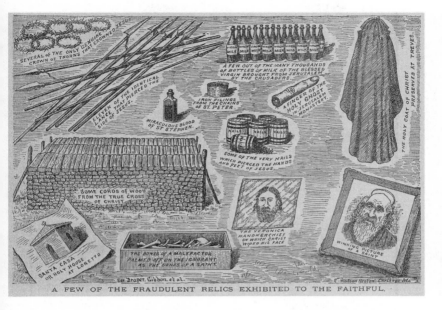

A FEW OF THE FRAUDULENT RELICS EXHIBITED TO THE FAITHFUL.

FIG. 1.1. The cartoonist Watson Heston provided an influential visual repertory for American freethinkers at the end of the nineteenth century. Among the objects of his barbed satire were the material elements of Roman Catholic devotion—particularly the bones, blood, and flesh of the saints. Watson Heston, "A Few of the Fraudulent Relics Exhibited to the Faithful," *Truth Seeker*, June 7, 1890, 353. General Research Division, The New York Public Library.

newborn secularist identity on having shorn their lives of the religious rot of "old bone bunco men."[2]

Strange then, it would appear, how much and for how long the bones of the anticlerical revolutionary Thomas Paine haunted American freethinkers. No founding figure occupied a more canonized role in the nineteenth-century secularist imagination than Paine, whose bold deistic critique of the Bible in *The Age of Reason* had made him the ogre of evangelicals and the hero of infidels. Denied burial in a Quaker cemetery—a religious fellowship with which he had a lingering familial

A WORSHIPER OF MOLDY RELICS—WHY THE CHRISTIAN CANNOT SEE THE TRUTH.

FIG. 1.2. Watson Heston aimed his mockery equally at Protestant piety, treating it as laden with its own barbarous relics and fetishes. A fundamental promise of secular enlightenment, Heston made plain, was emancipation from the debased corporeality of sacred things. Watson Heston, "A Worshiper of Moldy Relics— Why the Christian Cannot See the Truth," *Truth Seeker*, Nov. 10, 1894, 705. General Research Division, The New York Public Library.

affinity—he was interred in June 1809 on his farm in New Rochelle, New York, with little ceremony and few at all in attendance. Then, in 1819 the British radical William Cobbett, a one-time detractor turned ardent admirer of Paine, decided to dig up the remains and return them to England as a catalyst for protest and reform back in the motherland. With that act of grave robbery, Cobbett set Paine's bones in motion; sardonically dubbed a "resurrection man" by the British press, Cobbett had created an empty tomb of sorts for American freethinkers. That the stolen remains eventually went missing after Cobbett's own death in

Paine's bones

1835 made Paine's bones the doubly lost relics of nineteenth-century secularism. Dreams of reclamation, memorialization, and recompense would preoccupy Paine's freethinking disciples for decades. As late as 1908, one frustrated pursuer of the vanished bones waxed biblical to explain his failed search. Paine's "final resting-place" would remain, he concluded, as shrouded in mystery "as that of Moses": "No man knoweth of his sepulchre unto this day."[3]

Under the banner of the religion of humanity, the nineteenth-century architects of organized secularism built their disenthralled identities out of multifaceted religious engagements—by turns, fanciful, ironical, and earnest; at once, cosmopolitan in ambition and parochial in practice. When the British freethinker John Sholto Douglas made his plea in 1881 for secularists to be recognized as a *"religious body,"* he instinctively turned to Paine's revered place in the movement for validation of his claim. Those who dismissed freethinkers as irreligious, as having "no religion at all," he argued, were simply uninformed about the noble history of "the religion of secularism"—"a religion," he insisted, that "was long ago clearly defined by Thomas Paine." The very tangible veneration of Paine is a good conduit for reconsidering secularism, rather literally, as a religious body. While Paine's bones stayed missing—or, more precisely, were reported found and then lost in what amounted to a repeated cycle of secularist hope and disappointment—a portion of his brain and some of his hair (so several prominent American freethinkers professed) were eventually recovered for memorializing in New Rochelle in the early twentieth century. Even then, with the long quest at least partially fulfilled, Paine's sepulchral relics continued to draw inquirers into the chase and into secularist mythology. The abiding reverence for Paine among his American devotees reveals a more complexly religious, densely material version of secularism—one concerned as much with a localized shrine of a saint as with a prescriptive regime of disenchantment. Whatever political program secularists dreamed of enacting to limit Christianity's public power, they subsisted on minority allegiances and practices, seen quite clearly in this peculiar sect of American "Paineites," with its commemorative rituals and long-sought relics.[4]

Thomas Paine's reputation as an American patriot would have been far more secure had he stuck to politics and left religion alone. Arriving in the colonies from England in 1774 with scant resources, he quickly established himself as an editor and propagandist. A singularly influential pamphleteer in defense of revolution and independence, he became the most widely read advocate of a new social and political order swept clean of aristocratic privilege and monarchic tyranny. His exhortations in *Common Sense* and *The Crisis* steeled patriot resistance, and later his *Rights of Man* made the universalistic reach of his democratic politics all the more apparent. The hitch was that Paine came to believe that "a revolution in the system of government" needed to be paired with "a revolution in the system of religion"—that after throwing off the despotisms of monarchy and aristocracy, citizens of the new republic should now cast aside the superstitions of Christianity, the impostures of priests, and the fables of the Bible. Once his ferocious pen turned against the scriptures and the church in *The Age of Reason*, his contributions to the patriot cause were almost totally beclouded by charges of infidelity, blasphemy, licentiousness, and moral monstrosity. "All his services were instantly forgotten, disparaged or denied," Ingersoll lamented in a lecture eulogizing

nothing deep—
can diving)

Paine. "He was shunned as though he had been a pestilence. . . .
He was regarded as a moral plague, and at the bare mention
of his name the bloody hands of the church were raised in
horror."[5]

Precisely because Protestant resentment drove so much of
the enduring animus against Paine, those who would defend his
reputation felt doubly compelled to vindicate him on religious
terms. Against the chorus of his Christian critics, Paine's admirers routinely pointed to the positive thrust of his deism with its
vision of benevolent reform, cosmopolitan fellowship, and pu-
rified monotheism. "I believe in one God, and no more; and I
hope for happiness beyond this life," Paine had explained at the
outset of *The Age of Reason*. "I believe that religious duties con-
sist in doing justice, loving mercy, and endeavoring to make our
fellow-creatures happy." His disciples dwelled on that passage,
but they also pointed out that Paine had embraced the label of
Theophilanthropists for his communion of organized deists (it
was a group with French Enlightenment roots that had small
offshoots in the United States by 1800). Surely, that name indicated the moral conscientiousness of Paine's humanitarian
faith; in that altruistic light, Paine could be seen as a religious
draftsman more than a slashing iconoclast—as an opponent of
an unprincipled atheism, not its filthy abettor. Paine's Society
of Theophilanthropists, subsequent freethinkers suggested,
provided the practical groundwork for the religion of humanity.
Seen as "a cross between a church and a society formed for the
advancement of morals," it was counted a harbinger of the Ethical Culture associations and the archly liberal Unitarian congregations of their own day. As one dedicated Paineite declared, "On
this rock the Church of Man was to be built."[6]

In rescuing Paine from religious critique, his disciples accorded canonical significance to a single line from the second

easy
no edge

Public health

part of *Rights of Man*: "My country is the world, and my religion is to do good." By the 1840s, American Paineites had reworked that phrase and turned it into their hero's shibboleth: "The world is my country, and to do good my religion." Dubbed Paine's motto, the revised expression became a watchword for nineteenth-century celebrants of Paine's memory; it embellished banners, portraits, mastheads, monuments, and title pages; it was counted the "golden rule" that Paine had bequeathed to his followers. "There is no creed that can be compared with it for a moment," Ingersoll proclaimed. "It should be wrought in gold, adorned with jewels, and impressed upon every human heart." Distressed at the abuse Paine received as the author of *The Age of Reason*, his admirers were intent on restoring his reputation not only as a herald of democratic freedom and revolution but also as the bearer of an enlightened religion vastly superior to that of his Christian critics. Indeed, through the repeated invocation of Paine's motto, his disciples defined him by his cosmopolitan, philanthropic faith—the oracle of "the best religion that could be furnished to man." For nineteenth-century Paineites, no utterance was more associated with their namesake than this saying adapted from *Rights of Man*. The motto was their mantra—an epigrammatic conflation of liberal secularism with a religion of humanitarian universalism.[7]

Warding off Paine's detractors proved a nearly impossible task for the remaining years of his life. Patriotic gratitude was little match for Christian umbrage in popular estimations of him. When the old revolutionary returned to the United States from France in 1802, his pious antagonists poured out the vitriol and reveled in the scorned isolation of his final years. Sensationalized stories about his terribly poor health, his heavy drinking, his squalor, his deathbed torments, and his indifferent burial—all became fodder for decades of evangelical moralizing. One favored tale, repeatedly told, was that "an old negro," struck by how few had showed up at Paine's interment and "astonished at the coldness of the scene," had offered an impromptu rhyme as he shoveled dirt over the coffin:

> Poor Tom Paine! here he lies,
> Nobody laughs, nobody cries!
> Where he has gone, or how he fares,
> Nobody knows, and nobody cares!

Recollecting how forgotten Paine had become by the time of his neglected funeral was a commonplace of nineteenth-century Protestant memory—a well-worn narrative that exasperated those disciples who wanted to reclaim and celebrate him. "Not content with following him to his grave, they pursued him after death with redoubled fury," Ingersoll remarked indignantly of Paine's unrelenting critics. They "gloried in the fact that he was forlorn and friendless, and gloated like fiends over what they supposed to be the agonizing remorse of his lonely death."[8]

That Americans had given Paine such an unceremonious burial in such a nondescript place, that they had kept heaping libelous insults upon his character even in death—these wrongs the British political commentator William Cobbett wanted to set right. A late convert to Paine's principles, Cobbett was remorseful about his prior part in the Tory demonization of Paine as a treasonous apostate and had, upon a return visit to the United States in 1817, committed himself to a brazen act of repentance. In late September 1819, after months of anticipation, Cobbett and his fellow radical William Benbow launched a covert nighttime mission in which they dug up Paine's coffin and hauled it to New York City. Within the week, they had the remains loaded on a ship bound for England. "I have just done here a thing," Cobbett rejoiced, "which I have always, since I came to the country, vowed that I would do: that is, *taken up the remains of our famous countryman, PAINE, in order to convey them to England!* . . . We will let the Americans see, that *we Englishmen* know how to do *justice to the memory* of our famous countryman." Cobbett bubbled over with hopefulness about all ways in which Paine would now be commemorated and reverenced—how his tomb would become "an object of pilgrimage with the people," how a colossal monument would be raised, how a fitting funeral would finally be staged replete with twenty wagon-loads of flowers. He was positively giddy over the power and allure of the relics he had reclaimed. "Every *hair* of that head, from which started the idea of *American Independence*, would be a treasure to the possessor; and this hair is in my possession," Cobbett crowed. Hair was indeed a valued memento of the era, a way of connecting to the heroic dead or, more intimately, to deceased family members. Locks of George Washington's hair were already highly prized tokens of the revolutionary cause, so Cobbett appeared to have good reason for his optimism. He even contemplated putting pieces of Paine's hair into gold rings as personal reliquaries for the pamphleteer's most devoted disciples. The public exhibition of Paine's disinterred remains, Cobbett predicted, would vivify social reformers from Manchester to London: "Those bones will effect the reformation of England in Church and State."[9]

Alas, none of these things came to pass. Instead all of the machinery that had turned Paine into a byword for sedition, revolutionary violence, atheism, blasphemy, and moral degradation now ground up Cobbett. Cartoonists, newspaper editors, and rhymesters reviled Cobbett's "precious Relics" and his hopes for their political efficaciousness. Typical was "Sonnet to the Bone-Juggler," published in January 1820, less than two months after Cobbett arrived in Liverpool with his macabre freight:

> What dark project brought you back
>   O'er the broad Atlantic surge?
> Did some Demon point the track,
>   Some ill wind the vessel urge?
> Are you come to be a scourge
>   To these hapless Isles again?
> Singing dire Sedition's dirge
>   O'er the bones of putrid Paine?

A cartoon a month earlier, entitled "The Political Champion Turned Resurrection Man," pictured Cobbett riding a dragon-like demon to England's shores, followed by another imp carrying Paine's *The Age of Reason* (fig. 1.3). Cobbett wraps an arm around Paine's skeleton, which protrudes from a box marked "Cobbett's long hidden Treasures or the Relics of Paine." A riotous, uncouth crowd stands ready to greet Cobbett and his cadaverous cargo, while on the American shore a group dances merrily, happy that Paine's "Evil Spirit hath departed from us." Cobbett's political designs were mocked as both dangerous and delusional—as if he planned "to carry the bones at the head of a Revolutionary army." And even when he disclaimed any solidarity with Paine's religious views, there was simply no way to hive them off from his politics. His fellow radical Richard Carlile had recently been imprisoned for blasphemy for republishing *The Age of Reason*; likewise, Cobbett looked like a "blasphemer" too just by showing up with Paine's remains. As one paper vented, "It is *truly disgusting*, that the *corpse* of the *Author* of *The Age of Reason* is to be hawked through the country, to stir up and inflame the unthinking multitude against the sacred truths of Christianity."[10]

FIG. 1.3. The British press roundly derided William Cobbett for reclaiming Thomas Paine's bones, the remains of a fiendish blasphemer and riotous revolutionary. Isaac Robert Cruikshank, "The Political Champion Turned Resurrection Man," December 1819. The British Museum, Prints and Drawings.

The attacks on Cobbett were in many ways a predictable re-hashing of the denunciations of Paine and his freethinking disciples, but they entailed as well a specific assault on Cobbett's investment in Paine's bones, on the power and genuineness he claimed for them. At one level, Cobbett's "favorite, & precious Relics" were simply laughable; he was pictured carrying around Paine's skeleton like a pack on his back, a shabby peddler with his own ridiculous peep show, a knave and a fool deserving brutal mockery (fig. 1.4). As one member of the House of Lords asked less than a month after Cobbett's landing, "Was there ever any subject treated with more laughter, contempt, and

FIG. 1.4. William Cobbett's public designs for Paine's bones occasioned severe and boisterous mockery as this satire made plain—a series of scenes promising him rough justice for his exhibitory folly. Cobbett's pledge to memorialize Paine with a grand funeral procession and monument was rendered asinine, though the devil's presence suggested that the skeleton nevertheless possessed an uncanny power that was not so easy to dispel. The key accompanying the image identified the various scenes in this way: **A.** Cobbett carrying off the bones of Paine; **B.** The Devil pursuing Cobbett to recover his Property; **C.** Bones exhibited at the Hustings in derision; **D.** Emblematical of the head of a Traitor; **E.** Watchman's rattle, used to arouse Mr. Cobbett's friends; **F.** Bell, used by the collector of Bones; **G.** Knaves-post, a friend of Cobbett's; **H.** An Ass, a present for Cobbett to ride upon from the Booth; **I.** The opponents of Cobbett amusing themselves at the Hustings; **K.** A mock Skeleton of Tom Paine; **L.** Faggots to remind Mr. Cobbett of one of his Botley maneuvers; **M.** Cobbett led away from the Hustings by his friends, fainting; **N.** An emblematical figure of Death (painted) to remind Mr. Cobbett of his latter end; **O.** A Radical with his staff exhibiting a Monster. "Cobbett at Coventry," 1820. Col. Richard Gimbel Collection of Thomas Paine Papers, American Philosophical Society.

derision, than the introduction of those miserable bones?" Viewing Cobbett's relics as "a bad joke" was not enough, though. Paine's skeleton retained a dangerous, even demonic cast: "Give me my Bones," the devil demands in the cartoon "Cobbett at Coventry." However much the retrieved relics were derided, Paine's remains possessed a powerful religious and political aura that made their demystification essential.[11]

Various reports immediately circulated that Cobbett's foray was all a humbug, that the skeleton was inauthentic and hence inconsequential. Cobbett had actually arrived with the bones of an "old woman," an "old negro," or a lowlife "malefactor," which he was palming off as Paine's own out of scheming opportunism. He was trying to use these bogus bones—"his American Sham Paine"—to intoxicate radicals and laborers; it was all "a cheat," an imposture played upon dupes. Relics as frauds had the familiar ring of Protestant satires of Catholic devotional objects, and, indeed, Cobbett was seen as borrowing his trickery from "Roman relic-mongers" who have "long carried on a lucrative trade in sham relics." That Cobbett soon wrote a highly critical history of the Protestant Reformation only made his detractors more suspicious that he was somehow "at heart a Papist," an unwitting Catholic as much as a deistic accomplice. After all, the way in which he venerated Paine's bones made him look like some "uninformed Romish devotee" who "hallows the rotten relics which he is taught to believe were once the bones of some favorite saint." What better way to deflate Cobbett's elevation of Paine's bones than to render his efforts apiece with the materiality of Catholic devotion, a species of piety that every good Protestant knew to dismiss out of hand as a hoax and a scam.[12]

It did not take long for Cobbett to realize that he had seriously miscalculated the reaction Paine's bones would generate.

While there was some initial excitement among the gathered crowd when he made a spectacle of them upon arriving in Liverpool, that flurry rapidly dissipated as the censures multiplied. (Cobbett estimated that over three hundred newspapers joined in the calumnies against him: "No one dared to move a pen or a tongue in my defence.") With even his friends falling silent on the wisdom of repatriating Paine's bones, Cobbett modulated his memorializing ambitions, coming to see a monument and a public funeral as long-term projects rather than immediate possibilities. Absorbed in other tasks and embarrassed by the persisting caricatures, Cobbett stopped calling attention to the bones after 1821 and stowed them away, awaiting a more auspicious time to resume his efforts.[13]

Within a decade, the whereabouts of Paine's skeleton was already in doubt. Had Cobbett's grave-robbing partner, William Benbow, moved the bones into his cellar? That was one report in 1827. But by 1833, they were said to have been packed off to Cobbett's farm in Surrey, where they remained until Cobbett's death two years later when they briefly passed into the hands of Cobbett's eldest son. His father's estate had to be sold off, though, as a result of debt, and the bones fell into the hands of a local farmer named George West, who, in 1844, conveyed them to an old associate of Cobbett's, a tailor named Benjamin Tilly, who wanted to carry through, all these years later, on the plans for a public funeral and a monument. At last, these "sacred remains," these "interesting relics," would receive a final resting place. Tilly, however, proved no better than Cobbett at realizing this commemorative project, and the location of the bones kept getting more muddled. Had the skull and the right hand been detached along the way, winding up in the possession of a dissenting minister in London? Had Cobbett left a finger bone in the United States with a friend on Long Island? Had Tilly already removed some of Paine's hair and a piece of his brain in 1833? Had a corn merchant pilfered some of the bones when transporting them for Tilly and then stored them in a porcelain jar? By the 1850s, Paine's remains could not be reliably traced, and their fate got ever more obscure in the proliferation of competing tales. As one inquirer into their whereabouts concluded when faced with this welter of claims, "History repeats itself here, with a difference. It is said that there are pieces of the true cross extant in various places sufficient to load a battleship! Also that relics of saints are scattered about at numerous distant shrines in a vast superabundance!" Paine's bones had entered a netherworld of dispersed relics at once lost and multiplying.[14]

Meanwhile, as Cobbett's memorial ambitions came to naught, Paine's American admirers took up the commemorative cause as their own. In 1825, a small group of deists—they came to prefer the name of either Moral Philanthropists or Free Enquirers, but their Protestant opponents stuck with the slurs infidels and atheists—held an inaugural celebration of Paine's birthday (January 29) in New York City. That initial foray grew over the next several years into an annual festival for freethinkers in several cities and towns across the country: Boston, Rochester, and Cincinnati prominent among them. Organized around a dinner, songs, toasts, and recited poems, usually held in a coffeehouse or public hall, the birthday observances were a mainstay of deistic, anticlerical sociability throughout the antebellum period and beyond. These late January festivities, filled with hagiographic reverence, laid the foundation for a secularist identity built upon apotheosizing Paine. One versifier in 1846, for example, offered a celebratory poem expressly dedicated to the birth of "my saviour Thomas Paine." Three years later an orator at the 112th anniversary of Paine's nativity, hosted by a group of "Liberals" in New York City, captured the way in which freethinking fellowship was constructed through the canonization of Paine: "It has been customary since the time of Constantine, for the church to canonize all such as were eminent for their piety and devotedness to her cause. And now, to follow the example set by the church, as talents and virtue were pre-eminently the attributes of Thomas Paine, I do hereby proclaim him St. Thomas of our Church."[15]

The birthday celebrations were the ritual hub for the secularist exaltation of "Immortal Paine" from one year to the next for a very long time. "Hail! the auspicious day, / Hail, hail the natal day / Of Thomas Paine," opened one anniversary hymn from 1877, sung with all due irony to the tune of "God Save the King." Still, in 1901, when the freethinkers of Silverton, Oregon, gathered to celebrate Paine's birthday in Liberal Hall, they were eager to consecrate the proceedings. So, one of their number, John Prescott Guild, who fancied himself a poet of the "New Atheism" of his day, happily contributed some fresh verse. Entitled "The Secular Saint Thomas," the poem lauded Paine as "our Freethought Saint," who took no stock in "the 'gospel plan'" and "set Church-prisoners free" through *The Age of Reason*:

> Then THOMAS PAINE shall be our Saint,
>   "Apostle" of all lands:—
> "Do good to all"—that was his plaint,—
>   With heart and head and hands:
> "Where lives true Liberty, 'tis well.
>   There Justice too, can reign;
> Where she is not, there help her dwell,"
>   So preached SAINT THOMAS PAINE.

Whatever the quality of Guild's poetry, "The Secular Saint Thomas" made plain how irresistible the impulse to sanctify Paine was for his American devotees. Indeed, as late as 1937, when American Paineites were marking the bicentennial of his birth, the presiding toastmaster gave delicious religious significance to why the banquet was being held the day before Paine's actual birthday: "Why January 28th and not 29th?—Christmas Eve. Blessed Event." That the timing was actually a matter of more prosaic scheduling conflicts only made the religious allusion more emblematic. As the advent ritual of the religion of humanity, these birthday celebrations long served to consecrate secularist allegiances through the hagiographic elevation of Paine.[16]

Not only his birth but also his death galvanized Paine's American disciples, and, by 1837, they had turned their attention to the violated grave at New Rochelle as a focus for memorialization and reclamation. The leader of this campaign was Gilbert Vale, a freethinking lecturer, publisher, and astronomer with unbounded enthusiasm for Paine's views on both religion and politics. In July 1837, Vale toured the site of the "tomb" and was dismayed at its condition: the stone wall around the plot was broken down, and the headstone was missing (fragments of which, Vale explained, had been chipped away as souvenirs by successive visitors until a local woman rescued a "last remnant," plastering it into the wall of her cottage). Vowing to raise funds to secure the land, restore the gravesite, and build a monument, Vale rounded up a substantial list of subscribers over the next two years. Those efforts came to fruition with the erection of a twelve-and-a-half-foot-high marble column with Paine's profile chiseled into the face of it, duly dedicated on Thanksgiving Day in 1839 (fig. 1.5). The freethinker Ernestine Rose informally addressed the group,

FIG. 1.5. The Thomas Paine monument in New Rochelle, New York, was dedicated in 1839, and it took on a hallowed aura for freethinking pilgrims who journeyed there to see it and to be present at Paine's empty grave. The monument is crowned in this engraving with "Paine's motto," which served as a watchword among his admirers: "The World is my Country. To do good my religion." By 1860, the motto had been added to the face of the monument itself above Paine's profile. Thomas Paine, *The Works of Thomas Paine*, 3 vols. (Philadelphia: E. Haskell, 1854), 1: title page. Col. Richard Gimbel Collection of Thomas Paine Papers, American Philosophical Society.

but there was no "stiff procession," Vale reported, just the conviviality of "philosophical friends" who afterward shared a "fine dinner" and "a few bottles of wine" at a nearby tavern. Before the evening was through, the group had made plans for a return visit the next summer for the Fourth of July, which then became a tradition in its own right. What Vale's project of formal memorialization had done was effectively establish a pilgrimage site for freethinkers. At a celebration of Paine's birthday in Camptown, New Jersey, in 1844, participants saluted the "beautiful monument" in New Rochelle in precisely those terms: "The Rock of Plymouth has its pilgrims—will not the tomb of Paine have its," so went one festive toast. "The goddess of Liberty and the march of mind, say yes." Here was a place of origin for American freethinkers and secularists, a pillar set up to pay tribute to Paine's age of reason against "the rocks and shoals of Superstition and Bigotry." Over the next half century and more, Paineites repeatedly found their way to the monument, "this sacred spot," for picnics, orations, holiday outings, and rededication ceremonies.[17]

Vale always had very grand designs for the memorial in New Rochelle. By 1851, those included building a larger commemorative park to honor a pantheon of infidels, maintaining a "country house" to host "rational banquets," establishing a school for young freethinkers, and carefully preserving the home and farm that had belonged to Paine. In addition to those plans, though, Vale had from the beginning wanted to use the monument to correct for Cobbett's thievery—to restore Paine's tomb and provide him with a "decent sepulchre." He was the first to pursue the unsubstantiated story of Cobbett having left one of Paine's fingers with a friend on Long Island; he actively traced the circuitous travels of the bones after the dissolution of Cobbett's estate; and he prodded Benjamin Tilly and his associates about the status of their own plans for a monument and reinterment. In 1847, he even republished for American freethinkers the primary British account of the burgeoning quest, *A Brief History of the Remains of the Late Thomas Paine*, in response to the "many enquiries" he had received on the subject. Vale's circulation of this pamphlet, which was then picked up by the *Boston Investigator* as well, heightened the interest among Paine's American admirers in "ferreting out the whereabouts of the relics of this republican martyr." Getting the bones back to the United States—"the only land beneath the sun congenial to the final repose of the great apostle of civil and religious liberty"—gained new appeal through Vale's publicizing of their unsettled fate.[18]

Vale's monument was increasingly envisioned as the impetus for the ingathering of Paine's remains. As one freethinker who visited the New Rochelle monument in 1851 suggested, "*There* should be deposited all the relics that can be collected of Paine." Nine years later another liberal, John Morey of Saratoga Springs, wrote of his trips to the Paine monument—"a spot I have often visited solitary and alone, and at times in company with other friends"—and mused about restoring Paine's bones to their original American grave: "'Tell it not in Gath, publish it not in the streets of Askelon,' that the remains of Paine shall continue forfeited," he exhorted in a biblical cadence, "without at least one desperate effort being made to restore them to their resting-place, from whence it was the most wanton sacrilege to have removed them." It was, Morey claimed, "a foul blot upon the escutcheon of our country" that Paine's "disinterred remains" should reside in England without "we Liberals" mobilizing to reclaim them. Surely, "this matter of restoration" had to occupy a high place on the American secularist agenda. It was certainly high on Morey's, who, like Vale, was a devoted celebrant of Paine's memory over several decades: "Let us rise as one man in our exertions to obtain these sacred relics," Morey urged, "and place them where they belong, viz., beneath the monument consecrated to his memory by the Infidels of our country!"[19]

The retrieval of Paine's bones certainly kept coming up as a secularist objective. In the early 1870s, with freethinkers in Boston working intently to dedicate the new Paine Memorial Hall in time for the nation's centennial, the search for the remains gained fresh attention. When William Henry Burr, a prominent freethinker in Washington, DC, heard a report in 1872 that Paine's bones had been rediscovered in London, he wrote to the *Boston Investigator* offering to purchase them for reburial at New Rochelle or for placement in the new Paine Hall once it was completed: "No hurry, though; July 4, 1876 will be the great occasion." It goes without saying that nothing came of Burr's excitement to find out who the secret owner was and negotiate a deal, but his proposal caught the eye of one reporter who called attention to the recent "translation of the relics of St. Justinus" from Rome to the Church of St. Paul the Apostle in New York City. These "holy relics," including a vial containing the blood of the martyred saint, had been "borne around the church in solemn procession" before being installed in "the repository prepared for them." The reporter then wryly alerted New York's Catholics "that they were not going to have a monopoly [on] this sort of thing. There is another saint, not exactly of their calendar, whose bones are going to be translated, and worshipped too, with less ceremony, but equal devotion." The reporter then rehearsed Burr's desire to get hold of Paine's remains with a wink of solidarity: he saw no reason why Paine's "apostles" should not reclaim his bones and "build an altar" for them. All of this sounded tongue-in-cheek, to be sure, but Burr was not kidding. In 1886, still on the trail of Paine's bones, he said he was no longer content with the prospect of reinterring them at New Rochelle or in Boston. Instead, he now wanted "an inclosure of the well-preserved skeleton in a glass case for a shrine." If Burr had his druthers, the reliquaries of St. Thomas the Apostle or St. Thomas Aquinas would give way to the enshrined bones of secularism's vastly superior St. Thomas.[20]

The uptick in secularist attention to Paine's memory in the 1870s did not sit well with most Protestant observers. One evangelical weekly, *The Christian at Work*, cast an especially wary eye on what it termed "the TOM PAINE renaissance" that the centennial of the American Revolution had helped spark. Any patriotic rehabilitation of "a drunkard and blasphemous infidel" the paper could not tolerate, and calls for renewed memorialization of him struck the journal, which was edited by the orthodox titan Thomas DeWitt Talmage, as particularly profane. That included efforts in 1876 by the organizers of the National Liberal League to have a marble bust of Paine placed in Independence Hall in Philadelphia in recognition of his heroic role in the nation's founding. "He who wars against the Holy Scriptures is not fit to have his picture, or bust, or monument in Independence Hall," the paper railed. "The righteous shall be held in everlasting remembrance, but the name of the wicked shall rot." Talmage and company won that battle over Paine's bust, but the journal did not rest with that victory. It was also on alert over Paine's bones and Burr's publicized ambitions to repatriate them. Go right ahead, the paper suggested, and "buy that skeleton," but "fix it on a pedestal of whiskey bottles, and erect it in the public square of some town where the Bible is tabooed, and where infidels alone abide. . . . The place to erect that ossiferous monument to TOM PAINE is some spot of earth—if there be such—where drunkenness and debauchery rule, where blasphemy and infidelity abound, where the name of GOD is never pronounced but in ribaldry and jest. But don't put up that skeleton in the midst of a Christian people." More than a half century after Cobbett had raised Paine's bones from the grave, they retained a striking capacity to fire enlightened hopes and stoke evangelical fears. Conflicts over Paine's memory, whether over a sculpted bust or his bodily remains, served time and again as proxies for larger battles over evangelical and secularist imaginings of the nation's history, religious identity, and constitutional order.[21]

It was an improbable act of secularist faith, especially by the 1870s and 1880s, to think that Paine's skeleton was intact somewhere awaiting restoration and enshrinement. And yet the quest for the bones proved undiminished, resilient in the face of their long absence and also in the face of all the grim stories in circulation about their fate—how they had been ground into powder, turned into buttons, hauled off by "a rag-and-bone collector," or disposed of by "a waste paper dealer." When the very originator and architect of British secularism, George Jacob Holyoake, visited the United States in 1879, he made the requisite pilgrimage to Paine's monument at New Rochelle. There he remarked on his own efforts "to trace up Paine's bones" and reaffirmed his belief that they were still extant, despite his own lack of success at locating them. He urged his American counterparts to form a memorial association—in part, at least, to try once again to redeem the bones and bring them back for burial under the monument. That suggestion sounded quixotic, but it turned out to be prophetic. A few years later, on the 147th anniversary of Paine's birth in 1884, the Thomas Paine National Historical Association (TPNHA) was organized out of a network of prominent secularists and free-speech activists in Manhattan. The group's announced purposes were to defend Paine's reputation "against the aspersions of the enemies of Freethought, to provide for keeping the monument at New Rochelle in good repair, and to collect and preserve such relics of the great writer as were still in existence." Key players in that association—Moncure Daniel Conway especially—would bring the long search for Paine's bones to its climax.[22]

The TPNHA would not have gotten very far in the collecting of Paine's relics without Moncure Conway, its eventual president. The son of Virginia Methodist slaveholders and a one-time itinerant himself, Conway dramatically broke from his family and headed to Harvard Divinity School, from which he graduated in 1854. There he became an abolitionist and a disciple of Ralph Waldo Emerson and Theodore Parker. Landing at a Unitarian church in Cincinnati in 1856, Conway moved deeper into antislavery networks and embraced a theological nonconformity expressly open to freethinking critiques of Christianity. Cincinnati was an epicenter for both liberal Judaism and irreligious radicalism, and Conway quickly gravitated toward those unorthodox circles. He expressly embraced the infidel legacy of Frances Wright, who had died there in 1852, and began quietly attending the Sunday afternoon meetings of a local society of freethinkers. Those gatherings introduced him to the secularist veneration of Paine, and in 1860 Conway took the unusual step of staging a celebration of the 123rd anniversary of Paine's birthday at his church—unusual, that is, for a minister in his pulpit but not for a budding disciple of freethought. Increasingly at odds with Unitarianism's denominational leadership, Conway left the United States in 1863 for England, where he ended up the minister to London's archetypal liberal congregation, South Place Chapel. Thereafter he spent the bulk of his career abroad, leading this British congregation from its universalistic Protestant roots into a secularist religion of humanity. He described this journey as his "earthward pilgrimage"—a shift away from Christianity's heavenly city to this-worldly humanitarianism, an inverted pilgrim's progress that he anchored in his deepening affinities with Paine. By the 1890s, Conway had become Paine's chief biographer, editor, and vindicator.[23]

Living in London with all the right connections, Conway was ideally situated to take the lead on pursuing Paine's bones for his American comrades in the TPNHA. He was already showing a keen curiosity about the subject as early as 1874, placing a query about the remains in a prominent secularist journal and writing for the *Cincinnati Commercial* about his efforts: "It is said on good authority that Paine's bones, after a pilgrimage which it would be interesting to know, are now resting in a mahogany box in the editorial office of Charles Bradlaugh." Conway's source must not have been too reliable since there was otherwise little indication that Bradlaugh, among the most notorious British atheists of his day, had somehow acquired Paine's remains. Not long thereafter, William Henry Burr reached out to Conway for help in his own reclamation efforts but received much more discouraging news: "We seem not to get along, I regret to say, in the matter of Thomas Paine's bones, owing to the determined silence of the man—one Ainslie, a Unitarian preacher—to whom they were last traced," so Conway related. Reverend Robert Ainslie's inscrutable claim to have the skull and right hand of Paine, which were then said to have been lost by his son, became an especially exasperating dead end for those searching for the remains. Conway still found Ainslie's old evasions vexing three decades later, when, in May 1902, he published the full account of his long inquiry, "Where Are Paine's Bones? Strange Adventures of the Freethinker's Remains." Months prior to its publication Conway had described that manuscript more accurately in terms of a personal odyssey—"a history of my strange adventures through many years in search after the bones of Paine." To Conway, so long engrossed in locating Paine's remains, the whole "mystery" came to seem "like some page of Mosaic mythology," the fabled lore of his earthward pilgrimage.[24]

Members of the TPNHA had made some progress in relic-collecting by the 1890s. When hundreds of freethinkers gathered at the New Rochelle monument for Memorial Day in 1894, the festivities were elaborate, with Robert Ingersoll among the orators for the occasion. Thaddeus B. Wakeman—an anti-Comstock activist, a Princeton-educated lawyer, and a founding member of the TPNHA—dressed the solemnities in borrowed religious garb. On this Decoration Day, "our great national festival of the dead," the work "we have gathered here" to perform, Wakeman proclaimed, "is to lift the soul of Thomas Paine out of purgatory! For there is where the stupid bigotry of his time left him at death." New York's freethinking liberals, as Wakeman saw it, had gathered to preach Paine into the only heaven that mattered, a "terrestrial heaven" of "liberty, science, and humanity" that would replace the one of "celestial myth." They had come to honor "the real St. Thomas," the deistic founder of a "Secular Republic" who was "far more useful" than any other saint "yet canonized." Following Wakeman to the platform was the sculptor Wilson MacDonald, long-time president of the TPNHA, who further sharpened the contrast between enlightened skepticism and pious credulity by telling a humorous tale about "the superstition that possesses religious minds." (It involved a bunch of rustics mistaking a meteor shower as a divine portent.) Then, to conclude his remarks, MacDonald unveiled a new relic that the TPNHA had recently obtained, "a fragment of the original headstone of Paine's grave," long ago destroyed but for this vestige now recovered. Thereafter, in the final speech of the day, Henry Rowley, president of the Brooklyn Philosophical Association, rehearsed the sad tale of "Cobbett's disinterment and removal of the bones." Happily, though, Rowley was able to offer a modest surrogate for those lost relics as he held up "a wood-bottomed chair of good dimensions" in which he said Paine had sat to do much of his writing. Although that object excited "great interest" among the crowd, surely American Paineites could do better, especially with Conway's help.[25]

The year after this large Decoration Day gathering, Conway's decades of inquiry bore fruit with the Thomas Paine Exhibition at South Place Chapel in December 1895. The catalogue ran to nearly five hundred items—not only portraits, engravings, coins, caricatures, autograph letters, and first editions, but also Paine's snuffbox, his death mask, photographs of the New Rochelle monument, a copy of Conway's sermon from 1860 celebrating Paine, and a "small piece of timber" from the house in which Paine was born. Entries 94 and 274 were especially eye-catching, though: Conway had located two locks of Paine's hair, the provenance of both supposedly traceable back to Benjamin Tilly, though now in separate hands. And then there was entry 93: "Paine. Part of his brain." It was under glass, "about two inches by one, leaden in color, and quite hard," and came with an authenticating note from Tilly saying that he had removed it directly from Paine's skull at Cobbett's house on January 7, 1833 (fig. 1.6). Many of the items in the exhibition were already part of Conway's personal collection, but the locks of hair and the piece of brain were only on loan to him from other devotees. Still, he had done it: he had found some tiny fragments of Paine's physical remains, and there they were finally on public display in London, if not yet reclaimed for American secularists. Rejoicing over the huge number of "relics" that he had collected for the exhibition, Conway nonetheless had no doubt about which one was most important: "Most impressive of all was the darkened bit of brain whence radiated the inner light of

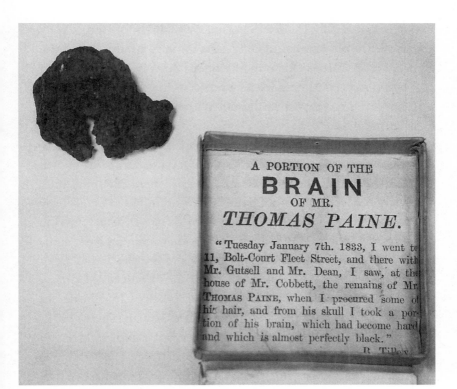

FIG. 1.6. The freethinker Moncure Conway located this portion of Paine's brain for display at his Thomas Paine Exhibition in London in 1895, subsequently purchased the relic in 1900, and then returned it to the United States to show to fellow Paineites at the Manhattan Liberal Club in 1902. The printed label was a mostly complete transcription of a handwritten note, attributed to William Cobbett's associate Benjamin Tilly, offering an explanation of the artifact's provenance. That original document had also come into Conway's possession with the relic itself. "A Portion of the Brain of Mr. Thomas Paine," photograph c. 1900. With permission of the Thomas Paine National Historical Association Collection, Institute for Thomas Paine Studies at Iona College, New Rochelle, New York.

that miraculous Thetford Quaker." With a relic of Paine's body in view, Conway made a noticeable shift toward the numinous. Although Paine's ties to the Religious Society of Friends were tenuous, especially so by the end of his life, Conway nonetheless mystified him as an illumined Quaker rather than a rationalistic deist.[26]

The London exhibition was a spectacular display of the secularist veneration of Paine, but Conway was not through yet. When, in 1900, the aged owner of the fragment of Paine's brain turned it over to a bookdealer in London for sale, Conway seized the opportunity, buying it for all of £5. Determined to end "the wanderings of the last-discoverable remnant of Paine's body," he brought his prized relic back to the United States for its final repose. But before letting Paine's brain rest, Conway wanted to show it off at the Manhattan Liberal Club, the parent body of the TPNHA, at its annual celebration of Paine's birthday. So he made his way there with his glass case and regaled those assembled with a valedictory speech about the closing of his long search for Paine's bones. "In the course of my researches into the history of Paine, I have pursued his skeleton through the houses of the great and in the homes of the humble; now in a tailor shop and then in a mansion," he narrated. His prolonged quest, he thought, had "ended with a certain success." He had come to believe that nearly all of Paine's remains had been quietly reinterred by a sympathetic Unitarian minister named Alexander Gordon. The evidence for that respectful burial was sketchy at best, but Conway's Paineite faith was strong. And now he had closure with this "little bit" of Paine's brain, "the last portion of the great man above ground," here on the table in front of him for all to see. This was a cerebral but devoted audience, and Conway could not resist indulging in one of his favorite stories about the talismanic effects of this particular relic. It had, along the way, passed through the hands of an orthodox Baptist minister who "subsequently became unorthodox," and Robert Ainslie had experienced the same "heretical symptoms" after his supposed exposure to Paine's skull. "If it were admissible for Paineites to believe in the potency of saintly relics," Conway awkwardly suggested, then "they might point" to the heterodoxy of these two ministers as signs of that power. It was, in some ways, the perfect story about his quest for Paine's bones, the paradoxes of a secular relic-hunter—a simultaneous affirmation of religious potency and its clumsy denial, a bit of poetic license used both to embrace and evade the palpability of his own reverence.[27]

It took a while for those associated with the TPNHA to get the final ceremony in place for the reburial of the fragment of Paine's brain, but on October 14, 1905, New York's leading free-thinkers gathered at the monument in New Rochelle for "the climax of all Paine celebrations." A few years earlier, in 1899, Wilson MacDonald had used his sculpting talents to add a "Colossal Bronze Bust" atop the old column that Vale had erected in 1839, and local leaders (some at least) had warmed over the last few years to their controversial townsman's revolutionary fame. The whole scene now had a celebratory, patriotic atmosphere with a thirteen-gun salute and a procession featuring a delegation of Minutemen and Washington Continental Guards (fig. 1.7). Conway himself had gone abroad again and had to send a letter of greetings from Paris, where he was still luxuriating in Paine's memory by frequenting the places associated with him during the French Revolution, including those where Paine had authored *The Age of Reason*. Despite his absence, Conway was able to emphasize his treasured gift for the occasion: "No brain ever lived who more completely incarnated the principles of justice, liberty, peace, and humanity than that of

Ideals

FIG. 1.7. Moncure Conway provided the portion of Paine's brain for this commemorative celebration at the New Rochelle monument in October 1905 during which the free-speech activist Edward Bond Foote displayed the box containing it to the crowd. James B. Elliott, ed., *Rededication of the Paine Monument and Assignment of Its Custody to the City of New Rochelle* (Philadelphia: Paine Memorial Association, 1909), 26. American Philosophical Society.

which I send you a little remnant to be enshrined in his monument." Edward Bond Foote, who, along with his father Edward Bliss Foote, had a sterling record of bankrolling Paine memorialization projects as well as free-speech causes, took the ceremonial lead in Conway's stead. When Foote rose to give the chairman's address, he saw this as "the last chapter" of a long story that had begun with Paine's burial there in 1809 and Cobbett's grave robbery in 1819. Knowing well the details of the long search for Paine's bones, Foote was able to rehearse those inquiries for the crowd, culminating in Conway's success in finally acquiring a piece of Paine's brain. "This relic of Paine is here in this small box," Foote explained, lifting up the TPNHA's secularist treasure, and now it was going to be "placed within this monument; then we can say the remains of Paine, all that we have, are to be found here." For his American disciples, Paine was the great embodiment of the religion of humanity, and at last they had brought a little bit of his actual body home to the shrine in New Rochelle.[28]

The TPNHA remained active in the years ahead. In 1909, on June 5, it celebrated the centennial of Paine's death with appropriate fanfare. In 1910, on Decoration Day, it opened the Thomas Paine National Museum in New Rochelle in Paine's old farmhouse near Vale's monument. The museum was to be a repository of the various relics that Conway and the TPNHA had amassed over the years—the gravestone fragment, the chair, a number of portraits, plus a new life-size wax figure of Paine with quill in hand. Conway had died in Paris in 1907, and his torch had passed to the photographer William M. van der Weyde, who became the new president of the TPNHA and the new authority on the protracted quest to recover Paine's bones. Van der Weyde took his job seriously, and by 1914, he excitedly reported a fresh breakthrough to the *New York Times*. It was the arrival from overseas of "a small wooden box" marked "of no commercial value" but the contents of which, he exulted, were actually of "incalculable" worth to "every patriotic American." Inside were two small envelopes each containing a lock of Paine's hair, both of which had been part of Conway's exhibition in 1895 and came with authenticating notes to establish provenance (fig. 1.8). The 1905 ceremony with Paine's brain had seemed like the end point, but now van der Weyde offered closure upon closure. Here were the final vestiges of Paine's remains; here terminated "the remarkable travels of Paine's body." This, van der Weyde assured, was "no doubt the last chapter in the story"; "certain it is that all the

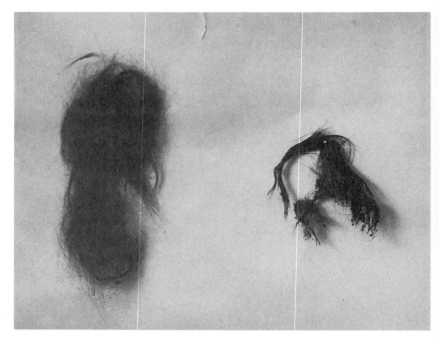

FIG. 1.8. As the inheritor of Moncure Conway's long quest to locate Paine's remains, the photographer William M. van der Weyde orchestrated the return of these two locks of Paine's hair to New Rochelle in 1914. "Locks of Paine's Hair," photograph c. 1914. With permission of the Thomas Paine National Historical Association Collection, Institute for Thomas Paine Studies at Iona College, New Rochelle, New York.

bones," even the skull, were lost and unrecoverable; there would be no more finds. After almost a century of hoping to reclaim the bones, it was time for Paine's American disciples to declare the search done. Van der Weyde's breathless description notwithstanding, the quest had ended—somewhat anticlimactically—with two locks of hair in a parcel-post box.[29]

Given how dedicated van der Weyde had been to collecting Paine's relics, it was hard for him to let go of the search. He published his official account of the end of the long quest for Paine's

remains in the *Times* on May 31, 1914, and then the very next day
drew up a "secret" memorandum for the officers of the TPNHA,
the contents of which were to be "kept undivulged . . . to the general public." Conway had actively circulated the story that one of
Cobbett's sons after his father's death had inscribed his name,
with "another word or two," on Paine's skull and larger bones.
Conway also claimed to be keeping those other words secret, so
that they could be used to authenticate the remains, should they
reappear. Along the way, van der Weyde had come to share in
Conway's privileged knowledge. In the *Times* piece, van der
Weyde had made the loss of the skeleton, and specifically the
skull, sound certain, but his clandestine memorandum revealed
that he still had a glimmer of faith in the ultimate restoration of
Paine's remains—enough to pass on the secret in order to prevent "the imposition of false relics of Paine on our Association or
on posterity by some trickster." What was the confidence—the
skeleton in the cupboard—that he and Conway had been keeping? They had both been intentionally lying in print about which
son was said to have inscribed his name on parts of Paine's remains. "It was <u>William Cobbett, jr.</u>, (William Cobbett's other
son,) who inscribed his name on the skull and on the larger
bones, <u>not James Paul Cobbett</u>. This is the 'secret.'" Deceit met
self-deception. The profession of closure was a dodge. Publicly
van der Weyde had been ready to bury the search, but privately
Paine's missing bones continued to haunt him.[30]

———

Through their absence the bones had gained an oversized presence in the nineteenth-century secularist imagination, so perhaps the failure to find Paine's skeleton was actually of benefit to
the cause. Conway had anticipated the symbolic potential in the
bones remaining lost despite all his inquiries: "As to his bones,

no man knows the place of their rest to this day. His principles rest not," Conway wrote toward the close of his two-volume biography of Paine in 1892. "Like his dust," they are "blown about the world." The trope—the dispersed bones as the sign of the universality of Paine's democratic principles and humanistic faith—proved hard to resist. "His bones may be scattered about the earth, but his soul goes marching on," Edward Bond Foote averred in 1905, leaping from Paine's vanished skeleton to his world-altering spirit. The very failure to reclaim the bones was an emblem of the diffusion of Paine's radical politics and philanthropic credo: "The world is my country, and to do good is my religion." The cosmopolitanism of that ever-present deistic motto, necessarily engraved on the monument in New Rochelle, found amplification in the symbolism of the empty grave the memorial recognized. "The earth would not hold him," Conway once poeticized in recalling the fanciful story about Paine's bones being turned into buttons. "Now his bones are traveling about the world"; strewn hither and thither, they were "the perfect charm," the far-flung "amulets" of *The Age of Reason* and *Rights of Man*.[31]

In the end, it would seem that the bones better served Paineite ideals by remaining lost rather than by being found. For freethinkers, who wanted nothing to do with "old bone bunco men," with the "religious rubbish" of "moldy relics," it never quite made sense, this quest for Paine's remains. To be a secularist relic-hunter had always been a delicate proposition. When Edward Bond Foote spoke at the dedication of the "Colossal Bronze Bust" in 1899—six years before he led the observance memorializing the fragment of Paine's brain—he retold the story about the removal of the bones and then disclaimed the loss as "a small matter," certainly not worth calling down a "curse" upon Cobbett's head. "It is the soul of Paine that we stand for, his principles and purpose," Foote pledged; it was not his earthly body, but his unleashed spirit that mattered. Perhaps then Paine's relics were never really sacrosanct—the locks of hair, the piece of brain, the long-pursued bones. What powers could they possess among those who were sure that they had thoroughly broken with the past of religious superstition and Christian materiality? Conway knew all along that it was impermissible for secularists "to believe in the potency of saintly relics," even as he recurrently indulged in the fancy that contact with pieces of Paine's remains had hastened the enlightenment of two fellow ministers. He knew all along, too, that Paine's bones had not been turned into buttons and that, even if they had, they possessed no talismanic power in the spread of Paine's philosophy. Perhaps, then, the borrowed religious rhetoric was all used with a wink and a nod, with a wry awareness of the artifice of such talk. As Conway professed elsewhere of his own disenchanted universe, he no longer "lived in days when saints could be real." In the religion of secularism, quite possibly, saints were not saints; relics were not relics; disciples were not disciples; pilgrimages were not pilgrimages; the empty tomb was not the empty tomb. And religion was not religion. The words were residues and traces; they were artful, but deceptive equivalences; they never eluded irony, incongruity, and discrepancy; they were the imaginative excursions of those who knew they were merely playing with bygone myths.[32]

And angels were not angels. In 1901, at the Manhattan Liberal Club's celebration of Paine's 164th birthday, Thaddeus B. Wakeman was looking for a new perspective to offer for this ritualized cycle of remembrance, for what he liked to call "St. Thomas's Day." He opted to pay tribute to Paine as a winged angel. He had hung a portrait of Paine in his parlor and had decided to preserve "the wings of a beautiful bird" by attaching the feathers to Paine's shoulders. As he contemplated his handiwork, Wakeman began to wonder if it was not time to consider Paine "as an angel—an angel on this earth" who had inspired both American independence and "the Religion of Humanity." His "angelship," Wakeman elaborated, had prepared the way for "the emancipation of the human soul from superstition. . . . Wherever the struggle for intellectual, social, and political liberty occurs, there his angelic influence, example, and inspiration will continually be found ever-growing through ages to come." Wakeman's effusions about Paine's "port-mortem angelship"—to say nothing of his avian handicraft—crossed the line for some in the audience. It was "strange," the *Truth Seeker* admitted in its report on the evening, that "a sworn foe of heavenly things" would "suggest wings and harps for Paine; but let us not forget that Mr. Wakeman is a poet as well as a philosopher, and poets, as we all know, are privileged persons, and should not be called to account for anything they may say." Whatever apotheosis Wakeman had glimpsed in his feathered portrait of Paine, the *Truth Seeker* marked his religious language down as poetic and strained before issuing a sardonic disclaimer: "No wings of Raphael or of any other angel were visible at the Manhattan Liberal Club." The hero worship accorded Paine came with a hedge against its too spirited manifestations. A portrait decorated with feathers and a meditation on Paine as an angel made freethinkers uncomfortably aware of the incongruities of their own devotion to the secular Saint Thomas. The religion of secularism inevitably faced secularist equivocality about the very notion of religion itself.[33]

Bedecking Paine's portrait with bird feathers and imagining them as angel wings certainly constituted an unusual decorative choice and an unexpected interpretive move for a disenthralled freethinker. Wakeman's credentials as an enlightened anti-fetishist could hardly be doubted; he knew more than enough about the period's emergent field for the scientific study of religion to hold forth knowingly on "Fetichism" as the lowest stage of religion's evolutionary development—a phase that unfortunately continued to be characteristic of "the tribes of Africa, the Indians of America, the hosts of China and of Asia, of Australia, and of the Isles of the Sea." This classificatory tool was such a common part of rationalistic, civilizing wisdom that one freethinker, M. M. Mangasarian, wrote the fetish into his *New Catechism*, a didactic guide intended to initiate the young into the ways of secular enlightenment, the first edition of which appeared the same year as Wakeman's seraphic meditation:

33. Q. What do we call the faith that is unintelligent?
    A. Superstition.
34. Q. Analyze and define superstition?
    A. To attribute to an object virtues or powers which it does not possess, is a superstition. . . .
36. Q. What is an object called when invested with imaginary virtues?
    A. A fetish.

A mastering knowledge of "Fetich-men" and "Fetichistic tribes" was a prerequisite of enlightened progress, civilizing uplift, and racial order. "Never shall we know what to do with, or how to treat, either Negro, Indian or Chinese," Wakeman warned, until "our statesmen" understood this "great religious evolutional fact" about the unmitigated persistence of fetishism, the devotion to objects imbued with imaginary significance.[34]

Civilizing politics and racialized hierarchies were written into Wakeman's origin myth for the religion of humanity—that Paine was its founding prophet, not Auguste Comte or anyone else. After combing his sources, Wakeman had concluded (inaccurately) that Paine deserved singular credit for the portentous coinage of the phrase *the religion of humanity*—those "magic words" that betokened "the brotherhood of man" and redounded to "the welfare of all the rest of the world." Wakeman's assertion of Paine's oracular priority rested on a single passage from *The Crisis* in 1778, which indicted the British pretense of being the imperial preserver of Protestant civilization in its prosecution of the war against America's revolutionaries. "The arm of Britain has been spoken of as the arm of the Almighty," Paine protested, "and she has lived of late as if she thought the whole world created for her diversion. Her politics, instead of civilizing, has tended to brutalize mankind, and under the vain unmeaning title of '*Defender of the Faith*,' she has made war like an Indian against the religion of humanity." Wakeman, Conway, and company all took that lone extract as establishing Paine as the originator of the religion of humanity more than a half century ahead of Comte. It was Paineite scripture. None of them, however, paused over the "like an Indian" phrase, which restricted the cosmopolitan universalism they saw in Paine's religion of humanity and established it instead on a familiar civilizational juxtaposition of the enlightened and the savage, an anti-colonial critique still wedded to the imperial hubris it impugned. The British, using an Anglican conceit to sanctify an inhumane monarchy, were behaving like Indians and hence set themselves against the true religion of freethinking civility. American Paineites rejoiced in the world-embracing sweep of their philanthropic creed—the international comradeship that the religion of humanity promised—but their excitement never hid the narrowness of their own evolutionary presumptions. Religion began in fetishism; it worked its way up through star worship, polytheism, and monotheism; it ended in their own religion of humanity in all its altruistic, republican, scientific, and civilizing splendor.[35]

When Wakeman made an angel of Paine, it was not simply that he was unaware of the contradiction: that as a standard-bearer for the fully evolved and supremely enlightened religion of humanity, he should not be making a fetish of Paine's portrait. Having grown up in the Presbyterian Church, Wakeman had imagined himself on a path to the ministry when in college at Princeton in the early 1850s and had attended lectures at the nearby seminary. Despite giving a senior oration titled "The Necessity of Faith," he soon decided against a ministerial vocation and turned to the law. Even as he lost his religion, he never let go of religion. Drawn after leaving Christianity to the religious positivism of Comte, he eventually switched allegiances to Paine as a far better embodiment of the religion of humanity for the American republic. Taking his lead from Holyoake and Ingersoll, Wakeman became as convinced as anyone that secularism itself should be understood in universalistic religious terms. "Secularism—Our Religion—Why Not?" was the title of a short piece he wrote in 1903 explaining why he accepted secularism not as a religion, but as "THE religion," "the most general, scientific, intelligent religion" with "the greatest benefits for mankind on this planet." Acknowledging the word *religion* to be "an old coin," Wakeman nonetheless wanted it "reminted and put in circulation again" among freethinkers, liberals, and secularists. So, when he reverenced Paine as an angel or saint, he meant that gesture to demonstrate just how seriously, how devotedly he took the religion of humanity—how consequential he imagined that commitment to be. He was staring down the equivocations and denials of his colleagues, those who wanted to purge secularism of sacral allusions and associations. Finding such religious representations too compelling to relinquish,

Wakeman kept multiplying them. At an Ingersoll Memorial Meeting in Cincinnati in 1900, he framed the gathering as "a Secular Canonization" for "the New Secular church." The assembled freethinkers were bent on the solemn work of glorifying "the second great Secular saint of America, Thomas Paine being always accounted the first."[36]

Wakeman had company in trying to circumvent, through his elevation of "the real St. Thomas," those who insisted on religion's across-the-board irrelevance for the enlightened. At the same gathering in 1901 where Wakeman had offered his riff on Paine as a winged angel, Conway reminisced about how he had first been drawn to "the mourners' bench" of infidelity through those Cincinnati freethinkers he had encountered in the late 1850s. Their "fervor of feeling towards Paine," Conway testified, had converted him to "a kind of Paine religion—a warm adherence to Paine and him crucified." The ex-Methodist's equivocation—it was only sort of a religion, this Paine religion—was subsumed into Christianity's structuring narratives to interpret his reverse conversion to rational enlightenment, his "ungodly inclination for the goats" rather than "the orthodox sheep." But Conway's testimonial was also to the sectarian distinctiveness involved in tending to "the posthumous life of Paine," the dedicated protection of his memory from his "persecutors." It reminded Conway of how the Methodists hallowed John Wesley or how the Quakers revered George Fox—the devoted recollection of an inspired founder often jeered at by opponents. Such reverence for the sect's forefather had, over the years, grown hoary with familiarity among Paineites. As the freethinker Susan Wixon observed in 1876, "While I never had, and never expect to have, a knowledge of what is termed experimental, ecclesiastical, evangelical religion, I confess to being a devout believer in that faith so grandly expressed in word and deed by that great moral hero and brave patriot, Thomas Paine, who said, 'The world is my country; to do good, my religion.'" Only "a kind of Paine religion"? Only like a religion, only loosely analogous to a religion? Such squeamishness often proved difficult to sustain, as Wixon's confession of faith made plain.[37]

Another of Wakeman's colleagues, the freethought orator John Emerson Roberts, who founded the Church of This World in Kansas City in 1897, also joined the company of devout Paineites. At the close of a lecture on "the sublime creed of Thomas Paine" in 1905, Roberts fully embraced Paine as a Christlike figure:

> Thomas Paine was a citizen of the world and loved humanity. He was a lone, wayfaring man, acquainted with grief. He died in poverty and deserted by friends, as Christ died. And like the grave of Christ, so that of Thomas Paine is unknown, and no man knoweth to this day where his bones repose. But his monument, more enduring than granite, more glorious than any ever built by hands, stands in the religion that he made humane.

Like Conway, Roberts gladly traded on the religious force of Christianity, on its scriptures and symbols, to interpret the secularist devotion to Paine crucified, dead, and buried—to his incarnational humanizing of religion. He gestured as well to the empty grave and missing bones, the tokens once again of the diffused influence of Paine's enduring spirit. Roberts surely would have agreed with a fellow Paineite who had gushed some years earlier: "Paine was better than Jesus." Paine, not Christ, was the bearer of "the most valuable and lasting blessings to man." Sometimes, at least, it was not all artifice, irony, or poetry—this religious language, this devotion: saints were saints; relics were relics; and shrines were shrines. And the religion of humanity, for its most serious adherents, was not simply like a religion; it was the real religion—not a surrogate, but a supersession.[38]

———

Even with the bulk of Paine's remains lost and irretrievable, the bones had been pursued and emblematized for so long as not to permit their final disappearance. During the country's bicentennial in 1976, there was a brief, nation-wide flurry of news reports that Paine's tombstone had been uncovered in upstate New York in Tivoli, a small town considerably north of New Rochelle. A seven-foot-high marble obelisk with Paine's birth and death dates on it had been "unearthed by a backhoe operator digging a ditch for a septic system," and suddenly the "mystery" of the whereabouts of Paine's remains became the subject of renewed attention. Perhaps this exhumed column was an indication that the revolutionary pamphleteer's grave—or, at least his gravestone—had been secretly moved up the Hudson River Valley. It certainly seemed to be an old gravesite, and the obelisk was very definitely a monument dedicated to the memory of Paine. On the other side of the tombstone, though, was another man's name, John Lasher, who had died in 1877, which made the significance of the pillar more puzzling and ambiguous. In short order a student of local history stepped forward with a newspaper article from 1874 that noted Lasher was "a staunch follower of Tom Paine" who had recently visited a nearby quarry to commission a memorial that would visibly express his admiration, which he then set up in front of his house. When Lasher died three years later, the obelisk honoring Paine doubled as his own gravestone. While the episode momentarily revived interest in Paine's missing bones, it was another red herring in a long history of them. What the backhoe operator had accidently excavated was not Paine's gravestone or his grave, but the archaeological remains of the nineteenth-century religion of humanity—or, rather, the Paineite version of it. Like Vale, Burr, and Conway, Lasher wanted to enshrine Paine and hallow his memory, so he had taken matters into his own hands and erected a well-hewn cenotaph.[39]

Unsurprisingly by now, even Lasher's bicentennial-boosted tale was not the end of the lost bones. An enterprising couple in Australia, John and Hazel Burgess, claimed (improbably) to have come across Paine's skull among the treasures of an antiques dealer in Sydney in 1988. Absorbed in trying to establish the authenticity of their find—the results of their efforts, including DNA testing, were predictably inconclusive—the couple became media curiosities for a time, particularly Hazel, who enjoyed posing with the newly recovered relic in a scene that reproduced Conway's exhibitory zeal (fig. 1.9). Always eager to publicize their prized artifact, the couple loaned the skull to the University of Sydney's Rare Books Library for display alongside an early edition of *The Age of Reason*. Joining a putative remnant of Paine's body to a quintessential text of enlightened demystification paid homage to all those nineteenth-century Paineites who had dreamed of similar spectacles of reverential illumination—a marvel that tacked between clarified rationality and faithful adoration. As in prior episodes, it remained an open question whose credulity was being exposed in this reappearance of Paine's skull alongside his infamous unmasking of mystery, miracle, and prophecy.[40]

Similarly revealing of these persisting fascinations was the literary travelogue of the writer Paul Collins, who pursued Paine's "strange afterlife" with a dedication worthy of the old

FIG. 1.9. Hazel and John Burgess discovered what was purported to be Paine's skull among the holdings of an antiques dealer in Sydney, Australia, in 1988. Much like Moncure Conway before them, the couple became dedicated aficionados of the lore surrounding Paine's bones. "Hazel Burgess Poses with Tom Paine Skull," Jan. 12, 1996, Sydney, Australia. Reuters/Megan Lewis.

Paineites. "Like saint's relics," Collins concluded in *The Trouble with Tom* (2005), Paine's remains had "passed from one idealistic reformer to another" in a finally impenetrable itinerancy—a dispersal that he presented, borrowing directly from Conway's reverential lore, as emblematic of the spread of Paine's democratic politics and enlightened creed. These relic-seeking devotees, Collins assured, "always came back to that call to common sense—to our sense of rationality, of hope, of kindness—against tradition and fearful irrationality, against the dead authority of the past. . . . We are the unseen future that they progressed toward." The *our* and the *we* are remarkable flourishes—that all of us share in Paine's age of reason, that all of us have shed the morbid weight of tradition and superstition, and that all of us somehow signal those progressive commitments through vicarious participation in the search for his mythologized bones. After roaming about Britain and the United States, following up nearly two centuries of clues about Paine's remains, Collins certainly knew how materially distinct the commitments of Cobbett, Conway, and company were—what "dead authority" they accorded his relics. But somewhere between New Rochelle and London, Collins had turned his whimsical curiosity into a secularist pilgrimage and closed with a genuflection to the universality of Paine's political and religious projects. "*Where is Tom Paine?*" Collins asks with an italicized urgency in his last lines. "Reader, where is he not?" With his own circuitous and otherwise lighthearted journey concluded, Collins is left contemplating the empty sepulcher of liberal democracy's globalized faith, the world-transforming spirit made manifest through Paine's missing body. All these years later the fables of Conway's odyssey continue to enchant a secularism at once cosmopolitan and imperial, emancipatory and civilizing.[41]

The disciples of "the real St. Thomas" made plain how secularists—or, more accurately, a distinct faction of them—were long attracted to sacred things in spite of themselves, to the complex associative significance of religion to interpret the depth of their fidelities. Paine's admirers participated, through annual celebrations of his birthday, in the mythic advent of a hallowed liberator whose reputation had been sacrificed to Christian ignorance and whose vision pointed to a perfected future freed of such superstition. They were drawn as well to a singularly radiant "prophet of democracy"—a prophet, they invariably lamented, who had been too long without honor in the country he helped invent. They were no more than a small sect, these American Paineites, and at no other point was their marked particularity more evident than in their attraction to their hero's remains, their search for a miscellany of relics that would render their reverence palpable. The forward march of secular enlightenment, they were convinced, was ushering in the universal religion of humanity—a sweeping commitment to liberty, equality, comradeship, science, reason, and free inquiry of global consequence. They could see on the horizon the world-conquering religion of the future: it would override all provincial gods and all parochial differences—all the tribal fetishes of the past and present, all the beads and ablutions of embodied devotion. But their own allegiances were surely more local and material, more ancestral and corporeal, more enshrined and ritualized, than those universalistic fantasies of expurgation suggested. Their humanistic cosmopolitanism, their globalized secularism was in the bones.[42]

CHAPTER 2

Positivist Rites and Secular Funerals

Courtlandt Palmer was a man of wealth and respectability in New York City in the Gilded Age. Of Dutch Reformed background himself, his wife and children reflected the family's social station in their membership in a prominent Episcopal church. Familiar with patrician privilege and ecclesial status, Palmer had nonetheless become an avowed freethinker and laborite sympathizer. He had also become an early disciple of Auguste Comte's religion of humanity—a devotion that had landed him in the late 1870s in the First Congregation of the Society of the Church of Humanity, one of a small handful of positivist religious fellowships that cropped up in the United States and Britain in the late nineteenth century. Presenting himself as part of a vanguard of constructive liberals, Palmer glimpsed in the Church of Humanity a way to reinvent and reritualize religion for a new age of science and progressive reform. However embryonic, this new earthbound religion, he hoped, would ultimately become the universal temple for all humanity.

The doctrines of the Christian church, Palmer was sure, were dead or dying fast. Heaven and hell, the soul and immortality,

God and the devil—all of the old theology was in decay. And yet, Palmer admitted, the church continued to hold considerable sway "within the *hearts* of men":

> Its arched and oriel windows, with their dim and holy light, evoke a calm repose; its choirs impel the worshipers through song and praise to nobler emulations; it takes the babe within its outstretched arms, admitting it to fellowship through baptism; it weds the blushing maiden to the manly youth; and when the last sad tragedy of death comes nigh it holds the cup of sacrament to dying lips and chants its solemn requiem o'er the grave. . . . And if I thought that Liberalism was impotent to yield such consolations or other equal ones, I am free to say, with all my detestation of the errors of theology, I believe my *heart* would keep me in the church. But we constructive liberals, believers in the new faith of Humanity, . . . *know* we satisfy the heart as well as [the] head. This nowhere can be better shown than in the new religion's fitness to give the dead a solemn burial and bear its messages of peace and resignation to stricken relatives and friends.

Palmer suggested that for liberal secularism really to take hold in people's hearts, it would need to replace Christianity's richly elaborated liturgies with humanistic ceremonies that were equally solemn and affective. The religion of humanity had to nurture tender feelings and altruistic sympathies as much as expunge outworn theologies and fetishistic superstitions, and it would have to do this through the creative reimagining of ritual. For Palmer, the enlightened were presented with a sacramental test that they had to find a way to pass—one that centered especially on how they navigated death and funerals.[1]

Palmer had made this plea for secular ritualism in 1881, and, by then, this "little band" of devout positivists, formally incorporated five years earlier in 1876, already had a fair bit of hard experience with conducting memorial services among its coterie. The year before they had organized themselves into a congregation, the group's leading lights had made it plain that being able to conduct appropriate funerals was a central part of what galvanized them: "When our time comes to take the quiet sleep of death, we want no reverend gentleman, no professional priest to pray or talk over us. We find ourselves able to live without their services, and we trust we will be able to die without them." That conviction was brought to bear when freethinker G. L. Henderson, one of the congregation's founders, lost two daughters in the space of two months in 1875. Another leader in this circle, the journalist Hugh Byron Brown, served as the chief liturgist for both of the funerals and thereafter put together a "little manual" for conducting "rational ceremonies" in lieu of the usual Christian solemnities, which he hoped to publish for the use of "Liberal Societies and Churches of Humanity." Comte had presented directives for rituals to bless the dying and commemorate the heroic dead, but Brown and his fellow positivists were nonetheless left to improvise the rubrics of local observances. Under the shadow of death they became quite practiced at memorializing their own "calendar of real saints," "the choir invisible of those immortal dead who live again in minds made better by their presence." By 1881, Palmer found ample room for hope in how well this little Church of Humanity was re-ritualizing bereavement on secularist terms. The emotional resonance of these positivist funerals was taken as a sign of the new religion's ultimate potential to supersede Christianity.[2]

Palmer had clearly given a lot of thought to a freethinker's last rites, so it came as little surprise to find out—upon his own death in July 1888—that he had a script in place. He had arranged well in advance for Robert Ingersoll to offer an elegy and had picked out appropriate music and poetry. He had also made it plain, including to his churchgoing wife and children, that "I shall not be buried from any Christian church, nor do I wish any Christian hymn sung." It was not only the funeral service that he had carefully considered but also the deathbed scene. Given how much Christian ink had been spilled depicting the imagined horrors of dying infidels—Thomas Paine always enjoyed special prominence in this regard—Palmer knew that he had to manage his deathbed with particular composure as a rebuke to such pious narratives. Among his last words to those gathered around him were: "The general impression is that Freethinkers are afraid of death. I want you one and all to tell the whole world that you have seen a Freethinker die without the least fear of what the hereafter may be." Newspapers around the country picked up on the manner of Palmer's death as well as the structure of his funeral. "How an Agnostic Died" was the headline in the *Cleveland Plain Dealer*; "A Sign of the Times? The Funeral of the Late Mr. Courtlandt Palmer" was the banner in the *Aberdeen Daily News* in South Dakota. It looked like Palmer had staged the perfect infidel death and funeral, so resolutely secular—with Ingersoll himself as officiant at the memorial service—as to gain national attention. And yet the funeral ended in telling disarray.[3]

The memorial service began well enough. With Palmer's Gramercy Park home filled with freethinking friends, including Paine's prominent disciples Moncure Conway and Thaddeus B. Wakeman, Ingersoll faced a like-minded audience as he spoke from the steps of the main stairway. In a voice that ranged from the soaring to the tremulous, Ingersoll paid tribute to Palmer's intellectual independence, to his emancipation from "the supernatural—the phantoms and the ghosts that filled the twilight-land of fear." Ingersoll offered only a vague note about Palmer's religious positivism—how he had discovered in Auguste Comte's philosophy the framework for his own constructive liberalism: "In the conclusions of that great, sublime, and tender soul he found the rest, the serenity, and the certainty he sought." Ingersoll dwelled primarily on more generalized notions of what constituted Palmer's humanistic faith, his "religion of Hope and Help"—more George Jacob Holyoake's streamlined secularism than Comte's robust ritualism. Palmer's allegiance, Ingersoll explained, was to "the gospel of this world," to "the religion of humanity," but the famed orator presented that adherence as having more to do with Paine's noble example than with Comte's sacramental system. "'The world was his country—to do good his religion.' There is no language to express a nobler creed than this," Ingersoll averred, using Paine's accustomed motto rather than Comte's positivist catechism to sum up Palmer's secular religion. Turning back to bereavement at the close, Ingersoll sounded a blankly agnostic note about death's mystery: "By the grave of man stands the angel of Silence. A heart breaks, a man dies, a leaf falls in the far forest, a babe is born, and the great world sweeps on." His own eyes "moist with tears," Ingersoll brought the memorializing of his friend to a close, and most attendees then departed.[4]

The problem was that most of those people were leaving in protest. Palmer's Christian family had not been content with a wholly secular funeral, and his wife had prevailed upon him the day before he died to add her Episcopal priest, R. Heber Newton, as a supplementary officiant at the memorial service. Thaddeus B. Wakeman, an old friend also active in the Church of Humanity, had been slated to speak alongside Ingersoll, but Palmer had submitted to his wife's wishes and allowed the substitution of Newton for Wakeman. Word of the last-minute switch, and the reasons for it, had not circulated among Palmer's freethinking comrades; so when Newton—a well-known liberal Protestant minister—began to lead a religious service after Ingersoll's performance, most of the assemblage left in anger. "I did not stay to hear the mockery of prayer and burial cant which were read over the remains of this brave man," the women's rights activist Helen Gardener wrote shortly afterward. "What mockery of all that was most dear to Courtlandt Palmer," she continued, a preacher "babbling of Gods and of a future life. . . . There are no words at present at my command to give the gorge of indignation force and scope. How dare a Christian wag his tongue at such a time and place as this." The Episcopal service of psalms and prayers that Newton led was no doubt expressly Christian, but his respectful elegy focused especially on Palmer's philanthropic endeavors and aimed at offering comfort to his grieving family. Newton did not attempt to reclaim Palmer posthumously for a faith he had renounced. Still, Gardener and company saw only desecration in the clergyman's presence and refused to listen to him: "There is no middle ground," she asserted. Palmer's well-planned funeral had ended in pronounced conflict and confusion, an open rift between genteel Protestants and aggrieved freethinkers.[5]

The failure of Palmer's studied ritualism, even at his own funeral, revealed many of the quandaries that secularists faced as they tried to create new commemorations to structure their lives apart from Christianity. The liturgical experimentation that Comte's religious positivism invited—he had called for a whole new calendar of festivals, a whole new set of sacraments, and a whole new priesthood of scientists, philosophers, physicians, and artists—got obscured by secularists who found Comte's ritualism alien and artificial, an unacceptable mimicking of Roman Catholicism. Palmer's story very much demonstrated that eclipse: he had embraced religious positivism with the hope of creating a new sacramental framework for liberal secularism, but few American freethinkers followed the Comtean path beyond elusive invocations of the religion of humanity. Even when employing that construct, most preferred to associate it with Paine rather than Comte, as Ingersoll had done in Palmer's elegy. Religious positivism had offered freethinking liberals the prospect of an expansive ritualism, but what prevailed instead was a far narrower set of what Holyoake called "secularist ceremonies." Despite their liturgical differences, religious positivists and Ingersollian freethinkers always agreed on this much—how important it was to establish their own funeral rites distinct from the expected Christian practices. For all his planning, Palmer's story revealed how challenging that disentanglement proved to be. Having once witnessed the "sacrilege" of a Christian service being performed over the remains of a dead freethinker, Palmer had vowed never to let that happen to him. Christian worship had nonetheless pursued him in death—a sign of the limited appeal of secularist liturgies even in Palmer's own family, let alone in the wider culture. The mask of universality that the new religion of humanity wore never disguised its sectarian oddity—the social peculiarity of secularist rites performed in the face of Christianity's deeply etched conventions.[6]

———

Herbert Croly, a founder of the *New Republic* and a leading progressive intellectual of his day, claimed a religious upbringing unfamiliar to most of his contemporaries. His parents were, in Croly's childhood in the 1870s, members of "a tiny but pretentious religious sect" in New York City that "proclaimed allegiance to Auguste Comte and his religion of humanity." The family's positivism, as Croly remembered it decades later, "was an atheism which was also a religion. It exalted social service, altruism and human love, but it would not allow its followers to love both God and their fellow-men." His parents, David Goodman Croly and Jane Cunningham Croly, were both New York intellectuals who found in Comte a way out, at least for a time, of a "religiously indifferent liberalism," a system to stave off nihilistic skepticism and imbue "the arts of secular life" with a sense of "religious aspiration." To that end, they were even ready to follow Comte in recomposing Roman Catholic ritual in the pursuit of a consecrated secularism. As Croly recalled, his parents had made him a rare beneficiary of that sacramental ingenuity: "I was, so I have been told, the only child of any professing Positivist who was officially initiated as a member of the sect by the holy rite of baptism." Croly exaggerated his singularity as a baptized positivist—though not by much in North America (he also mislabeled the Comtean version of the rite, which was known as the sacrament of presentation). Still, for all his sardonicism over his parents' sectarian proclivities, Croly had little doubt that his childhood "immersion in this shower of humanitarian ideas" had been "the most important single influence in my education." It gave him a lasting sense of "the importance of religion, of its necessary association with a valid body of knowledge, and of the impossibility of carrying on the work of human emancipation without a religious clue and a religious fortification."[7]

Herbert Croly's father, the journalist David Goodman Croly, had become quite the enthusiast for Comte in the decade after the Civil War. In 1871, under the pseudonym C. G. David, he even published an evangelistic tract for his new faith, *A Positivist Primer: Being a Series of Familiar Conversations on the Religion of*

Humanity. Not long into that piece, the elder Croly's imagined interlocutor receives an especially vigorous reply to the question, "Does your religion involve a ritual?"

> Certainly; and the noblest and most elaborate of which the human mind can conceive. It is our intention to use all the resources of art in magnifying the Deity we worship,—the fair Humanity; all the effect and grandeur that music can lend to our praise, all that art can do by statuary and painting to elevate our conceptions and ennoble our ideals, all that poesie can do to enkindle our imaginations, all will be used to adorn and glorify and magnify the Being to whom we owe everything, our whole service and our whole heart.

That spirited answer surprises Croly's conversation partner who presumes "a scientific religion would be a very cold and heartless affair,—a religion simply of the intellect, an argumentative religion,—a religion of formulae and demonstration, as one might say, a methodical thing involving mathematical proof by curves and lines and algebraic signs." Croly acknowledges that "our religion includes all that" but aims for far more. Somehow a religion based on demonstrable science and "this-world-ism"— "the most marked characteristic" of the religion of humanity "is its secularity," Croly tells his inquirer—would become, through ritual and art, "the most emotional of all religions." It would, in short, effectively meld enlightened rationality with romantic feeling and sentiment.[8]

Herbert Croly's mother, Jane Cunningham Croly, was quite the enthusiast too in her own right. In an article for the *Modern Thinker* in 1870, "Love-Life of Auguste Comte," she exalted Comte's rapturous affection for a thirty-year-old woman named Clotilde de Vaux. Comte, whose painfully bad marriage had ended with his wife's leaving him in 1842, became enthralled with de Vaux three years later. Flattered by Comte's attention, de Vaux embraced his philosophical musings but resisted becoming his mistress (she was already married, but her gambling-indebted husband had deserted her). When she died a year into their emotionally charged relationship, Comte developed a sustained devotion to her, in Jane Croly's phrasing, as "a revelation of the power, purity, genius, and suffering of woman." Idealized in death, de Vaux became "the Virgin-Mother" of Comte's emergent religion, "the representative of the noblest attributes of humanity." It was through de Vaux's "education of the heart" that Comte shifted the weight of his positivist enterprise toward the unfolding of "a new religion." And, indeed, his relationship with her—and the practices of veneration that he cultivated upon her death—became a major inspiration for the ritualization of the religion of humanity. Comte's thrice-daily prayer life—"positivist prayer" was understood as "the calling up to the mind's eye of some ideal of human excellence"—focused for years on recollecting "St. Clotilde" and all their unconsummated union had meant to him. Beyond serving as a spur for the domestic worship of religious positivism, de Vaux also left a critical mark on Comte's public calendar of saints and festivals in its apotheosizing of women as moral paragons. As Jane Croly's account made plain, Comte's "love-life" led him to set up an altar not so much to a goddess of reason as to a goddess of pure womanhood and sublimated sexuality. The intimate friendship of Comte and de Vaux became the symbol of the aroused emotions the fledgling movement sought to cultivate. Among the earliest items that the New York positivists offered for sale were paired portraits of the new religion's high priest and priestess.[9]

Comte was still putting together his religion of humanity in multiple volumes in the early to mid-1850s (he died in 1857), but he had already attracted one fervent disciple eager to bring religious positivism to the United States. Henry Edger, arriving in New York City from London in 1851, dreamed of enacting elaborate Comtean rituals the way others of his era imagined staging dramatic Masonic initiations or richly festooned Christmas pageants. His missionary efforts inspired the Crolys to organize the First Positivist Society of New York, which began meeting in their home in the late 1860s, and several members of that group, in turn, went on to help create the First Congregation of the Society of the Church of Humanity in the mid-1870s. Like Croly after him, Edger offered his own primer on religious positivism, leading with its liturgical significance, *The Positivist Calendar: Or, Transitional System of Public Commemoration Instituted by Auguste Comte, Founder of the Positive Religion of Humanity* (1856). The "New Worship," as Edger saw it, was at the heart of the new religion, the salve for the anarchic confusions of the era, the ritualistic performance of social unity and altruistic munificence. The new religion's imagined universality was embodied in the range of prophets, saints, philosophers, and poets it honored in its calendar; it claimed to synthesize the entire history of religion— from fetishism to polytheism to monotheism—into its week-to-week adoration of an enlightened humanity, the culminating cultus of all the previous stages; it matched a highly schematized vision of public worship with assiduous personal and domestic devotions centered on Comte's own archetypal devotion to the "feminine heart" as incarnated in Clotilde de Vaux; it offered a full panoply of rites of passage—"nine Social Sacraments"—that spanned birth to death. For Edger, "positive worship" was the regenerative answer for those who, emancipated from Christian supernaturalism, longed for a tangible alternative to having no religion at all—a religion after the loss of religion.[10]

Just how much of Comte's ritual system New York's small band of devout positivists actually put into practice is unclear, but it was certainly never more than a small fraction of the fully elaborated whole. Comte had architectural designs for temples of humanity and memorial parks that his American disciples never came close to realizing. Edger himself added a small chapel for private worship to his log cabin on Long Island, but he was for the most part without a community to enact his positivist calendar (he participated only marginally in the Manhattan fellowships of the Crolys, Palmer, Wakeman, and company). Most in these circles never intended their corporate ritual to become highly wrought—certainly, no smells and bells, no vestments, no baroque aestheticism. As one leading British adherent explained in defense of Comte's nine sacraments, there was "nothing mystical or fanciful" about them; they recognized critical epochs of life and made manifest important social obligations and virtues; there was no hocus pocus, no "crude imitation" of Roman Catholicism, nothing at odds with secularism's religion of ethical responsibility, its artless creed of deed and duty. Most of New York's devout positivists would have agreed with that apologetic. They seemed to want little more than a congregational fellowship for lectures and discussions—one that was only periodically leavened with a "sacrament" or "festival" intended to rededicate the group to its humanistic ideals. Such rites would never have been mistaken for Anglo-Catholic dramaturgy.[11]

Take, for example, the Festival of Humanity that New York's gathered positivists celebrated in 1872, which may have been the occasion for Herbert Croly undergoing the sacrament of presentation (the rite was performed for an unnamed infant as part of the festival). One member, Henry Evans, acted "as priest," offering an invocation that gestured at entering into "the arcana of thy mysteries," but the secrecy was safely rhetorical—it served only to mystify the social collectivity of "the Great

Being, Humanity." Evans proceeded to conjure up, mundanely enough, "the examples of heroic men and women, the work of statesmen and warriors, poets and philosophers, artists or artisans," all those who had embodied the virtues the new religion celebrated. "We ask to be among those who have added something to the sum of the world's happiness, to the welfare of individuals, to the honor of Humanity," this American positivist priest intoned. Laden with humanitarian commonplaces, the ceremony also had its distinct positivist markers—a toast honoring Comte's birthday, another recognizing Clotilde de Vaux as the "eternal companion" of the new faith's founder. But as festivals go, it was free of pageantry and effervescence, a bunch of gentlemanly toasts commending the new religion of humanity, all with an air of social conservatism, especially when invoking familial and gender norms. Women were celebrated as "the queen and priestess of the home"; men as bearers of science, philosophy, art, and the new priesthood. As public worship, the festival repeatedly pointed back to domestic worship—to women's superintendence of "home life" and the "family hearth," to confining women's work to that ostensibly private sphere. Clearly, a ritual of limited spectacle did not make it a ritual of limited social import. The festival's conventional, tightly laced script did mean, though, that New York's religious positivists failed to achieve through ritual what David Croly imagined they could—a religion of artistic magnificence and trembling emotion.[12]

Croly had been as optimistic as any of the American positivists about generating new forms of artful worship for secularists, but even he gradually lost faith in that project and in the capacity of positivism to serve as an alternative religion. As Herbert recalled, his father gave ground late in life to those freethinkers skeptical of the very idea of a religion for secularists:

he "ceased to talk as if he believed in a religion." In the son's view, the "obvious artificiality" of the new religion's sacraments and festivals proved unattractive to most inquirers; to Herbert, it was no surprise that the small band of New Yorkers who identified with religious positivism eventually dispersed, along with his parents, into other societies and clubs. When it came time for the elder Croly to offer his son advice for college in 1886, he still hoped that Herbert would read widely in Comte and his English interpreters, but his liturgical guidance for cultivating the "religious emotions" of "reverence, awe, and aspiration" had settled elsewhere: "Go to Catholic and Episcopal churches and surrender yourself to the inspiration of soul-inspiring religious music," he now advised his son. Religious positivism might make for interesting philosophical reading, but its ritualized expression, Croly admitted, was not the place to "learn the secret of tears and ecstasy." Dispirited by how little he had achieved through propagating the new religion of humanity, he suggested a bleak epitaph for his gravestone: "I meant well, tried a little, failed much." And, as for his own funeral in 1889, his directions were sparing to the point of self-effacement, entirely unadorned by the sacramental structure that Comte had prescribed for both the dying and the dead: "If any one thinks enough of me to bring me flowers, let them; but have no elaborate mourning, and bury me close to the earth, near the pines, and facing the sea." Even among its most ardent admirers, Comte's new worship—his "sacred sociological ecclesiasticism"—had proven a washout in the United States.[13]

The new religion did have greater success in England, although the positivist communities there still remained modest in size and number—these were congregations, one humorist remarked, of "three persons, but no God." The Church of Humanity had communions in London, Liverpool, and Newcastle, each of which approximated Comte's decorative instructions for temple interiors and managed to embody many of his liturgical directives through the turn of the twentieth century. (The appurtenances, in all three cases, included a central portrait of the Virgin Mother, a symbolic fusion of the Madonna and Clotilde de Vaux, as well as numerous busts of philosophers, poets, and saints integral to the positivist calendar—Aristotle, Dante, Shakespeare, and the like.) Among the cadre of English positivists devoted to the notion of building up the Church of Humanity, three stood out for their commitment to elaborating the worship practices these assemblies were to enact: Richard Congreve, Albert Crompton, and Malcolm Quin. An ordained Anglican in background, Congreve systematized the liturgy for Comte's nine sacraments with a volume of readings designed to stand in for the *Book of Common Prayer*, and Crompton built a particularly elaborate domestic devotion to his own deceased wife, which was modeled on Comte's daily prayers to Clotilde de Vaux. For years, both men served, in effect, as the vicars of their small congregations in London and Liverpool respectively. And then, in Newcastle, there was Quin who, liturgically speaking, was the most byzantine of the three and who left an unusually rich memoir detailing his quest for a religion beyond both Protestant Christianity and organized secularism. Quin's long career as a devout positivist serves as an indicator of what the religion of humanity might have looked like had it gained fuller ritual expression in the United States. No one spent more time imagining a liturgy for a religion after the loss of religion than Quin did.[14]

Born in 1854 into a churchgoing Anglican family, Quin recalled even as a boy a love of artful worship. Sitting there Sunday to Sunday in a church with a relatively spare Protestant interior dominated by a "towering pulpit" and with a lot of hymn singing, he nonetheless felt an attraction to the litanies and architecture: "Young as I was, I was not too young to gain from it a sense of religion as at any rate a thing of beauty." His father died when Quin was twelve, and his mother moved the family to Leicester, where they attended St. Matthew's, a church with a more "ritualistic clergy" who dressed in surplices rather than black Genevan gowns and who bowed before the communion table. Quin was transfixed: he became "a youthful 'High Churchman,'" for whom "worship was transformed into a poem of Heaven." Growing up with a view of religion as a good and beautiful thing, he developed none of the usual freethinking animus toward Protestant orthodoxy—no recoiling from hellfire sermons, "black Calvinism," Sabbatarian tedium, or biblical literalism. "To this day," he wrote at age seventy, "the sound of the church bells—or even the monotonous clang of a single bell—ringing for service stirs in me sensibilities which I am not in the least sorry to possess. If, therefore, I left the life of Belief behind me and passed into 'Unbelief,' this was not at all because Belief was a dismal tyranny and Unbelief the joy of freedom." Quin knew that most of his freethinking contemporaries—"the pure bloods of Unbelief"—did not feel "the slightest need for religion in any conception of it, supernatural or natural," but he was never attracted to that total emancipation and expungement. Even as a secularist, when it came to religion, he remained indelibly musical.[15]

By his early twenties, Quin was an unbeliever who had left the Anglican Church but who remained committed to finding a religion—some "unifying conception" by which he could see human life as a whole "integer" rather than mere "disordered fractions." Not sure what to call himself in his unbelief—freethinker, agnostic, atheist, or infidel—he was drawn into the organized secularist movement, first hearing George Jacob

Holyoake lecture in Leicester in 1873. With the benefit of hindsight, Quin claimed to have felt no deep affinity with Leicester's formal body of secularists—"a home of forlorn souls"—but he became a dedicated lecturer for them all the same, emphasizing secularism as a constructive rather than a destructive movement, broadly humanitarian rather than aggressively atheistic. He even began composing "hymns of ethical platitude" for use in secularist meetings, youthful productions that he mostly found trifling and vacuous in old age: "People who believed in nothing else believed in hymns," he wryly remarked. Heavily involved in the movement as a lecturer, hymnist, and essayist, he nonetheless found that he was unlike most other freethinkers. For starters, he relished visiting the Church of the Holy Cross to see the Mass celebrated—"an unusual thing" for a Protestant, let alone a card-carrying secularist—and then there was an Easter excursion to a Trappist monastery outside Leicester. The monks, the chanting, the cloisters, all seemed entirely agreeable to the freethinking Quin.[16]

A secularist with the disposition of a spiritual seeker, Quin began to sharpen his identity as a religious positivist in the early 1880s. Having by then settled in Newcastle, he started paying much closer attention to Comte's religion of humanity as the answer to his longing for a religion for unbelievers. He began carrying around Comte's *Catechism of the Positive Religion* as if it were his New Testament, eager to expatiate upon it among his secularist colleagues. With the blessing of Richard Congreve in London, he started experimenting in 1882 with congregational services in a "Positivist Room" decorated with an image of the Madonna and thirteen busts of personages celebrated in "Comte's Historic Calendar." Setting up his own branch of the Church of Humanity, Quin was quickly drawn into the inner circle of England's religious positivists in London and Liverpool.

From the beginning, his eye was on how the religion of humanity could find fuller expression in ritual. He liked, for example, what his colleagues in Liverpool were doing with the festival in honor of Comte's death (September 5): they had added a communion rite of dry bread and water as a sacramental sign of solidarity with the poor—with those who lacked adequate sustenance. He admired as well Albert Crompton's steady, prayerful, and lyrical devotion to his deceased wife. By contrast, Congreve's relative lack of an artistic and musical sensibility left Quin with "a chill of disappointment" on his first visit to the London congregation; the place looked like a "phrenologist's shop" with a bunch of busts on display and with "a small projecting sign" identifying it as the Church of Humanity. Quin also wanted Congreve to dress the part of the priest—to don vestments or colorful ribbons—but his mentor always administered the new religion's sacraments in "an ordinary morning coat." Receiving the sacrament ordaining him as a priest of the new religion in 1885, Quin took it as his sacerdotal calling to enrich the ritual life of these budding positivist churches. Worship, he said, was "the secret and centre of religion."[17]

By 1887, Quin and his small flock had managed to acquire an unused Anglican church with all its furnishings, a cast-off building that the positivists acquired after the Church of England had completed a larger edifice nearby. Quin ministered in that building for the next eighteen years. Any pastor would be busy with multiple tasks, but Quin managed to see almost everything he did through the lens of ritualism: decorating the "High Altar" with six candles and a red lamp to represent the "master-sciences," improving the music through a new pipe organ and new hymns, establishing an Order of Public Worship that included kneeling for prayer, adding "a liturgical poem" in Italian to intone every Sunday, and inserting whatever "Catholic morsels" he could to give drama to the proceedings. He also added two "side altars": one dedicated to Auguste Comte, the other to Comte's "Three Angels—his mother, his adopted daughter, and Clotilde de Vaux, who was the presiding figure on it." Amid the profusion of new emblems and pictures, Quin eventually redecorated himself as well with an array of "vestments"—a cassock, a surplice, and an academic hood that "combined certain symbolic Positivist colours." His old frock coat "had become an artistic solecism," unbefitting the rich symbolism he had created for the religion of humanity. He admitted that it was "too much to expect my 'emancipated' congregation," primarily freethinkers from Protestant backgrounds, to take kindly to all this ritualism. Most found one innovation or another objectionable, and from time to time a congregant or two reached a breaking point and decided to disaffiliate. On the whole, though, his "long-suffering tribe" let Quin go on with his "orgy of ritual." He instituted a Festival of Machines and a Festival of St. Francis of Assisi; he decorated the church "elaborately with evergreens and flowers" for the year-end Festival of All the Dead; and, amid the profusion, most of his small flock kept coming. For Quin, however meager the congregation's resources and numbers, there was a splendor in these rituals that revealed just how religiously evocative a humanistic faith could be.[18]

Quin only became more "Catholic" in practice toward the end of his career as a positivist priest. Like Comte, Quin saw Protestantism as a source of anomic disorder and recurred to Roman Catholicism as an emblem of the social whole. Hence Quin's announced aim was "positivizing Catholicism"; that is, to take "possession" of its sacramental structure and liturgical art "in the name of science." He became increasingly absorbed with the possibility of creating a "Positivist Mass," a secular

Eucharist that remained somehow "emancipated" from Christian supernaturalism. For that celebration, he added new vestments to his wardrobe and put a large crucifix over the altar (a particularly incongruous innovation since Comte had enshrined Paul, not Jesus, in his pantheon of historical saints). Explicitly following Catholic precedent again, Quin even "provided a receptacle in the altar for a 'relic,' the relic which I chose and placed in it was an original copy of one of Comte's 'Annual Circulars,' which he had despatched with his own hands." The paradoxes in all these borrowings were hard to plumb. What power did this associative relic, an autograph document touched by Comte himself, have for a religious positivist like Quin? Was it any wonder that "a thinking Freethinker" in his congregation decided that all these ceremonial additions had finally gone too far and stopped attending the church? Was it at all surprising that many of his secularist comrades would conclude that Quin had failed at secularism, that what was on display in Newcastle was not a religion of demonstrable science but a humanistic simulation of Catholicism, that his imaginative synthesis was a confused mess? Most unbelievers remained highly skeptical of Quin's conviction that the liturgical arts of Christianity were too important to be left to believers alone.[19]

Quin carried on his ritualistic experiments for a generation in Newcastle, but he was never able to extend his "apostolate" much beyond that. In the late 1890s he tried his hand at missionary work, concocting "a little portable altar" to take on the road and inviting the curious to come to his services. He won few converts in his itinerancy. "The harvest," he confessed, "was an exceedingly scanty one." Quin had taken the templates that Comte and Congreve had provided and run with them, but he was never able to make religious positivism into anything more than an idiosyncratic sect. In 1910, he finally closed his church for good with a feeling of "dreary resignation"; he sold the organ to a local convent; his vestments and altar decorations went to St. Dominic's Priory; the sculptural busts were donated to a grammar school; and the site itself was repurposed for a synagogue. Two years later, adrift with no positivist community left for him to pastor, Quin went "on pilgrimage" to France to retrace Comte's life from his birthplace to his grave. Along the way he stopped in Paris at "the empty Positivist church" there, which had been built on the site where Clotilde de Vaux had lived and died—another temple of humanity with a thinned-out congregation. Quin's experiment with an artful, worshipful, emotive atheism had lasted a lot longer than David Croly's, but both men felt at the end of their lives the weight of failure upon their projects to propagate Comte's religion of humanity.[20]

Few American positivists seriously entertained the notion that secularism would find its fulfillment by draping demonstrable science and ethical humanism in the robes of Catholic liturgy and art. Indeed, among Comte's American admirers, his Catholic sympathies, especially any notion of submitting to a new priestly hierarchy, were scorned, often vehemently so. Wakeman, for example, overtly resisted such elements in Comte's religion of humanity and talked instead of a republican positivism that lined up seamlessly with Ingersoll's "religion of Hope and Help." Wakeman later described this early period of collaborating with the Crolys as "The Positivist Episode"—a fondly remembered, but relatively brief phase on the way to the improved secularism he found in the Manhattan Liberal Club, the National Liberal League, and the Thomas Paine National Historical Association. Indeed, Wakeman eventually became quite adept at downplaying Comte's significance as the founder of the religion of humanity. Like Ingersoll, he preferred instead to link it to Paine as a hero of the American republic—a move that indigenized this secularist faith and diminished its status as a French positivist import. It was, by this reading, quite expressly the disciples of Paine who were responsible for instituting this new cosmopolitan religion, not the disciples of Comte. Increasingly, the very idea of a religion of humanity floated free from specific positivist rubrics and liturgical designs; it became instead an all-purpose aspiration of humanistic secularists, post-Christian liberals, and cosmopolitan idealists.[21]

Courtlandt Palmer, too, had shown diminishing enthusiasm for explicitly positivist rituals; the plans he drew up for his own funeral displayed little obeisance to Comte's sacerdotal sociology. Instead, Palmer's death was solemnized under the auspices of Ingersoll's freethinking secularism and his wife's genteel Protestantism. Not even an eschatological glimmer remained of Comte's grand vision in which the tombs of illustrious positivists would adorn the "sacred wood" surrounding his fully realized temples. Religious positivists entertained a lot of utopian fantasies about humanity's future, but Palmer's colleagues knew better than to imagine that Comte's "final Sacrament of INCORPORATION" into an embowered pantheon of saints would ever come to pass for his American disciples. By the mid-1880s, the First Congregation of the Society of the Church of Humanity was a thing of the past. Congreve, Crompton, and Quin had no obvious American counterparts in sustaining the Church of Humanity. The Crolys had moved on; Edger had left for Europe years earlier; Hugh Byron Brown never published his planned manual of positivist rituals; and G. L. Henderson, far removed from his old New York fellowship, was tending to a lemon grove in California rather than a temple of humanity. Religious positivism's sacramental program failed in the United States as it ultimately did in England and France as well. The movement's ardor for ritual as a humanistic art attracted a dedicated cadre of practitioners, but its liturgical virtuosity seemed misbegotten to most secularists—an "atheistical parody" of Roman Catholicism that proved largely untenable to Protestant-descended unbelievers. If new humanistic ceremonies were to be created, that task would fall primarily to unadorned freethinkers, not positivist priests.[22]

————

Romanus Emerson, an infidel in South Boston, wrote his own funeral address in 1849, three years before it was needed. Born in Hancock, New Hampshire, in 1782, he had studied for the ministry along with his three brothers, all of whom became orthodox Congregational ministers, but he had decided to become a carpenter and tradesman instead. Emerson had stayed in the church for a time as a Unitarian, but he eventually became an outright freethinker after reading Paine's *The Age of Reason.* He underlined his new identity through helping to organize annual celebrations toasting Paine's birthday as well as anniversary observances honoring the blasphemer Abner Kneeland's release from jail. He presided over the Boston Infidel Relief Society and displayed a social reformer's ardor for temperance, public education, antislavery, and the care of orphans. Given his avowed irreligion, he thought it unlikely that his devout extended family would do well by him in death and thus left very explicit directions that there should be no Christian observances surrounding his burial—"that no priest or minister of the Gospel or pious religionist be allowed to speak, address, or exhort . . . during any part of the funeral ceremonies." Only fellow freethinkers were to have any performative role in the proceedings, with one of their number being appointed to read the funeral address that Emerson himself had taken care to write out in advance.[23]

The address Emerson had crafted was a parting shot at Christian theology as "a system of deception and fraud" perpetrated by clerical swindlers, those who obtained a "rich living" preying on the hopes and fears of their fellow citizens. Typical anticlerical fare, it was not a generous estimate of the profession his brothers had pursued, but Emerson wanted to speak forthrightly from the grave. He had similarly negative views to express about "a book called the Bible" as well as Christian views of the afterlife, whether "future bliss" or "eternal damnation." Death was annihilation—he wanted his friends and relatives to know that. The speech had its gentler moments in its philanthropic invocation of the golden rule and "universal brotherhood," but it was not the kind of enlightened funeral address a family overstuffed with Congregational ministers was inclined to let stand. His freethinking friends, however strong their objections, conceded to the family's wishes. The reading of Emerson's address "*was prohibited*"; the service was moved into Hawes Place Church; a minister gave the funeral sermon, in which he noted not only Emerson's honorable qualities but also his "mistaken" unbelief; he closed with a prayer over the deceased. Emerson had done all he could to make sure he received a wholly secular funeral, led by a "well-disposed freethinker," but his plans came to naught in October 1852. His friends tried to compensate for this ritual derailment by memorializing him at subsequent celebrations of Paine's birthday, but those toasts hardly reversed the indignity of his canceled funeral address and his preempted wishes about keeping the ceremony out of the hands of the clergy.[24]

A generation later, the chances of pulling off a secular funeral were much improved. In the British freethinker G. W. Foote's compendium *Infidel Death-Beds*, the first American imprint of which appeared in 1892, the hopefulness was plain. Not only were the Christian bugaboos about Paine's death—the horror stories of fear, suffering, and recantation—gradually losing their force through repeated refutation, but also new stories about the composed deaths of more recent freethinkers, such as Courtlandt Palmer, had begun to displace the old canards. Foote found cause for optimism as well in how many infidel funerals were now being conducted free of the Christian intrusions that had marred Palmer's (and Romanus Emerson's). "Every week the Freethought journals report quietly, and as a matter of course, the peaceful end of 'infidels' who, having lived without hypocrisy, have died without fear," Foote observed. "They are frequently buried by their heterodox friends, and never a week passes without the Secular Burial Service, or some other appropriate words, being read by sceptics over a sceptic's grave." Foote was right about that development. While in the 1850s there were no recognizable forms for the funerals of infidels, by the 1890s there were several possibilities at hand for freethinkers. "Forty years ago," a self-described liberal in Ridgeway, New York, wrote in 1892, "Secular funerals were impossible. But the world moves." Indeed, the *Truth Seeker* tracked their spread in small towns and big cities: Petaluma, California; St. Louis, Missouri; Delphos, Ohio; San Antonio, Texas; Rogers, Arkansas. The paper monitored their growth globally as well—in Canada, England, Belgium, Spain, and France. At the International Freethought Congress, held in Madrid in October 1892, "secular funerals" had even become their own agenda item. Seeing these rites as "the proper thing" for freethinkers, the delegates urged them "upon the different nations." Among the things secularism clearly stood for by the end of the nineteenth century were distinct "secularist ceremonies," particularly "secular funerals," the ritualizing of an infidel way of death and interment.[25]

the form

Foote's commentary pointed to "the Secular Burial Service" as a leading resource that had made it easier for skeptics to memorialize their own with an appropriate funeral. Austin Holyoake, the younger brother of George Holyoake, had first published that text in 1868 in the *National Reformer*, a freethought journal associated with the renowned atheist Charles Bradlaugh. Within the year, Holyoake's service was circulating as an eight-page pamphlet under the title *Secular Ceremonies: A Burial Service*—a one-penny, pocket-size reference for conducting a suitably secular funeral. Then in 1871, Holyoake included it in *The Secularist's Manual of Songs and Ceremonies*, a joint production with his compatriot Charles Watts, a collection that Bradlaugh heralded as "the first of its kind" for unbelievers. That compilation, already in its fourth edition by 1877, became a standard guide for secularists invested in creating ceremonial alternatives to prevailing Christian practices. Significant portions of it, including Holyoake's burial service, were included in D. M. Bennett's *The Truth Seeker Collection of Forms, Hymns, and Recitations* (1877), which constituted the first American manual of rites and ceremonies designed "for the use of liberals." In the next decade additional entrants emerged for burying freethinkers—a service by Charles Watts, one by George Hill, still others that favored cribbing the various elegies given by Robert Ingersoll as oratorical templates. Also, among the new materials was A. R. Ayres's *A Secular Funeral and Marriage Hand-Book* (1886), a collection produced for the Society of Moralists in Hannibal, Missouri, and promoted as a ritual tool for freethinkers across the country. With such resources, secularists sought to wrest the ceremonial supervision of death and burial from the hands of the clergy.[26]

Compared with Comte's religion of humanity, there was a sparing frugality to secularist ritual as it emerged in these Anglo-American freethought circles. These were rites driven first and foremost by what was left out. As the itinerant lecturer and convicted blasphemer C. B. Reynolds observed of a funeral he conducted in 1889 for a young woman from an infidel family in North Dakota, "Many for the first time witnessed a burial service without priest, parson, or prayer; without Bible or any reference to God, Christ, heaven, or hell." It was the absence of such allusions and such authorities that marked the secularity of Austin Holyoake's initial experiments; "secular ceremonies" were defined by what they eschewed: scripture, hymns, and clergy. As would other freethinking officiants, Holyoake relied entirely on words to frame the ritual; there were no prescribed gestures, no rubrics for the orchestration of grief or burial, and no visual imagery or special dress, only a short oration framing death from "a Secular point of view." What Holyoake offered, in effect, was a secularist substitute for a Protestant minister's funeral sermon. The deceased was praised for having "fought the good fight of Free Inquiry," for being firmly committed to the "religion . . . of this world—the service of humanity," for being free of "sacred Scripture" and "ancient Church." Also, the ceremony presumed that the memorialized freethinker had exemplified the tranquility and intransigence of the infidel's model deathbed scene. As the hour of death approached, "the principles of Secularism" had been triumphantly and serenely maintained, yet another reproof of all those Christian tales that featured unbelievers trembling with terror when faced with their mortality. It was a point that Austin Holyoake made not only in his burial service but also at his own death, in 1874, dictating for publication his final thoughts from the sickroom—a testimonial to his continued refusal of Christian belief and his "perfect mental repose" to the very end. No God, no heaven, no hell, no Bible, no pastor, no problem—that was, for Holyoake and company, the secularist way of dying and being buried.[27]

Austin Holyoake insisted that his Secular Burial Service stemmed from a desire to console the sorrowing, intensified by his own hard experience with bereavement, but his words dwelled on duty and resignation, not feelings of loss or anguish. Bradlaugh had presented Holyoake's service as a necessary secularist device, a way to manage emotions by providing a formulaic text to anchor a grieving speaker: "The last funeral I attended—in which emotion prevented me from completing my address at the grave—convinced me of the need to have some form of words always at hand for such occasions," Bradlaugh explained in his preface to *The Secularist's Manual*. One critic, looking over the liturgical efforts of Holyoake and Watts, concluded that they had "succeeded in excluding every element of sentiment and imagination from their solemn ceremonies." Indeed, unlike the affective ideal of religious positivists, emotional austerity was frequently the point of secularist funerals. "From the blank chaos of the past we spring into existence like a bubble on the ocean," explained the author of "Form 2" for funerals in *The Truth Seeker Collection*. "The earth we tread is a vast cemetery: . . . According to scientific speculation the whole surface of the globe has been dug over one hundred and twenty-eight times to bury its dead." Submitting to inexorable realities, banishing superstitious fears, while yet living virtuously and laboring for humanity's future—these were the values that secularists extolled as they bid their final farewells. If they allowed a "romantic" or "spiritual" crack in this edifice of enlightened rationality, it usually came through an agnostic incomprehension about any world beyond this one. Since they could know nothing about a future existence one way or another, they did not necessarily have to negate it. "Improbability does not imply impossibility," so went a line in one of George Holyoake's "secularist ceremonies" for the dead.[28]

Secularists were certainly in earnest about providing themselves with "a true Secular liturgy," but how far did their functional, down-to-earth substitutions take them in finding "ritual
answers" to Christianity? A closer look at the work of A. R.
Ayres and the community of freethinkers in Hannibal, Missouri, provides some specificity to how these efforts worked out
in local practice. In October 1875, a small group of about a dozen
liberals began meeting in that Mississippi River town. Struggling "against an overwhelming current of orthodoxy," they
called themselves the Society of Moralists. They gained enough
traction over the next few years that they decided in 1881 to incorporate the larger Association of Moralists, with the ambition
of attracting members well beyond their immediate environs
and creating other local societies. At its peak, the fellowship in
Hannibal had about forty members, and the larger association
claimed about twelve hundred members around the country.
Dedicated to free inquiry, mutual support, and philanthropic
benevolence, the Association of Moralists remained agnostic
on questions about the existence of God and a future life; by
leaving certain questions open, they hoped that they would be
able to appeal to "all classes of Liberals." The fledgling organization pledged itself to helping the orphaned, the sick, and the
destitute, but its most specific object was providing secular
burials for its members upon their death and for anyone else
who desired such a rite.[29]

A. R. Ayres, a physician and pharmacist well respected in
town despite his heterodoxy, led the Society of Moralists in its
weekly Sunday meetings, served as its treasurer, and became its
chief officiant. When called upon to perform "a strictly secular
funeral" for a local farmer in 1882, Ayres relied on selections
from *The Truth Seeker Collection*, which he personalized by adding a brief life-sketch of the deceased. Over the next few years,

he compiled his own manual, *A Secular Funeral and Marriage Hand-Book*, which received favorable notice in the *Index*, the *Boston Investigator*, and the *Truth Seeker*, the three major freethought journals of the era. Ayres's collection, especially the way he orchestrated secular funerals, became the trademark of these associated moralists (the offering of secular marriages was hardly a footnote by comparison). As the group's secretary averred, "A well conducted Secular funeral does more to elevate and advance the cause than can possibly be done in any other way."[30]

Ayres's Universal Secular Funeral Service included eight concise elegiac sections, plus a collection of sixteen hymns, poems, and meditations, which could be used in combination with the short addresses or spoken separately at the grave. The first section framed the secularist inclination for ritual in an anthropological universalism—that everyone, even freethinkers, must have their hallowed ceremonies: "The funeral rite is a natural sacrament which has been observed in some form by all people, even barbarians, from the earliest periods of the world's history; and we are assembled here to-day in accordance with an impulse as universal as the human race." The second and fourth sections insisted that the secularist had been emancipated from all superstitious fears of hell and damnation but could yet hold out an agnostic's hope that there might be some undetermined future life beyond the grave—just not one "indebted to any priesthood, to any church, or to any book." The third, fifth, and sixth sections stressed serene resignation in the face of death's grim inevitability alongside the imperative to live nonetheless with conscientious moral purpose and humanitarian resolve. The final two parts then added some age-specific reflections on the death of a child or an old person. The hymns and short meditations echoed the same scripts. Once at the grave, the assembled secularists usually closed on a note of earthly splendor by invoking the natural landscape that surrounded them: "With changing clouds and changeless stars; with grass, with trees and birds; with leaf and bud; with flowers and blossoming vines; with all the sweet influences of nature, we leave our dead. Farewell." Ridding itself of scripture and Christian liturgical forms, Ayres's compendium provided freethinkers with twenty-five pages of "valuable hints and suggestions of the most sensible kind" for arranging a strictly secular funeral.[31]

For a very modest volume from an unassuming little society, *A Secular Funeral and Marriage Hand-Book* nonetheless got put to good use. Mary G. Trabue, a youthful freethinker in Hannibal, wrote to the *Boston Investigator* in July 1886, to relate how her family had already (sadly enough) employed Ayres's new guide twice. "My little brother, Jo Trabue, died, and we buried him with the form set down in the book; and my uncle, Robert Trabue died, and we buried him by the book." Ayres became known as the go-to local officiant for secular funerals—the one to call upon to conduct ceremonies in "his usual dignified manner" when "a lifelong Agnostic" required memorializing. His ceremonial blueprint ended up traveling widely, frequently cropping up in accounts of secular funerals far from northeast Missouri: for example, in Pittsburgh, Pennsylvania; Marion, Ohio; Nipomo, California; Ridgeway, New York; and Washington, DC. An old freethinker in Ashland, Oregon, wrote for a copy of Ayres's book in 1890, knowing that he was "liable to pass in my checks" all too soon. "I do not want any preaching over me, for they will be sure to lie about me," he explained of his need for the handbook. The same sense of urgency motivated a Michigan freethinker; he had been sick for weeks and wanted to make sure his "funeral ceremonies" were "clear of orthodoxy."

vs,
Sat NightClub

Such requests were exactly the kind that Ayres was hoping to receive and wanted to address. He had made it, after all, his announced mission to keep secularists from being "buried with the meaningless mummery of priests" and to prevent Christian families from sacrificing the "dead bodies" of their freethinking relatives "on the altar of superstition." It was not an easy errand to perform, especially when family members wanted a minister present and balked at a secular funeral, but such challenges only underlined the importance of the work. "There is no individual right more sacred," Ayres claimed, "than the right not to be misrepresented at one's own funeral."[32]

What success this small Society of Moralists had enjoyed in Hannibal did not last much more than a decade, and that was because of a fault line that they had papered over at their founding. In trying to maintain a quorum when they first organized themselves, the "liberals" of Hannibal had decided to adopt an agnostic posture on the afterlife. That way they could sustain an alliance between freethinking spiritualists and atheistic materialists; there were, after all, only a half dozen of each when the fellowship formed. (It was a balancing act that D. M. Bennett had also tried to strike with his *Truth Seeker Collection*; he hoped to keep a variety of contrarian dissenters working in union with one another but had similarly uneven success.) Even though the two "liberal" camps in Hannibal—the "Spiritualists" and the "Materialists," as they identified themselves— differed dramatically on the metaphysical reality of a spirit world, they enjoyed a certain heterodox, anticlerical solidarity against the orthodox. Ayres was in the materialist faction, and his secular funerals had no truck with spiritualist sensibilities beyond a mild agnosticism about a future life. Still, he considered himself a broad-minded liberal who was ready to work with spiritualists to find common ground for mutual association, even though he admitted growing "weary of listening to discourses on 'Harmonial Philosophy,' and being regaled with wonderful accounts of *séance* experiences." That cooperative impulse worked well for a time, but the strains eventually pulled the society apart. It was the starkly different interpretations of death that ultimately doomed the group.[33]

Already in 1883, one Hannibal freethinker, Frank O'Mahony, complained that the town needed a new association with much tighter boundaries than the Society of Moralists had: "I cannot indulge in the credulity of the Spiritualists belonging to said society. . . . I would just as soon believe in the real presence of the 'body and blood' of a God in the Romish sacramental wafer and wine, as accept as truth the fanciful spook developments palmed off as communications from the dead!" By mid-1887, a schism had set in with the materialists excommunicating the spiritualists and renaming the group the Society of Agnostic Moralists (they used *agnostic* as a signal of their materialist turn, but it was more confusing than clarifying; they soon dropped it and returned to the original name). The reorganized society was still dedicated to its old program of promoting secular funerals, but it had added a new animus—the eradication of "all belief in spirits." The spiritualists objected, of course, and thought the new name a misnomer: this was not a Society of Agnostic Moralists but instead a Death Ends All Society. By 1890, Ayres and his collaborators had gone all the way on this materialist point. They were ready to dismiss the American Secular Union, the organizational successor to the National Liberal League, as not secular enough because it was willing to embrace alliances with liberal Protestants, Jews, and spiritualists in pursuit of its demands for strict church-state separation. As the Society of Agnostic Moralists redefined itself in exclusive terms as the home of "non-spiritual Freethinkers," it

managed to sink itself in a sectarian dispute. Like those devotees of Paine who ran up against their own enlightened disci-
plines in consecrating his memory—no, he was not an angel;
no, he was not a saint; no, his relics did not possess efficacious
power—Hannibal's liberal secularists turned reason's regula-
tions on themselves and banished every last conduit of ghostly
manifestations. Whether the society had become "a bigoted
sect," as the spiritualists claimed, or a disinfected bastion of the
fully enlightened, as Ayres believed, was a question that soon
enough mattered very little. The cleansed association sputtered
out of existence by the mid-1890s. Purity had its dangers, not
least that the policing of spirits upstaged the practical matter of
secular funerals.[34]

Although Hannibal's Society of Moralists faltered in the early
1890s, the custom of secular funerals that it had promoted endured. In 1892, a freethinker in western New York named
George L. Pratt proposed a new organization dedicated to "conducting Secular funeral services." He had already chosen the
hymns and readings for his own burial ceremony and had gotten his family to commit to carrying out his wishes; by secularist formula at this point, he stipulated that no minister be on
hand. Pratt's primary inspiration for proposing a new group of
freethinking ritualists and for elaborating his own liturgy was
Ayres's *A Secular Funeral and Marriage Hand-Book*. Pratt per-
sisted in his campaign over the next several years, but what success he had at propagating such secularist ceremonies remained
entirely ad hoc: he offered to officiate at the funerals of freethinkers whenever he could, but his reach only went so far in
the region. However improvised and local, Pratt's efforts clearly
followed some well-established grooves by the 1890s. Eschew-
ing the intricacies that religious positivists brought to their sacramental inventions, secularists like Pratt emphasized a

workable set of ceremonies—solemn, functional, humanistic rites untethered from the Christian ministry and from Christian eschatology. "Don't Let the Priest Get You at Death" was the headline on one of Pratt's letters to the *Truth Seeker*. Plan a secular funeral, and plan it now, or risk a clerical farce in which the freethinker's entire life would be rewritten through Christian burial. By the 1890s, secularism—its meaning, its scope, its import—had been rescripted through the practical imperatives of properly ritualizing death and disentangling it from routine Christian practices. The religion of secularism was, quite tangibly, a way of memorializing the dead, but the Universal Secular Funeral Service it promoted was clearly anything but universal. Pratt, like Ayres or the Holyoakes, was part of a tiny sect, battling its own divisions and dwarfed by Christianity, and the secular funerals that Pratt designed for himself and others remained ineluctably minority rites.[35]

Properly staging funerals remained a preoccupation for secularists and freethinkers going forward, and rubrics from the nineteenth century continued to shape humanist ceremonies well into the next century. When the acclaimed novelist and notorious skeptic Sinclair Lewis died in 1951 at a nursing home in Rome, the manner of his death and the plan for his funeral became news, much akin to Courtlandt Palmer's decease in 1888. A sharp satirist of evangelical hypocrisies, most famously in *Elmer Gantry* (1927), Lewis was an old-school antagonist of Christian orthodoxy in the mold of Ingersoll and Clarence Darrow. Once when speaking at a church in Kansas City, he had infamously pulled out a watch and given God ten minutes to strike him dead for his unbelief—a story that secularists took delight in retelling as a humorous rebuke of fundamentalist yokels. So it was with utter incredulity that his humanist friends heard tales that a nun attending to Lewis on his deathbed had witnessed his repentance and his last-minute confession of faith. They knew that to be another pious legend of the kind they were used to debunking; for Lewis, there had obviously been no wavering from his "naturalistic humanism." The very specific instructions that the novelist had left "for a secular funeral" was further proof of this point—a service "without sermons, prayers, or hymns," to be led by a fellow nonbeliever with no clergy on hand. The story stayed true to the nineteenth-century script in another regard as well: namely, that at the graveyard Lewis's Episcopalian brother had closed the gathering with the Lord's Prayer, thus marring what was otherwise an "entirely humanistic service." Secular funerals in the mid-twentieth century—their ritualistic and cultural framing—still owed a lot to the secular funerals forged in the previous century. That included the dread of Christianity's enduring capacity to spoil the best-laid plans of even the most determined freethinkers.[36]

The entwined stories of Edwin H. Wilson, a leading light of the American Humanist Association (AHA), and Christian H. Roman, an isolated freethinker in small-town Ohio, reveal the persistence of these nineteenth-century legacies with particular clarity. A Unitarian minister, Wilson helped spearhead the growth of humanist fellowships and publications from the late 1920s onward—activities that laid the foundation for the formal organization of the AHA in 1941 and later for the Fellowship of Religious Humanists in 1963. As a churchgoing humanist, Wilson had an aesthetic appreciation of ritual. Like Charles Francis Potter and Kenneth Patton, among others in these circles, he was invested in the elaboration of what he called "liturgical agnosticism." Based in Yellow Springs, Ohio, Wilson lived about fifty miles south of Sidney, Ohio, where C. H. Roman had made his way, by turns, as a teacher, farmer, traveling salesman, and lawyer. Feeling thoroughly alienated from his Christian neighbors—there were seventeen churches in town, and Roman cared for none of them—he had joined the AHA and connected with Wilson. It was the imminent prospect of Roman's death and his quite tangible plans for the memorialization of his secularist commitments that brought Wilson and Roman together.[37]

In the mid-1940s, Roman found himself in the hospital with severe heart problems and a grim prognosis. Told he was dying, he began counting up his final regrets, and the one that gnawed at him the most was that he had done nothing over his six-plus decades to advance the cause of freethought. Fearing the damage that an open avowal of unbelief would do locally to his business and reputation, he had long kept his irreligious opinions concealed from his fellow townspeople. Now, seemingly in his last days, with various ministers stopping by to offer their blessings and prayers, Roman wanted to die forthrightly as a confirmed freethinker. An inheritor of the stories of the infidel deathbed, he needed to make sure that there was no way of mistaking his dying profession. So he decided that he would commission a large cemetery monument through which he would finally "speak my mind without reservation." The monument—and the funeral service dedicating it—would bear unequivocal witness to his secularist credo. With Wilson, humanist emissary, slated as the officiant, the memorial ceremonies would be in safe hands and would surely make plain Roman's convictions.[38]

Roman's heart did not fail him this time; it would a few years later, in March 1951. Still, he wanted to make good on his hospital pledge and saw no need now to wait for a posthumous testimonial. Why not proactively erect his "Agnostic Monument" in Graceland Cemetery and have Wilson stage its dedication "regardless of public censure"? Investing much of his savings in the project, Roman wanted it to be the largest monument in the Sidney graveyard and pulled off the installation in August 1948. The result was imposing: a giant granite block heralding the canonized triumvirate of Paine, Ingersoll, and Cornell president Andrew Dickson White, who was famed for his work highlighting the "warfare" between science and religion (fig. 2.1). "READ THEIR WORKS," the megalith advised. An anti-sermon in stone, Roman's monument declared science the "SOLE REVELATION" and included, true to form, Paine's ubiquitous motto on its front: "THE WORLD IS MY COUNTRY AND TO DO GOOD IS MY RELIGION." On the reverse side, it added Ingersoll's agnostic thoughts on death—a faint glimmer of otherworldly hope that remained necessarily locked as a "TONGUELESS SECRET"; it also invoked the great orator's deathbed as a model: Ingersoll, Roman related, had met death on July 21, 1899, with serene assurance "JUST AS HE HAD LIVED, AN AGNOSTIC." Finally, as his beloved Ingersoll was wont to do as well, Roman slipped in some bourgeois moralizing with his irreligious polemic: "EVILS OF MY DAY; USE OF TOBACCO, ALCOHOLIC BEVERAGES AND RELIGIOUS SUPERSTITION." He wanted his neighbors to know that he could be good—and just as abstemious as a Methodist teetotaler—without God. Roman's monument was, in many ways, a capsule of nineteenth-century freethought put on display in mid-twentieth-century Ohio.[39]

The monument certainly got the community talking, attracting "a constant stream" of curious visitors to ponder its oppositional message. The pastor of the First Presbyterian Church, John W. Meister, devoted a whole sermon to the subject of

FIG. 2.1. The freethinker C. H. Roman erected his Agnostic Monument in a
cemetery in Sidney, Ohio, in 1948, three years before his death, as a public
testimony to his admiration for Thomas Paine, Robert Ingersoll, and Andrew
Dickson White. It became a flashpoint of local controversy and an opportunity
for the humanist Edwin H. Wilson to stage a mid-twentieth-century solemnization
of the religion of humanity. Photograph courtesy of Jane Bailey, Curator,
Shelby County Historical Society, Sidney, Ohio.

Christian Roman's tombstone, which conjured to him a specter
of infidelity weirdly out of place amid America's postwar religious upswing. "I never seriously thought that in my generation
there would be cause for argument with a real, live agnostic,"
Meister preached to a crowded congregation. After two world
wars and the Great Depression, humanistic self-regard paled
before the sterner stuff of neoorthodox faith. Moreover, with
the dawning of the Cold War, there was little room for doubting
God, Jesus, and the Bible without seeming to underwrite Soviet
communism and atheism. Roman's objections to religion thus

seemed, to Meister, "a ghost of yesterday." "The thought tides are in the direction of God," he felt certain as he surveyed the American religious landscape of the late 1940s, so much so that he found it easy to cast Roman's tombstone into the oblivion of the readily forgotten. "That monument, pretentious as it is," Meister averred, "will be mouldering dust when the [word] of Jesus will still be drawing men unto God." Confident in his faith, Meister was no rabble-rouser; he framed the offense, "if not insult," of Roman's monument in judicious theological terms. "Let the church never substitute dogma for intellect; let us never laugh off a questioning mind," the pastor advised those Christians who were "up in arms" over Roman's gravestone. The intellectual tenor of Meister's criticism was lost at least on some in town, particularly on those who talked glibly about "dynamiting it" right out of the cemetery. "For Shame," scrawled a vandal across the base of the marker. The indignation ran high enough that Wilson thought any public dedication of the monument would only inflame local antagonisms and do nothing to advance the humanist cause. He was still temporizing on a public ceremony two years later, much to Roman's chagrin.[40]

After Roman's death on March 15, 1951, Wilson finally carried through on his promise to dedicate the monument and also to officiate at what amounted by then to a significantly delayed funeral ceremony. "I honestly believe that Christian Roman was amazed at the furor his monument occasioned when he was agreeably disappointed not to die, after he had erected it," Wilson ventured at the memorial service. He sought to contextualize Roman's deep attachment to Paine, Ingersoll, and White— the ways these men had been misunderstood in their day just as Roman had been in his community. His eulogy painted these freethinkers as truth-telling nonconformists who were hardly "crass" critics of all religion but instead prophetic proponents

of the religion of humanity. Wilson repositioned Roman's cantankerous, isolating antagonism toward Christianity in the
"positive" light of religious humanism: "Had there been near
here a Unitarian or Universalist [church] or an Ethical Society,
he would have had a home," Wilson ventured. What Roman
had instead was the "company" of the far-flung AHA, which
Wilson was trying to coordinate from Yellow Springs but which
provided Roman little camaraderie amid the uproar over his
monument. Wilson did what he could at the memorial service
to integrate Roman into a recognizable tradition—a community of freethinkers and humanists joined in their reverence for
Paine, Ingersoll, and White and the "real religion" for which
these men stood. Perhaps the surest indicator of that tradition
was the ceremonial form of the secular funeral itself. The "Last
Rites for Christian Henry Roman" that Wilson put together
would have been impossible without that inheritance. From a
passage borrowed from Moncure Conway's *Sacred Anthology*
to a line from George Eliot used also at Courtlandt Palmer's
memorial, Wilson performed a secular funeral in line with
those enacted by Austin Holyoake and A. R. Ayres.[41]

From the funeral home, the mourners made their way to
Graceland Cemetery for Roman's burial and also for Wilson's
belated dedication of the monument. "When Christian Roman
ordered this monument made, he expected not to live. I gave
him on several occasions my solemn pledge that at this hour, I
would formally dedicate this monument," Wilson explained at
the ceremony. "In the name of the Religion of Humanity, I shall
now fulfill that pledge." And thus he did, sanctifying the monument as an embodiment of the nineteenth-century religion of
secularism brought into the twentieth century by Roman's
conspicuous project of memorialization. First, Wilson invoked
the memory of Paine and credited him—as Wakeman had

done—with coining "the phrase Religion of Humanity, a religion whose duty required the service of all mankind." The erasure of religious positivism—the replacement of Comte by Paine—was complete: the religion of humanity was recalled and solemnized under the sign of Paine's philanthropic cosmopolitanism. Second, Wilson appealed to the legacy of Ingersoll, whose this-worldly religion located human fulfillment entirely "in the here and now." Secularism, Ingersoll had insisted in following George Holyoake, was a religion that gives no mind to heaven, and certainly Roman had created a monument that boldly declared an agnostic's indifference to Christian eschatology. Third, Wilson called upon the bequest of Andrew Dickson White, who had also anticipated "a purer and more universal religion," one harmonized with science in the service of humanity. "To these men, the heroes and mentors of Christian Henry Roman, we dedicate this monument," Wilson intoned, making clear at each step that there was a humanistic religion within secularism and beyond Christianity. It was a striking burial service and an odd monument, but the "Last Rites" Wilson performed were also an epitome of the conventions that had been formed for secularist ceremonies over the previous century. Secularism, practically embodied, was a recognizable liturgy of death and burial.[42]

CHAPTER 3

Churches of Humanity

In early 1896 it looked like two of the world's most famous infidels, Robert Ingersoll and George Jacob Holyoake, had gotten religion—thanks to a young minister named Caroline J. Bartlett, who led the People's Church in Kalamazoo, Michigan. A celebrated orator still unmatched in notoriety, Ingersoll came through Kalamazoo in January 1896 with the usual media hype that accompanied his lecture tours. There he met Bartlett and learned all about her independent, liberal congregation—a universalistic fellowship of Unitarian extraction that was ready to embrace the religious and nonreligious alike in a common humanitarian enterprise. "If all churches were like this, leaving the human mind free, and working seven days in the week to make people better in this world," Ingersoll told Bartlett after touring her church, "I never would say one word against churches or religion. If I lived here, I would join this church if it would receive me." Bartlett immediately "offered him the right hand of fellowship," caring not what creed Ingersoll affirmed or denied but recognizing instead their shared commitment to "the religion of character." By Bartlett's lights, she and Ingersoll might differ in their views about God, immortality, and prayer, but they were joined together in the pursuit of "practical religion," which included projects of education and social service.

Ingersoll agreed, and he gave the People's Church and Bartlett's ministry a very public endorsement from the lecture platform. News of Ingersoll's "conversion" quickly ricocheted from paper to paper around the country and across the Atlantic. When Holyoake heard the details of Ingersoll's testimonial, he decided to write Bartlett from Brighton, England, to ask if he could join the rolls as a "far-away" member. She happily obliged that April, adding the name of British secularism's founder to "the book of our church."[1]

Ingersoll's "conversion" caused considerable excitement among freethinkers and Christians alike. Some news reports tethered Ingersoll's expressed fondness for Bartlett's church to a long-running evangelical campaign to save "Pagan Bob" from his faithlessness. Recently, for example, the evangelical youth of Cleveland—members of Christian Endeavor and the Epworth League especially—had sent up "thousands of prayers" for Ingersoll to see the light, and perhaps the Kalamazoo affair was a sign that those petitions were being answered. The rumor even flew that Ingersoll was going to stop giving his freethought lectures—a speculation that was immediately contradicted by the orator's undiminished schedule. More ardent evangelicals, though, never gave much credence to the news of Ingersoll's supposed conversion. Bartlett's church was at best "sorry Christianity"; it was only "a semi-religious establishment" with a woman as a faux pastor; Ingersoll's awakening was nothing more than a "loud profession of humanitarianism," so the *Wesleyan Christian Advocate* argued. "He is willing to join a church provided it believes nothing," the paper sniffed. "It appears to us that the public will find here, not the conversion of the skeptic, but the perversion of 'the People's Church.'" Liberal Christians might be able to take solace in the Ingersoll-Bartlett rapprochement, but not orthodox evangelicals. "This church has nothing to do with the supernatural, or miraculous. It is for the good of people in this world," Ingersoll explained. "I believe that in a few years there will be hundreds of churches like the 'People's Church' all over this country."[2]

Freethinkers were torn over the Kalamazoo episode. They were united in dismissing the "myth" that Ingersoll had wavered in his agnosticism—that was an obvious canard, as illusory and wishful as tales of Paine's recantation. But they were divided over Ingersoll's flattering views of "religion" and "church" that his endorsement of Bartlett's ministry entailed. Bridge-building secularists like Holyoake had no problem with those positive estimates. A congregation devoted to deeds, not creeds, to the promotion of "human welfare in this world," was to Holyoake a model for a freethinking fellowship. That the People's Church had daily educational programs for the poor and dispossessed, that it crossed the color line with its Frederick Douglass Club, that it pursued public health reforms, that it embraced a woman as its leader—for Holyoake, these were all markers of secular progressivism. Hence he was delighted to become one of Bartlett's "non-resident members" as a sign that the People's Church hewed closely to what he imagined the religion of secularism should look like whatever one called it—by turns, a religion of duty, a religion of character, a religion of daily life, a religion of humanity. By contrast, purists among freethinkers wanted to explain away Ingersoll's endorsement of Bartlett's "religion" and her "church." Like evangelicals, they saw her liberal, independent congregation as representing a confusion of categories; it did not rightly fit within Christianity or even religion. As the *Truth Seeker* editor E. M. Macdonald rationalized, "The People's Church is not a 'church' at all, but an association of people for humanitarian purposes." It was a liberal club, not a religious body—certainly, not an ecclesial institution, Macdonald insisted. Ingersoll's endorsement had obviously muddied things up for the purists, and they wanted to redraw crisp, clean lines with freethinking secularism safely removed not simply from Christianity, but from the very notions of "religion" and "church." To Macdonald, these were contaminated words. If not quarantined outright, they at least needed to be handled with far more caution than Ingersoll's very public embrace of Bartlett's church had displayed.[3]

Macdonald's qualms were entirely understandable. Getting free of the church—its intellectual constraints, its Sabbatarian restrictions, its hellfire sermons—was an axiomatic part of the emancipation that secularists pursued. A world without churches loomed as a fantasy of the exalted future to which the enlightened were headed as an age of reason and science unfolded. That fundamental displacement was exemplified in one of the more remarkable experiments American freethinkers conducted, the utopian community of Liberal, Missouri, founded by a lawyer named George H. Walser in 1880. Liberal, by Walser's design, was to be "a town without a church," a place where freethinkers could live together free of the usual Christian harassments of infidels. "It is the only town of its size in the United States without a priest or preacher, church, saloon, God, Jesus, or hell," Walser boasted in 1883, when Liberal had grown to about four hundred people. "You will not hear the solemn and doleful sounds of the church bells here. . . . God is neither known, loved, nor feared here. The people stand upon their own merits; they want no scapegoat to bear off their sins." Instead of a church as a village focal point, Liberal had a lecture hall dedicated to "Universal Mental Liberty"; the community gathered to hear Sunday lectures on scientific topics promoting "useful, practical learning." As with most idealistic schemes, Walser's plans for Liberal were hard to sustain. Its infamous reputation as a godless town attracted unceasing evangelistic efforts to sabotage it; Walser's own openness to "all shades of Liberalism" meant that the factionalism that divided freethinkers almost everywhere soon became apparent in his utopia. Within the decade, the Methodists had taken over the village's freethought hall, and spiritualists had established a thriving camp-meeting ground on the edge of town. Still, Walser's quixotic ambition—to create a town without a church—was indicative of the purist impulse within secularist ranks. Why would a freethinker want to build one? Why had Ingersoll and Holyoake slipped up and endorsed any church, however hospitable its pastor?[4]

Those who wanted to keep organized secularism devoid of churches faced a growing number of challenges by the 1880s and 1890s. Post-Christian dissenters, mostly from within Unitarianism, had come together in 1867 to form the Free Religious Association (FRA)—a group that provided encouragement for a range of universalistic, deed-over-creed ministries like Bartlett's. Octavius Frothingham's Independent Liberal Church in New York City, which flourished in the immediate aftermath of the Civil War, was one bellwether of this humanistic ferment among Unitarian come-outers. The FRA's vaunted "free religion" also helped galvanize other liberal movements. Of particular note was Felix Adler's Society for Ethical Culture, initially devised in New York City in 1876, which by century's end had spawned modest-sized satellites in Chicago, Philadelphia, and St. Louis. The dissident son of a highly regarded rabbi, Adler had taken a leading role in the FRA and saw institutionalizing Ethical Culture as a practical upshot of that group's platform. In turn, one of Adler's early disciples, M. M. Mangasarian, left the Ethical Society to found the Independent Religious Society (Rationalist) in Chicago in 1900, one of the most successful ventures in congregation-building among freethinking, humanistic liberals. At the end of his career, Mangasarian struck up an alliance with the Unitarians, but some secularists insisted that they could maintain their own distinct churches apart from such connections. Two grassroots experiments stood out in that regard: Katie Kehm Smith's First Secular Church in Portland, Oregon, and W. H. Kerr's Church of Humanity in Great Bend, Kansas. Constituting secularism as a "church" was certainly a precarious endeavor, and none of these ventures broke any membership records. Almost as a matter of course, such upstart groups were of limited scope—and usually limited endurance, much like the Society of Moralists in Hannibal or the fellowship of ritualistic positivists in New York. That tenuousness went with the territory: the religion of secularism was always a minority practice, a sectarian peculiarity, within a God-blessed nation.

———

In *The Conduct of Life*, in 1860, Ralph Waldo Emerson had uttered a prophecy that became almost scriptural among those hoping to organize rationalistic, this-worldly, character-focused congregations in the decades following the Civil War:

> There will be a new church founded on moral science, at first cold and naked, a babe in a manger again, the algebra and mathematics of ethical law, the church of men to come, without shawms, or psaltery, or sackbut; but it will have heaven and earth for its beams and rafters; science for symbol and illustration; it will fast enough gather beauty, music, picture, poetry.

Like Paine's commendation of the deistic Society of Theophilanthropists or Comte's call for an organized religion of humanity,

Emerson's oracular musings were taken as a validation of efforts to forge liberal, enlightened, post-Christian fellowships—new churches for those who could no longer sit in the old pews. At the close of a lecture in 1891, for example, the leader of the Ethical Society in St. Louis, Walter L. Sheldon, adduced Emerson's words as "the most beautiful expression that has yet appeared in literature" about the imperative to create an up-to-date "Ethical Church." If the exalted sage of Concord could see so clearly the need for a new religious body—one with freshly minted forms of worship and song, one in harmony with science, one intently focused on moral ideals—then surely earnest inquirers who shared that aspiration, whether in St. Louis or elsewhere, were the advance agents of religion's future.[5]

Emerson's hopeful vision of a new church emerging from the ruins of the old came at the close of his chapter "Worship" in *The Conduct of Life*. He summoned that prophecy after an almost apocalyptic judgment of the contemporary religious scene. The Christian tradition had lost its hold on all too many people—"the stern old faiths have all pulverized," Emerson claimed, and his own journey had been one of jettisoning the Unitarian ministry for the philosophical club, literary salon, and lecture circuit. This widespread loss of faith, by Emerson's lights, had led to an unmoored seeking after new religions, the results of which were hardly commendable, certainly not productive of the newborn bards Emerson had anticipated. Drawn into "freak and extravagance," all too many wayfarers were latching onto a host of embarrassingly unintellectual religions, so Emerson alleged from his erudite perch: "the periodic 'revivals,' the Millennium mathematics, the peacock ritualism, the retrogression to Popery, the maundering of Mormons, the squalor of Mesmerism, the deliration of [Spiritualist] rappings, the rat and mouse revelation, thumps in table-drawers." Surrounded by this surplus of religious activity, Emerson nonetheless shifted to counting up religion's massive losses: "There is faith in chemistry, in meat, and wine, in wealth, in machinery, in the steam-engine, galvanic battery, turbine-wheels, sewing-machines, and in public opinion," Emerson observed, "but not in divine causes." Always the master of the distilled phrase, the ex-minister rendered his own experience of disenchantment into a single line: "There is a feeling that religion is gone." Not that Emerson thought anyone should rush rearward to the meetinghouse in hopes of getting religion back. Earlier in the chapter on worship, he had already sounded his essential commitment to religious individuality over ecclesial solidarity: "Souls are not saved in bundles," he vowed. "The Spirit saith to the man, 'How is it with thee? thee personally?'" As the Concord philosopher said elsewhere, "I go for Churches of one."[6]

If Emerson was the prophet of a post-Christian "Ethical Church," he was certainly an equivocal seer. "We must go alone," he had exhorted in his famous essay on self-reliance in 1841. "I like the silent church before the service begins, better than any preaching." Still, it was evident that Emerson wanted to reorient religion and revitalize the church rather than contribute to atheistic demolition. So it came as little surprise that late in his career he threw his lot in with the rebel Unitarians of the Free Religious Association, those who found the denomination's continued profession of discipleship to the "Lord Jesus Christ" antiquated and constraining but who still wanted "to increase fellowship in the spirit." Seeing themselves as post-Christian liberals rather than liberal Christians, leaders of the FRA were mostly cosmopolitan theists who wanted to cull from the scriptures of the world an anthology of timeless wisdom and moral insight. They had tired of the Christian church, even in its most liberal forms, but were hopeful about creating a new church to embody their conception of the pure, universal religion beyond any exclusive revelation. Addressing the FRA's organizational meeting in 1867, Emerson captured that combination of alienation and longing: "We are all very sensible—it is forced on us every day—of the feeling that churches are outgrown; that the creeds are outgrown; that a technical theology no longer suits us." Yet, despite that sense of religion's desuetude, Emerson saw these post-Christian dissidents as gathering together in order "to reanimate and reorganize for ourselves the true Church, the pure worship." If freethinking in spirit, the FRA's leadership had no interest in encouraging across-the-board attacks on religion and the churches. With Emerson, its chief supporters longed for a new church beyond Christianity—one that was intellectually elevating, ethically oriented, and broadly inclusive of theists and nontheists. However much orthodox Christians saw these Emersonian nonconformists as agents of infidelity, the FRA was intent on the work of reconstruction, not further destruction. They wanted to salvage religious sentiments, not savage pious frauds.[7]

Among the brightest lights of the FRA was Octavius Brooks Frothingham, a disciple of Emerson and Theodore Parker, who conducted his heterodox ministry under the banner of the religion of humanity. (Like Moncure Conway, he saw himself as using that phrase with more "spiritual comprehensiveness" than those who embraced Comte's specific sacerdotal designs, which Frothingham dismissed out of hand.) At the time of the FRA's formation, he was pastor of a breakaway Unitarian congregation in New York City that was in the midst of divorcing itself from the parent denomination and adopting an explicitly post-Christian identity. Originally known as the Third Unitarian Society, it eventually settled on the Independent Liberal Church for its name. Frothingham liked to describe it as "a church of the unchurched." While it included those from both Protestant and Catholic backgrounds, it counted many others with "no religious training whatever, materialists, atheists, secularists, positivists—always thinking people, with their minds uppermost." In 1869, the congregation left its old church edifice behind and moved into Lyric Hall, which was used as a dancehall during the week and then outfitted for Frothingham's "religious service" on Sunday. "The first sermon preached there was on 'Secular Religion,' and it indicated the whole character of the services," he later recalled. The liturgical props were predictably minimal—only a small organ and a plain platform from which Frothingham extemporized his addresses; he had already abandoned the sacraments several years earlier, though he had preserved prayer as a form of meditative awareness and focused aspiration. While he retained some Unitarian hymns, he openly demoted the Bible by replacing it with Moncure Conway's *Sacred Anthology* of moral verities and literary gems—an adoption of the "comparative Science of Religion" for the purpose of embellishing and advancing "the Religion of Humanity." Frothingham enjoyed a reputation as a refined, accomplished speaker; by the mid-1870s, when the congregation had moved on to a still larger hall, his audience usually counted six to seven hundred in attendance each week, sometimes more.[8]

Frothingham's self-described "secular religion" flowed from the same feelings of disenchantment that Emerson experienced: namely, that the church had been reduced to "a simulacrum, a spectre, a ghost of things departed, the reminiscence of a tradition." For all too many, religion was now little more than "a piece of harmless decoration on the walls of modern existence." As a preacher, Frothingham wanted to step into that breach and restore "religion" as a compelling concern for those who had come to see it as "an unmeaning phrase." Hence he would no longer address questions about the Trinity, the deity of Christ, Original Sin, the Atonement, or the Bible's authority. "Theological problems interest nobody," Frothingham declared. "My thought is fixed on themes of more universal interest," he explained of his sermons, "that should be engaging to people who have detached themselves from personal associations with all organized and instituted faith." The themes he identified were humanistic questions, all of which retained their significance apart from Christian theology—"the capacities and possibilities of man, the reach of his hopes, the range of his desires, the worth of his attributes, the weight of his will, the conditions of his expansion and elevation." Neither a priest offering the sacraments nor a minister preaching the gospel, Frothingham instead aligned himself with artists, poets, dramatists, and musicians—all those "earnest contemplators of the silent principles which preside over human affairs." Cultivating a variety of literary and artistic alliances, Frothingham made his church into "the haunt of eager, restless, unsatisfied spirits"; it was a congregation of Emersonian seekers more than unalloyed atheists.[9]

Still, Frothingham's church was very much open to unbelievers, even those who were happy to remain such. Like other leaders of the FRA, including Francis Ellingwood Abbot and Thomas Wentworth Higginson, he was explicit about the need to include atheists, agnostics, and secularists under the umbrella of "free religion." He had no interest in repeating "the silly denunciation of infidelity" that still routinely tripped off the tongues of orthodox Christians. His "reasonable religion" bestowed only honor on infidels—whether Thomas Paine, Theodore Parker, or Robert Ingersoll—as "earnest and conscientious men"; a scorned minority throughout history, they served as the "martyrs and pioneers of new thought." Frothingham

nonetheless wanted to rally his most ardent freethinking contemporaries around his particular form of secular religion. Directly addressing the atheists and materialists among his hearers, he urged them to rank themselves "with the affirmers, not
with the deniers; with the builders, not with the destroyers;
with the worshippers, not the desecrators." Like Holyoake,
whom he admired as a fellow apostle of the religion of humanity, Frothingham advised committed atheists not to waste time
ridiculing the idea of God or the "superhuman world" but instead to spend their days trying to make "the material and moral
world what it should be." Ever hopeful about the progress of
society and the individual, he had no patience with an unbelief
that ended in nihilistic pessimism. Whatever label was attached
to Frothingham's "new religion"—"liberal religion," "free religion,"
"secular religion," or "the religion of humanity"—he wanted to
be sure that it was written down on the affirmative, aspiring,
and ameliorative side of the ledger. This much was clear: he
thought that nontheists were right to move beyond Christianity
but that they should retain the comprehensive notions of "religion" and "church" as moorings for their own secularity.[10]

The Independent Liberal Church flourished until 1879, when
Frothingham's deteriorating health forced him to resign his
charge. Members could not agree upon a successor, so the
church wound up disbanding. By then, though, it had helped
establish a model for other liberal, post-Christian fellowships
on (and beyond) the edges of the Unitarian fold, several of
which would take hold over the next two decades. Caroline
Bartlett's People's Church was certainly one heir of the organized "free religion" that Frothingham championed, but there
were numerous others as well: Jenkin Lloyd Jones's All Souls
Church in Chicago, Anna Garlin Spencer's Bell Street Chapel
in Providence, Alfred W. Martin's First Free Church in Tacoma,

and Lewis J. Duncan's Church of Good-Will Towards Men in Streator, Illinois, to name four. The most proximate heir, though, was another New York-based experiment, the Society for Ethical Culture, which was being promoted by an equally prominent leader of the FRA, Felix Adler. Like Frothingham, Adler labeled his society "a church for the unchurched," but it was also a synagogue for the unsynagogued. Over the following decades, Adler's Ethical Society came to occupy a congregational niche similar to the one that Frothingham's Independent Liberal Church had in the late 1860s and 1870s. Indeed, by 1891, Frothingham himself was ready to proclaim the Ethical Society the fulfillment of "the church that Emerson had predicted."[11]

Groomed from a young age to succeed his father as the rabbi of Temple Emanu-El in New York City, Adler came back from his doctoral studies at the University of Heidelberg in 1873 with a grim sense that revealed religion was in ruins and that he could not in good conscience pursue the rabbinate. That decision caused considerable dismay in his own family as well as in New York's wider Jewish community, but Adler was unbowed as he threw himself into a series of scholarly ventures beyond the temple. Over the course of several months in 1873 and 1874, he presented a series of public lectures in Lyric Hall (the same venue Frothingham was utilizing) that demonstrated his expertise in the emergent discipline dedicated to the scientific study of religion. These lectures, which ranged from "The Fall of Jerusalem" to "The Life of Buddha," burnished his intellectual reputation, and Andrew Dickson White invited him to join the faculty at Cornell University as a professor of Hebrew and Oriental literature. That appointment quickly became mired in controversy over whether Adler's comparative approach to the study of religion was subversive of the Christian faith (one of his lectures on Buddhism had created particular concern among some faculty, students, and trustees). When the university failed to renew his contract in 1876, Adler found himself without an academic appointment and without an obvious career path. Returning to the public platform in New York City, he shifted his attention to inaugurating a new form of Sunday fellowship organized around the cultivation of ethical growth and social engagement. Closely allied with the FRA, Adler saw this new venture as a practical expression of the aspirations of that body—"a scheme of local organization" for embodying a universalized religion of elevated moral action. As Adler told his colleagues in the FRA in his presidential address in 1879, "*Ethical Culture*—the building up of character—that is to me the highest purpose of all religion."[12]

In his estimation of existing religious institutions, Adler started where Emerson and Frothingham did: the dramatic decline of their traditional authority required their total reconstruction on liberal, humanistic terms. "No one can fail to see that the power of the church to-day, among large portions of the community, is waning or gone," Adler proclaimed in an address in 1897. "Can the world get along without any institution like it? Do we need some equivalent of it? If we agree that some substitute is needed, then how far does the Ethical Society take the place?" There was the obvious parallel that the Ethical Society gathered at 11:00 a.m. on Sunday mornings, "at the hour when the church-bells ring"; Adler's weekly lecture clearly stood in for the minister's sermon. Sidestepping the Jewish Sabbath and adapting instead to the nation's prevailing custom of Sunday churchgoing, Adler focused his efforts on creating a convenient surrogate for those who wanted to consider "the most serious topics of human interest in solemn public assembly" in synchrony with the culture's Protestant norms of respectability. Also, the Ethical Society was "like a church" in that it attempted to provide ceremonial structure around life passages. Adler insisted that an Ethical Culture leader needed to be prepared to interpret those "occasions in life when new ties are formed, as in marriage, and when old ties are severed, as in the hour of bereavement." Having foresworn any form of prayer and any sanctity in ritual, Adler had only so much liturgical room with which to work to bring "charm and grace" to such ceremonies, but he nonetheless saw it as an institutional responsibility of the Ethical Society to furnish services that paralleled what other religious bodies offered. To that end, he even gladly embraced Easter, a seasonal festival of parading fashion and sumptuous adornment in New York's churches by the 1890s, as an occasion to substitute his own annual reflections in addresses such as "The Resurrection of Humanity," "The Miracle of Rejuvenation," and "The Ethical Interpretation of Easter."[13]

For Adler, the Ethical Society was also like a church in its striving to be "a center of good works"—an ameliorative institution devoted to practical engagement with the needs of the city's poor and laboring classes. Most freethinkers, Adler well knew, concentrated on the massive moral failings of Christianity—from the Inquisition to proslavery theologies—but he accentuated instead a "different set of facts" besides such violent enormities: namely, that the churches had regularly served as important institutions for inculcating such "primary virtues" as honesty, charity, humility, and self-sacrifice. Like Emerson and Frothingham, Adler was not interested in tearing old institutions down—they were crumbling already—but instead in finding a new vessel for his own moral idealism. So, as Adler saw it, the church, at its best, was "a school of virtue," and for the Ethical Society to serve as a sustainable substitute for the church, it

would have to fulfill that role. This, of course, was exactly the
domain in which Adler thought the Ethical Society excelled;
indeed, where he thought his new fellowship surpassed the
church. Routinely caught up in the prescription of right beliefs
rather than the inculcation of proper actions, the churches all
too often strayed from this crucial mission of moral formation.
Easily distracted by theological minutiae and doctrinal formu-
las, the churches resorted to defining the bounds of community
in terms of creeds rather than deeds—a criterion that the Ethical Society was intent on reversing. That deed-over-creed prem-
ise, which Adler emphasized over and over again, became con-
stitutive of the group's identity. At the celebration of the
society's tenth anniversary, in 1886, by which time it numbered
nearly six hundred members, a huge festoon of roses hung
above the platform, spelling out the motto "Deed, not Creed."
Adler built his "church of the unchurched" around a project of
ongoing moral education, self-mastery, and social engagement.
The singularly focused effort to create a "culture" of moral
growth among its members was, in Adler's view, what distin-
guished the Ethical Society and made it "as sacred as any
church."[14]

In organizing the Ethical Society around the ideal of moral
striving, Adler left out a lot that most people would have expected to find in a church. As with other freethinking liberals,
he measured life's meaning in terms of this world alone, not any
world to come; the belief in immortality had become far too
nebulous to provide a compelling horizon: "We must find
something right here, now, that shall give to life its worth, inde-
pendently of what may come after." Hence he threw the Ethical
Society behind a host of this-worldly projects of benevolence
and reform—from housing to nursing—but put particular emphasis on expanding educational opportunities, including the

creation of a Sunday school, a free kindergarten, and an industrial school for "working men and women." Focused squarely on deeds and moral character, Adler abandoned any notion of a personal God—an absence that made many suspect that the Society for Ethical Culture was simply a fancy name for a fellowship of atheists and agnostics. If atheism meant "the denial of a being conceived by superstitious mortals in the image of themselves, a 'big man' above the clouds," then by all means Adler wanted the Ethical Society to be counted as an atheist body. But if atheism meant "the denial of the transcendent importance of morality" or "the blasphemy against the Ideal," then surely the Ethical Society was its antithesis. Adler presented his faith in "the supreme excellence of righteousness" as sufficient refutation of "the charge of Atheism," but he mainly wanted to change the subject—from fruitless arguments about God's existence to the immediate needs of humanity. If the God of Christianity and Judaism had gone missing, so too had the hallowed authority of the Bible. Its revelatory force was dissolved in a bath of historical, critical, and comparative studies. Adler saw the Ethical Society as the equivalent of a church, but it was one without heaven and hell, without scripture, and without a personal deity.[15]

Adler could have claimed that he was primarily interested in creating an organization that embodied a philosophy of ethical responsibility rather than one that presented itself as a religious society. But that was not the path he pursued. "Have we still a religion?" was a question he posed time and again to his hearers in his Sunday lectures, and the answer was always in the affirmative. To make that positive assessment required a definition of religion compatible with Adler's vision, and he became quite adept at delineating the category on his terms. "Religion may be defined to be the pursuit of the moral Ideal," he told the FRA in 1879. Then he added another layer to his definition: "Religion is the going out of the soul toward the perfect,—*the homesickness of the finite for the Infinite,*—that is religion." What was the Infinite to which humans aspired in their obvious finitude, Adler posited, but the absolute moral ideals of justice and love? The "indisputable sovereignty of ethics" was what defined religion. "Justice," Adler pronounced in a lecture on the religion of humanity in 1878, "is fully adequate to be unto us a religion." For those who remained skeptical of his claims that the Ethical Society constituted a religious society, he gave no ground. "It has been believed by some that when we said 'Deed and not Creed,' we sought to abandon the religious issues, we sought to say: Let us confine ourselves to the practical good. But in this practical good is the very substance of religion." Adler saw the line between non-religion and religion as existential. On the one side was a life of aimless nihilism, and on the other was a life of meaningful purpose. When seen that way, he was confident that the Ethical Society had to be classed as a religious society—so much like a church as to be a church in function, if not in name.[16]

All of Adler's chief acolytes—William Mackintire Salter in Chicago, S. Burns Weston in Philadelphia, and Walter L. Sheldon in St. Louis—agreed with their mentor on this point: the Ethical Society incarnated an Ethical Religion or an Ethical Church. When Weston, for example, gave his inaugural lecture for the newly organized Ethical Society in Philadelphia on Easter morning in 1885, he chose for his title, "The Need of an Ethical Religion." Like his colleague in Chicago, William Salter, Weston was a graduate of Harvard Divinity School who had come to see the residual Christian affirmations within Unitarianism as too constraining and who had found in Adler's movement "the promise of a new religion." For those in his Philadelphia audience who saw religion merely as a superstition to be outgrown, who disliked "the very name religion," he was there to resurrect religion for them on ethical terms; it meant devotion to "the cause of personal and social righteousness." As Adler recalled later, it was the "distinctly religious natures" of the "little group of persons" who took the lead in founding the Ethical Society that stood out. "We were not primarily iconoclasts. Neither were we just altruists in the ordinary sense, saying: let us increase the comforts and well-being of the poor, and let that be to us in place of a religion. We set out to save our souls alive." Those "who simply cared for moral betterment" without "this religious feeling" were certainly welcome in this church for the unchurched, and Adler admitted that the word *religion* had "a somewhat flickering meaning . . . as we have used it." Nonetheless, for this cadre of early leaders, the Ethical Society remained haloed with religion and comparable to a church. Amounting to all of 1,064 members, spread over four fellowships in 1890, the Society for Ethical Culture, so Adler and his lieutenants believed, offered a tangible foreshadowing of "the religious temple of the future."[17]

Frothingham and Adler were frequently paired as the leading embodiments of "the radical pulpit." They were generally held in high regard among freethinkers; their complementary enterprises were covered favorably in the pages of the *Index*, the *Boston Investigator*, and the *Truth Seeker*; as much as Ingersoll and Abbot, they supported secularist demands for strict church-state separation. They were, however, moderating liberals more than aggressive activists; they mounted no soapbox and indulged in no crude ridicule but instead occupied platforms that were models of genteel refinement; they were driven by deep regret over the lost plausibility of Christianity and Judaism, not by bristling hostility toward benighted superstitions. They remained fond of the church and the synagogue, even nostalgic.

Late in life, retired from his independent ministry, Frothingham returned contentedly to the pews of the old Unitarian church in Boston where his father had once served as pastor—a sign to some freethinkers that he had "retrograded" and was no longer a reliable ally. Likewise, Adler continued on good terms with his rabbi father—a close relationship of mutual respect despite the son's drift away from the temple and the rabbinate. His was by no means an all-out rupture: "The Religion of Israel," Adler maintained in a lecture before the still emergent Ethical Society in 1877, was the original foundation of "the Religion of Humanity." Frothingham's Independent Liberal Church and Adler's Ethical Society occupied a space beyond familiar forms of religious liberalism—Unitarianism and Reform Judaism—but not beyond the aspiration for a new religion congruent with those ethical inheritances and congregational patterns.[18]

The mediating role that Frothingham and Adler performed—holding onto "religion" and "church" for those who had verged out of theism into agnosticism and atheism—was bound to excite opposition. Christian and Jewish critics saw so much missing from "free religion" and "ethical religion" that they could not see how such projects counted as religion at all. The fellowships that Frothingham and Adler led were philosophical clubs or philanthropic societies; they conducted lecture series, not divine services; they were in no way viable substitutes for actual churches and temples. That critique was fully expected, but the pair's humanistic religion also raised parallel suspicions among those freethinkers and secularists on the watch for any signs of ecclesial deference. Arguing in 1874 that Frothingham's "religion" was "about the same as our Infidelity," the *Boston Investigator* was willing to confer its ultimate blessing: "His kind of religion reminds us of that of Thomas Paine, who we think had about the best religion that ever was." But the next year, the paper struck a more judgmental tone: Frothingham too often pulled his punches, was overeager to disclaim atheism, and used religious rhetoric disingenuously. He was golden when expressing "his humanitarian, secular, moral, liberal, and social views," but he tended to "whitewash" his heresies with vague metaphysical talk in order to "curry favor with Christians." Why not have the courage to let "free religion" stand shoulder-to-shoulder with infidels and atheists for "no religion at all"? Adler's obvious fondness for religion drew similar skepticism from the *Boston Investigator*: "It seems very strange to us that a radical, like Mr. Adler, should cling to the word religion, which always misleads and amounts to nothing when used to signify anything else than morality, in which case it is entirely unnecessary." Adler and company kept insisting that freethinking liberals required the moral ballast of religion, but the paper found that an entirely needless concession, an unnecessary contamination of secularist purity. It was time for the word *religion* to be abandoned outright—or, even better, "abolished from the language."[19]

The challenges for those who tried to amalgamate religion and secularism were on full display in the ministry of M. M. Mangasarian. An Armenian immigrant who graduated from Princeton Theological Seminary in 1882 and who served for a time as a Presbyterian minister in Philadelphia, Mangasarian moved thereafter through a variety of liberal heterodoxies. His initial way out of Reformed theology was, predictably enough, through Unitarian influences. Drawn to the writings of William Ellery Channing and Theodore Parker, he found encouragement from Boston's Unitarian leadership to break with the Presbyterians and start his own independent, liberal congregation in Philadelphia. No longer bound to a church building, Mangasarian gathered his fledgling fellowship in "a secular hall" and gradually liberalized his theology through his new "free plat-form." Soon enough, though, he was dissatisfied with the per-sisting Christian elements within mainstream Unitarianism—too much emphasis, at minimum, on Jesus as "the wisest and best teacher." Still, he knew that it was one thing "to part with Presbyterianism" and quite another "to part also with Chris-tianity." When he gave a sermon entitled "Was Jesus God?" and answered the question explicitly in the negative, many of those in his audience grew pained; some left in the middle of it; sev-eral never came back. Mangasarian felt their indignation: "Did I bring them out of the Presbyterian church to make 'infidels' and 'blasphemers' of them?" Most of his members thought they had signed up for a distinctly liberal Protestant ministry, not an expressly post-Christian association; they expected their pastor to be more Henry Ward Beecher than Octavius Frothingham. It was a crisis point. Mangasarian found himself tossed on a "deep, dark sea of fear," trying to find safe passage "from Calvin-ism to Rationalism" but clearly not to dry land yet.[20]

In 1888, about three years after his exodus from Presbyterian-ism, with things going far from smoothly in his independent ministry, Mangasarian connected with the Ethical Society, a branch of which S. Burns Weston had recently launched in Philadelphia. It did not take long for Mangasarian to see the movement as a lifeline amid his vocational struggles. He began inviting the leaders of the Ethical Society—Adler, Weston, Salter, and Sheldon—to speak from his platform, and, in turn, they reciprocated with opportunities for him to lecture at their societies in New York, Philadelphia, Chicago, and St. Louis. By the early 1890s, Mangasarian had abandoned his own congre-gational venture in Philadelphia and joined the Ethical Society as one of its leaders, assuming charge of the Chicago fellowship. Here was the decisive passage out of Christianity; here was the clean break from God, Jesus, and the Bible that Mangasarian had desired; here, he thought, was a fearless and consistent rationalism. For the better part of a decade, Mangasarian felt very much at home in this new "fraternity of lecturers"—all of whom had also set out on a path toward conventional religious leadership before giving up on the rabbinate and the ministry. Ultimately, though, he came to see the Ethical Society as too compromising; it was a way station more than a final refuge. The movement's resistance to "aggressive radicalism," its desire to tame the "wild species" of freethought, began to grate on Mangasarian. As he had during his Philadelphia ministry, he felt increasingly constrained not to give offense. He worried that Adler's version of ethical religion put respectability ahead of candor: "It became the ambition of an Ethical lecturer to deliver only such lectures as no church-goer would object to hear. I do not mean that Orthodox doctrines were promulgated by the Ethical lecturers, but nothing was to be said against them, if nothing could be said in their favor." To Mangasarian, the Ethical Society had become so "harmless" that it essentially served as "an annex to the church."[21]

Mangasarian left the Ethical Society in the pursuit of a bolder freethinking platform—one that was willing to expose without compromise the "false teachings" and "degrading effects" of the churches. Adler and his colleagues did not want to fight over creeds—members of the Ethical Society could believe what they wanted to about God or Jesus; they could be theists, agnostics, or atheists—but Mangasarian still wanted to fight. Orthodox Calvinism had consumed his boyhood and early adulthood; his mother had raised him to be a minister from the beginning and had thus, as he saw it, vastly narrowed his horizons as "one set apart for God"; he was not going to give a pass to the "obsolete and obstructive dogmas" of Christianity.

"Nothing would please the priests and rabbis more," he argued, in another swipe at the "policy of silence" he saw governing the Ethical Society, "than to be assured that the efforts of the new teachers will be confined strictly to giving moral exhortations, and that they will leave church and dogma respectfully alone." Beyond the conciliations of "free religion" and "ethical religion," Mangasarian would lay claim to "a thoroughgoing and uncompromising Rationalism"—one entirely "free from gods, christs, bibles and churches." He would possess Ingersoll's boldness in calling out the "debasing superstitions" of Christianity and Judaism; he would thunder against the inquisitorial instincts of the churches in suppressing free speech and scientific inquiry; he would question the very historicity of Jesus in a public debate with an Episcopal priest. He would honor Thomas Paine with lectures on *The Age of Reason* and *Rights of Man*; he would fight to vindicate Paine's reputation against his latest slanderers, including Theodore Roosevelt. He would extol the martyrs of freethought—from Hypatia to Bruno—and decry the blood-drenched violence of Christianity. He would court sacrilege by mimicking the Lord's Prayer with a Human Prayer for the "reign of Reason." He would not hold back.[22]

For all the combativeness Mangasarian displayed after leaving the Ethical Society, he nonetheless continued to follow Adler and Frothingham in showing a noticeable deference to the notions of religion and church. A lecture he gave in 1894, "The Religion of Ethical Culture," when still a leader of the Chicago branch of the Ethical Society, made the movement's standard case for moral righteousness as the supreme end of religion. This basic gesture of casting Ethical Culture as religion, as providing a church for the unchurched, carried over to Mangasarian's new congregation, the Independent Religious Society (Rationalist), which he organized in 1900. A program for its

11:00 a.m. Sunday morning meeting on November 7, 1907, carried Emerson's familiar prophecy—one fully internalized in Adler's movement as a charter—about the dawning of a new church built on moral science: "No wiser or more beautiful words," Mangasarian observed, "could be found to describe what the Independent Religious Society aims to accomplish in Chicago" than those from Emerson. The utterance was so apt that Mangasarian frequently repeated it in his weekly programs, an epigraph intended to make plain that his own Independent Religious Society (Rationalist) had assumed the mantle of Emerson's new church from the Ethical Society. Much like Frothingham and Adler, Mangasarian pledged that his enlightened fellowship required no assent to any particular theology but welcomed all who were seeking "the religion of truth, righteousness, joy and freedom." The Independent Religious Society (Rationalist) embodied, Mangasarian said, "a *human* religion" focused on this world alone and dedicated to "the *free search* for Truth." Having passed through post-Christian Unitarianism and Ethical Culture, he continued to share in the larger quest for a religion after the loss of religion—a religion within irreligion, a religion of secularism. "It is not enough to profess Rationalism—make it your religion," Mangasarian advised his three children in the dedicatory preface to his memoir. Even in his new public role as an uncompromising freethinker, Mangasarian never set aside his own pursuit of the religion of humanity.[23]

Not surprisingly, Mangasarian faced the same critical questions that dogged Frothingham and Adler. Why was he holding onto the notion of religion and why was he making his Independent Religious Society (Rationalist) stand in for a church on Sunday mornings? "Our Society has been more than once seriously criticized—not by its enemies, but by its friends, for calling itself *religious*," Mangasarian acknowledged in 1911. The skeptical challenges had become so frequent that he made answering them the subject of a Sunday lecture: "Are We a *Religious* Society?" Unsurprisingly, the answer was in the affirmative; the name went unchanged through the remainder of Mangasarian's career, which lasted until 1925. His defense of his terminology was resolutely humanistic: "The Independent Religious Society is *religious*, not in the traditional, but in the ethical and scientific sense of the word,—*religious*, because it is an *earnest* and *constructive* movement devoted to the *Service of Man*." Mangasarian had gotten religion the way Ingersoll, Holyoake, Conway, and Wakeman had gotten religion. Citing Ingersoll's "creed" in his Sunday program for May 16, 1909, Mangasarian embraced it as his own:

> To love justice, to long for the right, to love mercy, to pity the suffering, to assist the weak, to forget wrongs and remember benefits—to love the truth, to be sincere, to utter honest words, to love liberty, to wage relentless war against slavery in all its forms, to love wife and child and friend, to make a happy home, to love the beautiful in art, in nature, to cultivate the mind, . . . to discard error, to destroy prejudice, to receive new truths with gladness, to cultivate hope, to see the calm beyond the storm, the dawn beyond the night, to do the best that can be done and then to be resigned—this is the religion of reason, the creed of science.

Mangasarian's Independent Religious Society (Rationalist) represented the religion within Ingersoll's secularism. When Holyoake took stock of Mangasarian's congregation, he accented the same hybridity of a devout humanism that remained at once emancipated from religion and yet wedded to it: the fellowship, he said, was filled with "spiritual and ethical inquirers" rather than "the children of dogma."[24]

Mangasarian had an unusually successful career as a lecturer to a freethinking congregation. The Independent Religious Society (Rationalist) met in a series of music halls and theaters—the Grand Opera House, Orchestra Hall, and the Studebaker Theatre—all of which boasted seating capacities well over one thousand and none of which Mangasarian had trouble populating on Sunday mornings. Near the end of his secularist ministry in the early 1920s, he would make the circuit back to a more churchly version of religious humanism through aligning his society with the Western Unitarian Conference and adopting its motto of Freedom, Fellowship, and Character in Religion as his own. Curtis W. Reese, one of the leaders of a burgeoning humanist movement within Unitarianism, boasted in the pages of the *Christian Register* about pulling off this rapprochement. Mangasarian, he reported, could claim "one of the largest liberal religious audiences in the world"—upward of fifteen hundred people had turned out for the Sunday service in February 1922 to hear him discuss the new alliance. Here he was, a graying lion of freethought, ready to join arms once again with the tradition of Channing, Emerson, and Parker, the very religious liberalism that had decades earlier led him out of the Presbyterian Church. From the platform, Mangasarian told the story of how he had named his only son after Parker and how he had once, "with all the devotion of a pilgrim," journeyed to Parker's grave in Florence, Italy. Unitarianism had earned his religious allegiance; it was a wholly progressive movement, he insisted—one that had come to identify most closely with its post-Christian heretics rather than with the cautious denominational leaders who had once scorned them. Mangasarian was thus confident in assuring his hearers that the new association with the Unitarians was fully consistent with the freethinking rationalism he had long espoused.[25]

Still, the alliance was at least a partial concession about the limited prospects he saw for his own type of religious society. "We are and should be proud to be associated with the Unitarians," he told his audience. "They bring to us more than we can give them. They have a history. They have institutions." Perhaps it was only the years catching up with him; he was in his early sixties and not far from retirement; he had been preaching and lecturing for forty years at this point. Still, it sounded like a depreciation of his own trajectory after leaving the Ethical Society, an admission that the Unitarians were far better equipped than unaligned secularists to sustain a religious fellowship like the one he had built. He was ready now to rename his Ingersollian religion in terms more resonant with a prominent wing of the tradition he was joining. The title he chose for the address explaining his new partnership with the Western Unitarian Conference was "Humanism: A Religion for Americans." It was one of his last published lectures, and his warm embrace of "the religion of Humanism" made him an express ally of ministers like John Dietrich in Minneapolis and Leon Birkhead in Kansas City, both well-known humanist leaders of prominent Unitarian churches. "Religion is the knowledge of man and of our duties toward one another," Mangasarian explained. "It means service in the cause of human welfare. . . . The one word which in my opinion fits the word religion as I have tried to define it, is *Humanism*." Was Mangasarian now trying to do what Adler and Frothingham had done before him—to domesticate the wild species of freethought with an ameliorative, humanistic faith amenable to familiar "ecclesiastical connections"? Was his Independent Religious Society (Rationalist) finally no different than a Unitarian church? Were such realignments inevitable? Certainly, some freethinkers and atheists thought they could build churches that would stand apart with undiminished defiance: Katie Kehm Smith's First Secular Church and W. H. Kerr's Church of Humanity were two grassroots efforts to prove that.[26]

———

A teenage convert to freethought and a schoolteacher by vocation, Katie Kehm Smith emerged as a leader among secularists in Oregon at a young age. In the fall of 1891, still in her early twenties, she delivered a paper entitled "What Shall Liberals Do to Be Saved?" at the annual convention of the Oregon State Secular Union, which had been founded two years earlier as a branch of the American Secular Union, the descendant of the National Liberal League with its litany of demands for strict church-state separation. Smith was there to diagnose an organizational infirmity in the secularist movement and to offer a remedy. While any number of prominent freethought lecturers had passed through the region during the previous two decades—Ingersoll, B. F. Underwood, and Samuel Putnam, among them—they showed up intermittently at best and built no lasting institutions. What liberals needed was a methodical "church plan" that would rely on settled lecturers and foster sustained community for otherwise isolated freethinkers: "How lonely it is for most of us to hear the church bells ring every Sunday, and see the people going to church, while we must stay at home or roam the fields, because we have no congenial church to attend," Smith lamented. "Is it true that we cannot have churches as well as the Christians?" The different denominations had succeeded in establishing congregations all over the place, and she wondered why secularists would spurn this tried-and-true technique for extending their own movement. "The idea is, to give our speakers a particular field in which to work, and deliver regular lectures, organize Sunday-schools, get up social and other entertainments, as the churches do," Smith explained.[27]

She was not naïve about the incredulity that this proposal for copying the churches would spark in at least some of her listeners. "We need not call it a church," she conceded. "Call it 'Secular Hall' if you wish." But that was not her recommendation: "To say 'Secular Church,' as 'The First Secular Church of Portland,' or 'The Morrison Street Secular Church,' would not sound objectionable; on the contrary, the word 'church' would, to some extent, modify the prejudices some now entertain toward our cause." Out on the lecture circuit, Smith extolled "aggressiveness" on the part of freethinking liberals and was happy to engage in sharp-edged public debate with the faithful: "We must overthrow and destroy the christian religion," she insisted. "We must kill it dead." Nonetheless, she saw considerable social benefit in organizing secularism into a church. Freethinkers needed, in effect, a standing ministry; they needed rooted lecturers expounding upon the principles of secularism from one Sunday to the next; they needed capable men and women ready to "officiate at funerals, solemnize marriages, visit the sick, and take the lead in all entertainments conducive to the pleasure of the congregation." Smith was clearly ready to turn her "church plan"—using "stationary lecturers and permanent congregations" to advance secularism—into a living experiment. "Let such of the Liberals of Portland who will get together, appoint a committee or trustees who will send a call to the lecturer of their choice to fill their pulpit in this city," she advised at the close of her paper. Let them rent a hall first with an eye toward building their own church later. Let them establish a respectable salary. "If you do this I have no doubt you can secure an able speaker who will take his or her chances with you in the venture," she predicted. "In fact, it would be no venture; it would be a success." A little over a year later, in late January 1893—timed, of course, to the celebration of Thomas Paine's birthday—the First Secular Church of Portland was inaugurated with Smith as its regular lecturer.[28]

For the next two years, Smith's new venture certainly looked like a success. She had good attendance at her lectures on Sunday evenings—estimates varied, on different occasions, from a little over a hundred to three times that. She graced her church with an accustomed repertory of discourses such as "Secular or Parochial School, Which?"; "Some Mistakes of the Christian Savior"; "The Christian Church and Slavery"; "Freethought the Fundamental Reform"; and "What Secularism Has Done for Women." That was a typical configuration for those looking to create a substitute for the churches—to organize Sunday meetings around a platform lecture in the place of a sermon; it is what Adler and his colleagues had done; it is what Mangasarian would do. Smith added to that lecture program a "Secular Sunday-school," which met earlier in the day and aimed "to stuff the attending children full of common sense instead of superstition." For that enterprise, she had the help of Nettie Olds, a musician and fellow secularist lecturer, who served as its superintendent. The Secular Sunday school, as Smith and Olds imagined it, would double as a library and a museum; they put out a call for the donation of "books, minerals, shells, fossils, insects, etc.," which they would use to enlighten young freethinkers. Lessons obviously steered clear of God, Bible verses, prayers, and hymns, but they also eschewed spiritualist teachings about mediums and "angel voices"; they dwelled entirely on "this world and the here and now" and not "some other world 'in the sweet by and by.'" Their pupils sang and marched; they did calisthenics; they were divided into groups named for famous freethinkers; they received badges; they recited the moral and scientific lessons they learned; they repeated gems of wisdom from Paine's writings. For Smith, the modeling of a Secular Sunday school was absolutely central to her church's mission. "The future of Secularism," she said, "depends upon the Secular Sunday-school."[29]

Smith had an especially good feel for pageantry and festival beyond the usual platform oratory. Take, for example, the Christmas celebration that she and her congregants staged in 1893, which Smith described with ebullience:

> The festival of the "sun-God" at the First Secular Church of Portland was a grand success. The members of this freethought organization never do anything by halves. The secular church is continually growing in popularity, and on this occasion more than three hundred people enjoyed the programme. The choir—always excellent—surpassed all preceding efforts. . . . I read an extract from Ingersoll's oration on "Bruno," following which came the tableau, "The Burning of Bruno," in which our philosophical friend, D. Priestly, represented Bruno, while W. W. Jesse, president O.S.S.U., and Mr. Spahn, whose happy, fat and "priest-like" face is seen every Sunday evening in the choir, were the two priests who stood, with crucifix in hand, before the dying martyr.

One congregant, Orville Lee, described the scene as "awe-inspiring"—with theatrical effect, the "red flames flashed up around Bruno as he burned"; his "dying agonies" were an unsettling reminder to all in attendance that the orthodox, if they had the power, would gladly "burn some of the Brunos of the nineteenth century," including "our brave Freethought speakers" like Smith. Lee said it was the "most enjoyable Christmas evening" he had ever experienced.[30]

"The Burning of Bruno" was a tough act to follow, but Smith did her best with the pointed address "The Origin of Christmas," on how the holiday really honored "the sun-God, and not the son of God." Claiming the season for secularists, she rejoiced in pagan merriment: "Thousands of years before cunning priestcraft wove the fiction that wedded its cruel God to one of the daughters of men—to bring forth a mythical Jesus—pagans held festivals of joy in commemoration of a well-known astronomical event. It was a beautiful festival. It was a natural festival, and we to-night pay tribute to pagan common sense." Christmas was all the better, in Smith's view, when Christ was kept out of it. "No truth is destroyed, no joy is lost, no goodness is suppressed, because we do not believe that Jesus was born at this time," Smith proclaimed. "So let us be happy on this day. Let us do our best to make others happy. This is the religion of the secular church." There followed a festooned ship named Progress, towed onto the platform and loaded with toys for the children of the Secular Sunday school. The whole pageant ended with Nettie Olds presenting Smith and her husband with a handsome clock, a gift from a grateful congregation. "May you hear this clock strike the hour," Olds toasted the Smiths, "when every orthodox church in the land will be turned [into] a temple of reason." The congregation was clearly smitten with Smith after her first year at the helm. "We consider her the woman Ingersoll of the world," one member effused after her theatrical staging of this secular Christmas. "There is no other *church* in the country like ours," so crowed another adherent, "founded on good common horse sense, instead of God, Jesus, Holy Ghost, & Co."[31]

Smith displayed a similar penchant for secularist festivity when celebrating Thomas Paine's birthday and Memorial Day; she also relished remaking Easter into a spring festival openly subversive of the Christian story of crucifixion and resurrection. She was a better impresario of secularism than Frothingham, Adler, and Mangasarian ever were; she had a feel for ritual and celebration to rival David Croly or Malcolm Quin. Her freethinking spectacles nonetheless proved short-lived. At the end of 1894, only two years into her leadership, Smith resigned from the First Secular Church and left it in the hands of her chief lieutenant, Nettie Olds. Why she left was unclear. There was some financial controversy over the creation of Oregon Secular Park, on the Willamette River twenty miles outside Portland; Smith had promoted it as a summer campground for freethinkers, a festive venue all its own. But funds were scarce for delivering on her elaborate plans for the property, and the accrued debt rankled one of her key members, the church's treasurer. The money problems dragged on unresolved, and her half-done improvements of the park, including a dance pavilion, were left to go to ruin. The financial wrangling over her collapsed plans might have been enough to make Smith shift her focus elsewhere.[32]

One thing, though, was clear: her dreams for Oregon Secular Park were symptomatic of her larger ambitions, which increasingly pulled her away from Portland. She wanted to extend her "church plan" and her Sunday-school model across Oregon, so she traveled and lectured widely, despite her own enjoinders about the importance of having a settled ministry. She was off to Corvallis, Medford, Ashland, Junction City, and Grant's Pass; she and Nettie Olds hosted a ten-day "Secular revival" in August 1894 in a small town across the border in Washington. As a result of her travels, a small handful of satellite fellowships emerged outside Portland; she emphasized the "circuit" in Mc-Minnville especially and worked hard to make sure that church also had a regular lecturer tending to it. Much of her energy was trained on the town of Silverton, not far from Salem; a tiny community of just over five hundred people, it had been for years a stopover on the liberal lecture circuit with its own meeting hall dedicated to "Universal Mental Liberty." By the spring of 1895, Smith identified herself as the lecturer for the Silverton Secular Church, but that new role did not last long either. Setting out that summer on a speaking tour in eastern Oregon, she contracted typhoid fever and died in September 1895, at age twenty-seven. It was a huge blow. Without her leadership, Oregon's nascent secular churches sputtered. Olds and a couple of other lecturers kept the First Secular Church of Portland in operation at least into 1896; the McMinnville Secular Church and the Silverton Secular Church lasted a bit longer, but neither endured for long.[33]

After Smith's premature death, the Oregon State Secularist Society devoted itself to other projects besides her church plan. One of them was commemorating Smith, "the brightest star of the Pacific coast." Her memory had to be safeguarded from the usual rumors of deathbed conversion and infidel recantation—how at the end she had "five preachers praying over her" and how they had pulled her onto the "Christian lifeboat" just in time. She had been cared for instead by a small knot of freethinkers in John Day, Oregon, with no minister on hand; she had "died as she had lived, a staunch Infidel and Liberal." Her friends and admirers had transported her body sixty miles to a little graveyard, known as "the Infidel cemetery," in the Haystack Valley, "an oasis of Secularism in the desert of superstition." There, in death, she would be "surrounded on all sides by friends of her own religion—the religion of humanity." However suitable, the location was remote—more than two hundred miles from Portland—and that distance made secularist plans to raise "a fine monument to her memory" a complicated undertaking. It took them almost three years to do it, but in July 1898, those attending the tenth annual convention of the Oregon State Secular Union gathered at the cemetery where Smith was buried. With ceremonial tributes, they unveiled a marble obelisk dedicated to "A WOMAN WITHOUT SUPERSTITION" and embellished with a chiseled badge of the torch of reason. The monument carried as well Paine's omnipresent motto, the same one that "the wee little folks" in Smith's Secular Sunday school learned to recite in unison for his birthday: "The world is my country. To do good is my religion." It was a pillar of cosmopolitan faith and secularist devotion set up on an isolated hillside far removed from Portland, let alone New York, London, and Paris.[34]

The monument that Smith did not leave as a testimony to her short life's work was a lasting secular church. At the dedication ceremony in the summer of 1898, one of her fellow lecturers, Kate DePeatt, remembered Smith as "a constructive Secularist"—the one who "organized our Sunday schools and churches and earnestly looked forward to the time when they should be organized in every city, village and hamlet in Oregon." Smith had faced many discouragements, DePeatt acknowledged, finding opposition to her church plan "not only from the orthodox, but from many persons who call themselves Liberal." DePeatt urged the gathered freethinkers to carry on Smith's organizational work, but by 1898, there was not much left to administer. Smith's colleagues back in Silverton had started a freethought weekly called the *Torch of Reason* in late 1896; they were in principle still supportive of her ideas about the secular church. The editor J. E. Hosmer revisited Smith's proposal in March 1897, arguing that freethinkers should seize the word *church* for their own purposes. "If we wish to knock the sacred, holy, humbug ideas out of the church," Hosmer reasoned, "the surest way to do it is to establish a church without any of the old mythical ideas in it." Even locally, though, resuscitating the Silverton Secular Church was a low priority for Hosmer and friends compared with other ventures. They were focused on keeping their new journal going, which was in itself time-consuming and costly, but even more, they were absorbed with launching a new institutional enterprise, Liberal University, which opened its doors in January 1897. Between fundraising, student recruitment, and teaching, there would be little to no space left on the agenda for Smith's "church plan." Her hope of dotting Oregon with secular churches, announced in 1891, was dead by decade's end.[35]

The *Torch of Reason* and Liberal University kept the secularist cause in Oregon alive into the new century, but both were precarious enterprises, hard-pressed for money and riven with in-fighting. One of the university's chief agents, Pearl W. Geer, had generated enough interest in the fledgling operation on his tours eastward to entice Thaddeus B. Wakeman, the longtime Paine devotee, to move from New York to Silverton in 1899 to serve as a professor. (Wakeman would then step in as president in 1901 after Hosmer resigned and would also take over as editor of the *Torch of Reason*.) Getting a freethinker of Wakeman's stature to sign on was a coup, but it was hardly a cure-all for the institution's internal conflicts and fiscal challenges. By early 1903, Wakeman and Geer had decided that the only way to save the *Torch of Reason* and Liberal University was to move both enterprises to Kansas City. Even with a new building secured, the change of venue did not work out as hoped. The university floundered, and the journal lasted only until December before being absorbed into the *Liberal Review*, one of M. M. Mangasarian's publishing projects in Chicago.[36]

As the *Torch of Reason* gradually flickered out in Kansas City, it started carrying occasional notices from a freethinker named

W. H. Kerr in Great Bend, Kansas, about his plans for a new Church of Humanity. Like Smith before him, Kerr thought it imperative to organize a church for otherwise isolated unbelievers. "When I see on every beautiful Sunday," he wrote to Wakeman in April 1903, "my neighbors in their fine turnouts going to the various churches, and my children going along, and hear them singing the religious hymns they hear at church, I feel so deeply the need of a church to whose teaching I can subscribe." Kerr stood ready with his own grandly ambitious church plan to replace the one that Oregon secularists had relinquished. He started publishing a monthly paper to promote his scheme in December 1903, the same month the *Torch of Reason* closed up shop 250 miles to the east. It was "Devoted to Teaching the New Discovery and Founding the Church of Humanity." What was Kerr's discovery? "That God is a fabulous being like Santa Claus." The Church of Humanity would be dedicated to publicizing the good news: "Christians, I bid you greeting," Kerr wrote on the front page of his first issue. "I bring you tidings of great joy. Not one of our race is suffering now in hell or ever will."[37]

William Henry Kerr moved to Barton County, Kansas, from Missouri in 1876 as a homesteader, when he was twenty-one, and over the next three decades he married, fathered eight children, and amassed considerable farmland around Great Bend. Persevering through lean years, he built up a local reputation as an enterprising farmer and respected citizen, which made his eventual anti-Christian broadsides more tolerable than they would have been otherwise. Kerr's alienation from his Protestant upbringing had begun at a young age, especially over the practices of prayer and Bible reading that his mother had taught him as a boy. While other evangelical habits stuck— Kerr remained a devout teetotaler and anti-tobacconist his whole life—he chafed at his mother's steadfast piety, especially the way she held onto her faith despite obviously unanswered prayers. Bedridden for several weeks at age twelve after a horse kicked him in the head, Kerr took his extended convalescence as "a good opportunity to read the bible through." The exercise did not have the uplifting effects he had anticipated: "I was often shocked by the ignorance, wickedness and immorality of God and his unfairness and partiality of his judgments in favor of the Israelites, his special pets." Kerr's public schooling had ended in eighth grade, but at age sixteen, mostly occupied with work on the family farm, he had joined a local debating society and honed his critical skills, which he soon turned against his Protestant inheritance: "Sermons, religious papers, tracts, books, all had to go through the debating mill of my mind," he recalled. That same year Kerr won a Sunday school prize for memorizing and reciting more Bible verses than any other youth in his church, but looking back on that feat, he was quite sure that he already had one foot out the door. In another decade, by the time he was in his late twenties, Kerr claimed to have settled into a thoroughgoing atheism, convinced that the Bible was full of savagery and delirium, that God was "a made-up character of fiction," that heaven and hell as much as angels and demons were all pipedreams, and that humans had no immortal soul.[38]

Kerr may well have been the village atheist of Great Bend by the 1880s, but he nonetheless mostly went about his business as a farmer and did not advertise his unbelief. His irreligion only became a matter of public record after June 29, 1900. On that day a lightning strike killed his twelve-year-old son, Albert, during the wheat harvest, and thereafter Kerr's relationship with his Protestant neighbors noticeably worsened. Two preachers came by the farm and offered to preside over Albert's funeral, but Kerr politely declined their help. His family "could not accept any religious services whatever," knowing as he did that "God is a myth and death the end of life forever." Even in his great sorrow, Kerr was certain "those nature truths remained unchanged"; with no suitable officiant around to conduct a secular funeral, Albert was buried without ceremony. "Those who knew him," the father wrote in a poignant memorial ten years later, "will always remember him as an industrious little soldier of the field." Word soon got back to the family that at least a few of their Christian neighbors were attributing Albert's death to God's wrath over his father's atheism. Those speculations only intensified when lightning also hit the family's house and badly damaged it. Angry and grieving, Kerr wrote a vituperative letter deploring such Christian gossip and sent a copy to nearly every newspaper in the county as well as to a number of freethought journals. Published in January 1901, Kerr's "public defense" assailed his neighbors for believing in a God capable of such atrocity and cruelty: "Christians, if I worshiped a God that had been accused of murdering your child upon any excuse, I would investigate the matter and try to find out if he really existed and was guilty. If he did not exist I would cease worshiping him. If he did exist I would repudiate him."[39]

After this public discord over Albert's death, Kerr became convinced that freethinkers, agnostics, and atheists very much needed their own local organizations to support them in their unbelief. To that end, he announced the founding of the Church of Humanity, which would provide a necessary sanctuary from Christian superstitions, teach his sobering discovery of God's nonexistence, and expose all the enormities of the Bible. Not ministers but qualified "instructors" would carry on the work of the church; they would offer "weekly orations" at Sunday meetings; they would promote a variety of auxiliary societies, educational programs, and entertainments; and they would "perform marriages, and christenings where desired, and conduct funerals with appropriate eulogies and song services." A successful farmer, nearing fifty, Kerr had some disposable resources by 1903 and was intent on putting whatever he had into the Church of Humanity. He began lobbying freethought editors around the country for support of his new venture and launched his own four-page monthly paper, which he initially called the *Christian Educator and God's Defender*. (The title struck many as odd, but Kerr thought he was educating Christians out of their idolatry and exonerating God from the barbarities ascribed to him by rendering him as fictitious as Santa Claus.) After a run-in with postal authorities in 1905 that sidelined his paper for six months, Kerr relaunched it as the *Truth about God* and kept it going for a decade thereafter. Unlike Smith, Kerr did not feel called to be a public lecturer. Although the Church of Humanity did meet locally in Great Bend, at least on occasion, most of Kerr's missionary work went on in the pages of his journal, where he tried from one month to the next to recruit new members from around the country. He also acquired an old hotel in downtown Great Bend, in which he hoped to house his own church college—an institution he envisaged becoming the headquarters of a worldwide educational and ecclesial project dedicated to his atheistic discoveries.[40]

Needless to say, few of Kerr's dreams for the Church of Humanity became a reality. The Great Bend Hotel never became a church college, and he never gathered nonbelievers into local congregations across Kansas and the rest of the country. The closest he came was one commissioned disciple named Emil Fredrich in Mount Sterling, Kentucky, who tried to launch a branch of the Church of Humanity in a town of four thousand people already boasting ten Christian churches. "I believe I live in the most stupid orthodox town in Uncle Sam's dominion,"

Fredrich wrote Kerr, describing the very hard row he was trying to hoe in setting up weekly meetings there. Drawn mostly from Midwestern states, membership in Kerr's church stood at 64 people in November 1904. That was after one full year of publishing the *Christian Educator and God's Defender*, with its urgent appeals to join and its ready-at-hand application forms. In another year, membership had climbed to 91; at the end of 1906, it stood at 136 (fig. 3.1). When Kerr called a national convention to incorporate the Church of Humanity in June 1908, sixteen people were on hand, including him and his wife. Fredrich made the trip from Kentucky to serve as the convention's chairman, but this was clearly not the inspiring organizational launch that Kerr had imagined. Nonetheless, the bare quorum of delegates tried to proceed with due solemnity as they drew up a charter and adopted a constitution for their atheistic church. As Article III proclaimed, "All people who learn the two discoveries that all Gods are myths and death the end of conscious life forever are eligible [for] membership in The Church of Humanity." Kerr reported 252 members at that point; Kansas led all other states with 33 adherents; farmer and rancher were the most common occupations of those who joined. Although Kerr kept circulating missionary tracts into the 1920s, the Church of Humanity never got much bigger than that.[41]

Part of Kerr's problem was how doctrinaire he was about his own atheistic formulations for establishing the bounds of his fellowship. He often accused other secularist editors of being too soft on Christianity and recurrently explained why he was unable to fellowship most freethinkers, including any who were deists, agnostics, or spiritualists. As one liberal from Hood River, Oregon, wrote Kerr, "I think there is something too narrow or limited when you cannot let me of the Paine or Ingersoll type into your church. Nearly all unbelievers are much like

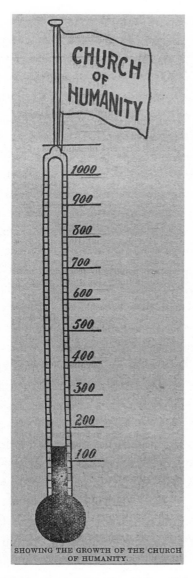

SHOWING THE GROWTH OF THE CHURCH
OF HUMANITY.

FIG. 3.1. The Kansas farmer W. H. Kerr frequently published an image of a
thermometer as a measure of the growth that he anticipated for his atheistic
Church of Humanity. It never heated up in the way that he hoped it would.
"Showing the Growth of the Church of Humanity," *Truth about God* 2
(Jan. 1907): 1. Author's collection.

them." Such unbelievers did not count as genuine unbelievers to Kerr; he required harmony on the fundamental questions— that all gods are proven deceptions and that conscious life ceases forever at death. "Deists and Agnostics like Paine and Ingersoll should have sense enough to not desire membership in the Church of Humanity for the purpose of teaching their errors," Kerr baldly asserted. "If they should attempt it they would have to be promptly expelled." Of all the secularist experiments in church-building, Kerr's was the most uncompromising. He wanted no one to join his association who had any agnostic equivocations or lingering deistic sentiments. At one point he had drawn up an atheistic catechism for the Church of Humanity based on his discoveries; he meant it to be memorized—as much as the Bible verses that had been drilled into his own brain as a youth. This was not a church for those who doubted; this was a tiny sect for true believers—or true unbelievers.[42]

As a cantankerous sectarian, Kerr attracted at best mixed support from other freethought activists and editors. Much of the time his fellow secularists viewed him as a puffed-up yokel, perversely confident in the unique importance of his purported discoveries. That Kerr did not pay appropriate deference to the usual saints—Paine and Ingersoll—only made him more vexing. Then, of course, there was his troubling insistence that what freethinkers really needed was their own church—a contention that set off the usual alarm bells about secularist mimicry of ecclesial foes. Kerr was clearly no Emerson or Frothingham on this point; he actually insisted that his church was not "a religious church," in any sense. That distinction did not compute with his critics. The freethinker W. F. Jamieson, well known on the secularist lecture circuit, simply could not understand why Kerr wanted to start a church instead of a debating society or a lyceum. "I frankly say I do not like the word *church*," Jamieson complained. He admitted that "any person who wants to start a 'church,' or join one, has that right," but he thought it was a bad idea for freethinking liberals, especially in this case given Kerr's stringent dogmatism. Unsurprisingly, Kerr was quick to defend his use of the word *church* from such objections. "It is the name of an organization to teach the people the facts about God. Now that we have learned more about him, we should teach it under the same name." He commended "the church-going habit" as a valuable form of sociability and popular pedagogy; it just needed to be switched over to his church, where people would learn the truth about God's fabrication. Most remained skeptical. The freethinker Singleton W. Davis, editor of the *Humanitarian Review*, found much that was "ludicrous" about Kerr's peculiar project, but he deemed the use of the word *church* especially inappropriate. Call it "An Association of Atheists" and be done with it, not the Church of Humanity. Getting liberal secularists to join a church was always a shaky proposition; for an unbending atheist like Kerr, it proved a well-nigh impossible one.[43]

———

Three years after his jovial visit to Caroline Bartlett's People's Church in Kalamazoo, Ingersoll found another church very much to his liking in Kansas City. "Ingersoll Goes to Church and Finds a Philosopher in the Pulpit" read the headline in the *Truth Seeker* about the orator's Sunday morning attendance at the Church of This World in January 1899. The congregation's leader, John Emerson Roberts, had started his career as a Baptist preacher in 1878. After being dismissed as pastor of the First Baptist Church in Kansas City in 1884 for denying the eternality of hell, he switched over to the Unitarian ministry. He lasted in that denomination until 1897, when he left to launch his own independent church, which met in an opera house. Ingersoll had paused toward the end of his lecture that Sunday evening to offer a testimonial to the dawning light that he had witnessed hours earlier at the Church of This World. "To-day I listened to a sermon. I don't often listen to a sermon," Ingersoll drolly observed. He heard in Roberts, who had spoken against the Christian cross as a benighted symbol, a bona fide freethinker. "He does not strive to frighten you with demons and hobgoblins. He asks you to think, to investigate, to inform yourself. He is a lover of the good, of the right, of the just." Ingersoll was as sold on Roberts as he had been on Bartlett; indeed, Roberts had produced the paragon of the "enlightened church"; he was, by Ingersoll's hyperbolic estimate, "the greatest man that stands in the pulpit in this country to-day!"[44]

However singular Ingersoll made Roberts's ministry sound, it had by 1899 a familiar appearance. That Roberts became a close collaborator with M. M. Mangasarian over the next decade was entirely fitting—two ex-Protestant ministers, each carving out a post-Christian fellowship for those who had likewise become alienated from evangelical orthodoxy. The Church of This World and the Independent Religious Society (Rationalist) were clearly cut from the same cloth. When Thaddeus B. Wakeman moved to Kansas City in 1903 in a last-ditch effort to save the institutional schemes of Oregon's secularists through transplantation, he and his family happily started attending the Church of This World. Nurtured on the practical designs of Comte's religious positivism and Paine's cosmopolitan deism, Wakeman immediately recognized a like-minded enthusiast in Roberts. When a local newspaper editorialized against Roberts's use of the word *church* to describe his congregation—deceptive window dressing for what was at best a "semi-religious" venture—Wakeman rushed to defend the ecclesial nomenclature. Roberts had reached, under Ingersoll's influence especially, "a truer religion of Liberty, Science and Humanity," so Wakeman argued. "Like the Christ of old," Wakeman went on, Roberts had come "not to destroy but to fulfill": that is, to bring religion to its evolutionary culmination in the universality of an enlightened humanism. He "need not drop the names and tools of old religious workshops," Wakeman argued, but was free to "use them when handy." That Roberts's congregants still liked to call him "reverend" was fine with Wakeman, who had long ago substituted his own youthful plans for the Presbyterian ministry with the secularist pursuit of Paine's religion of humanity. For Wakeman as much as Ingersoll, the Church of This World was a token of what the "real church" should be.[45]

Roberts presented the Church of This World as an exemplar of the "Liberal Church" generally. He did not draw a sharp line distinguishing his freethinking congregation from Unitarianism or Ethical Culture; he admired Henry Ward Beecher alongside Ingersoll. Still, he believed in the distinct mission of his church; he hoped that his Kansas City congregation would inspire the organization of additional Churches of This World in other cities and towns. In 1902, he even embarked on an evangelistic tour for organized agnosticism, although it was not (predictably enough) a raging success. He did manage to set up one other Church of This World, in St. Joseph, Missouri, but that did not exactly constitute a Pentecostal fire of church growth. He knew all along that there was considerable prejudice "against the word 'church'" among freethinkers and admitted that he himself sometimes felt "rimmed in" by the designation. For a time in the early to mid-1910s, he lectured instead for a group called the Chicago Society of Rationalism (which was distinct from Mangasarian's fellowship). For many freethinking liberals, the notion of a secular church, a humanistic church, or an ethical church seemed anomalous and ill-fitting—as unappealing as it was incongruous. Roberts had an impressive run with the Church of This World; apart from his hiatus in Chicago, he kept its doors open until his retirement in 1930. But he never put to rest the suspicion that true secularists did not need a church, a religion, or a reverend. They were, after all, unchurched for a reason.[46]

Those involved in this project of making a secular religion—a religion of this world, a religion of humanity, a religion after the loss of religion—kept trying to negotiate an in-between space for themselves, one in which they were no longer Christian but not simply nonbelieving or disaffiliated. They were still something rather than nothing, religiously speaking; they still belonged, but to what exactly—that was an unsolved puzzle. The ex-Methodist minister J. D. Shaw had built a Sunday lecture platform in Waco, Texas, in the 1880s that looked like it fit right in with the experiments that stretched from Frothingham to Roberts. But he labeled the new meeting space he built Liberal Hall and was careful to specify to an inquiring journalist in 1888: "We do not consider ourselves a church." Still, he called his new journal the *Independent Pulpit* and claimed to "feel as much called to preach as I ever did," only now as a freethinker; for good measure, he also announced to the reporter his interest in promoting "a system of ethical culture." Adding to the confusion of categories, Shaw called his new society the Religious and Benevolent Association. So, it was a freethought hall, not a church, but still a religious association; he gave lectures, not sermons, but still had a pulpit. Cutting through the muddle, the *Waco Daily Examiner* continued to list Shaw's Sunday meetings under "Church Notices," alongside St. Paul's Episcopal Church, Austin Street Presbyterian Church, and New Hope Baptist Church, among numerous other options in town, including his erstwhile employer, Fifth Street Methodist Episcopal Church South. Shaw may not have had "church" in the title of his break-away fellowship, but it was not a simple misrecognition that his "Liberal Congregation" ended up classified that way. Frothing-ham's Independent Liberal Church, Adler's Ethical Society, Mangasarian's Independent Religious Society (Rationalist), Smith's First Secular Church, Kerr's Church of Humanity, and Roberts's Church of This World—they all received similar rec-ognition among the Sunday notices in local newspapers. Shaw's Religious and Benevolent Association looked the part too.[47]

Nineteenth-century secularism had its own churches and religious societies, just as it had its own relics and rites. Did that mean that secularism was a religion as leaders like Ingersoll, Holyoake, and Wakeman all claimed at one point or another? On that issue, secularists themselves never agreed, but how that question was answered ended up carrying considerable legal and cultural consequence going forward. For many of those who left Christianity and Judaism for liberal secularism, the no-tion that their humanistic commitments counted as religion mattered deeply. They wanted to be recognized on religious terms—as devotees of Paine's religion of humanity, as ritual specialists who could marry and bury people, as members of ethical fellowships that possessed the same religious gravity as churches or temples. In the middle decades of the twentieth century, such religious recognition would become a two-edged sword. It would solidify the tax-exempt status of their institu-tions; it would sustain their rights as conscientious objectors to military service; it would, in short, offer them constitutional

protections as a religious minority. However, it would also provide conservative critics with a weapon for the culture wars:
that liberal secularists, far from supporting a posture of genuine
neutrality, were actually taking over American schools and
much of public life with a nontheistic religion all their own—
the religion of secular humanism.

Beyond Secular Humanism

In the 1910s and 1920s, Reverend A. D. Faupell served as a dedicated Methodist preacher in Michigan, Kansas, and Colorado. When faced with a choice of going to "Heaven with Moody" or going to "Hell with Ingersoll," he had chosen the evangelist's path. His resolve to side with the old-time religion wavered, though, once he had actually read Ingersoll's works. By the early 1930s, Faupell had retooled himself as an active member of the First Unitarian Church in Oakland, California, where he led a popular adult class that addressed political, economic, and philosophical issues of the day, all sharpened by the privations of the Great Depression. He also occasionally filled the pulpit at his home church and at other Unitarian congregations in the region, but he eventually grew restive with that denominational connection as well and began contemplating a separate form of liberal fellowship. In January 1935, Faupell and a cadre of supporters inaugurated what they called the Church of Humanity, which met on Sunday mornings. Although he still often had his old vocational title attached to him as "pastor" or "reverend," he preferred the simple designation as "leader" of this new society. But what his role was exactly as the head of this humanistic church remained hard to label: one announcement in 1940 referred to him as a "lecturer on sociology and humanitarianism."

The group's name also fluctuated over the first few years—from the Church of Humanity to the Liberal Fellowship to the Fellowship of Humanity, with the last eventually winning out. Initially relying on rented venues, the society managed to purchase its own meeting hall in 1941, a space that it repurposed from local Lutherans. The American Humanist Association was also launched that year, and Faupell's Fellowship of Humanity would become an early affiliate.[1]

That Faupell's new venture was incorporated under the familiar moniker of the Church of Humanity suggested his indebtedness to the previous century's projects aimed at creating a religion of humanity. In the fellowship's first year, Faupell gave a pair of addresses on nineteenth-century prophets who deserved particular notice as augurs of the "new religion." The first focused on Edward Bellamy, whose *Looking Backward* (1888) was a portent of the socialist utopia that Faupell and company were also imagining as a way out of the massive breakdown of America's capitalist system. To Faupell, Bellamy's vision of an alternative to the class conflicts of the Gilded Age displayed the foresight necessary to help inspire the progressive economic programs of the New Deal. The second nineteenth-century prophet that Faupell lifted up was Robert Ingersoll, whom he hailed as "the Forerunner of Modern Religion." Maligned in his own day as an infidel, Ingersoll had actually "laid the foundations for the modern and rational concepts" of religion that were now ascendant among most religious liberals, so Faupell claimed in 1935. Several years later, in August 1944, now enfeebled by a stroke, he managed a final Sunday morning lecture to the fellowship he had founded: "Ingersoll, the Great Humanitarian." Faupell's backward glance did not stop with Bellamy and Ingersoll. Early in 1936 he gave the lecture "The Religion of Thomas Paine versus That of Jonathan Edwards"—the latter standing for arbitrary authority and divine terror; the former for deistic reason and this-worldly benevolence. Paine's example long continued to inform the society. Indeed, in the 1950s, the fellowship would emblazon the old Paineite motto across the front of its meeting hall, the focal decorative element in an otherwise plain interior: "THE WORLD IS MY COUNTRY. TO DO GOOD IS MY RELIGION" (fig. E.1).[2]

The historical inheritances behind Faupell's enterprise explained a lot about the form this emergent fellowship in Oakland took, but there were certainly a variety of more contemporary influences. "The New Era Demands a New Religion" was the title of Faupell's first address to his freshly organized Church of Humanity on January 6, 1935, and newness for convinced modernists always sold at a premium. Faupell took immediate inspiration from the social and religious thought of Upton Sinclair, especially his book *The Profits of Religion* (1917), which offered a proletarian critique of religion's alliance with caste and plutocracy. A prominent figure among socialists and progressive Democrats, at the peak of his influence in California electoral politics in the early to mid-1930s, Sinclair joined the coming economic revolution to "a new religion" of prophetic righteousness—"the Church of the future, the Church redeemed by the spirit of Brotherhood, the Church which we Socialists will join." Sinclair knew well the work of the religious positivists and had even visited "their imitation church in London," and while he found no more satisfaction in their worship than did most freethinkers who sampled it, he did get one thing from them—a name for his socialist church yet to come: "We pioneers and propagandists," he wrote near the close of his book skewering capitalist religion, "may not live to see the birth of the new Church of Humanity; but our children will see it, and the dream of it is in our hearts." It was that passage from Sinclair

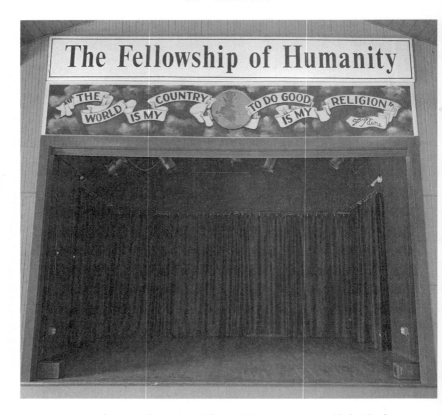

FIG. E.1. A large panel containing Thomas Paine's motto was added at the front of the Fellowship of Humanity's meeting hall in Oakland, California, in 1958, the year after the group won an important court case establishing its religious status for purposes of tax exemption. Photograph courtesy of Grace Goudiss.

that had given Faupell and company a tag for their new church—one that owed a debt less to Auguste Comte's direct progeny than to current social prophets like Sinclair, Edwin Markham, and Eugene Debs, all of whom Faupell lectured on in his first two years at the helm of this new fellowship. When he posed the question to his congregation in February 1935 of whether Sinclair's "prediction of a 'Church of Humanity'" would "become a reality," he was asking about the specific prospects of their new community—whether they would make a lasting difference for social justice.[3]

Depression-era politics surrounding poverty and unemployment profoundly shaped Faupell's Church of Humanity, but increasingly the umbrella designation for a venture like this was "religious humanism" or the "new humanism," liberal buzzwords for the up-to-date worldview that the twentieth century demanded. The signs of the times were legion. The philosopher Roy Wood Sellars at the University of Michigan offered a pair of influential humanistic prognostications about religion's future, *The Next Step in Religion* (1918) and *Religion Coming of Age* (1928), both of which made prior predictions of supernaturalism's eclipse seem almost humble. Sellars became a principal author and signatory of the Humanist Manifesto, the fifteen-part credo of the movement, which appeared in a Chicago-based journal called the *New Humanist* in 1933. The philosopher John Dewey signed the manifesto as well and soon offered his own rendering of an emancipated religion in *A Common Faith* (1934), a resolute ethical sensibility shorn of archaic "survivals" and "madcap ghosts." In tandem lectures in 1935 and 1936 that focused on Dewey's account of humanistic purposefulness, Faupell contrasted the new religion with the old fundamentalism and saw it as the culmination of humanity's long "religious quest." Even among the philosophy's highbrow academic proponents, the revision of religion drove the discussion—how all the religions of the world, in the face of science and secularity, had to be transformed by "a candid and explicit humanism." As the Humanist Manifesto warned, "the word *religion*" itself had been almost fatally wounded by a whole host of outmoded associations; salvaging it required "a new statement of the means and purposes of religion"—the articulation of "a vital, fearless, and frank religion" in which abiding human values were sustained without "any supernatural or cosmic guarantees." Calling for here-and-now "social passion" rather than the "wishful thinking" of heavenly deferral, these religious humanists placed the responsibility for realizing a better world squarely on their own shoulders.[4]

Faupell's interest in religious humanism was always as much organizational as it was intellectual: he hoped that his Church of Humanity would become part of a larger network of humanistic congregations and wrote that ambition into the group's founding articles. In that practical emphasis he had significant company: Charles Francis Potter had inaugurated the First Humanist Society of New York, and Theodore Curtis Abell had launched the Hollywood Humanist Society, both in 1929. Within Unitarian ranks especially, a growing number of ministers had adopted the religion of humanism as their badge. John H. Dietrich led the way in turning the First Unitarian Society of Minneapolis into a "humanist pulpit" of wide influence; one of Dietrich's chief allies, Curtis W. Reese, served as secretary of the Western Unitarian Conference and was well positioned in Chicago to pull others into this orbit; that included M. M. Mangasarian and his Independent Religious Society (Rationalist). Tucked into the Humanist Manifesto was a call for such institutional realignments, an exhortation to harness existing religious associations for "the purpose and program of humanism." The enjoinder came with typical overconfidence: "Certainly religious institutions, their ritualistic forms, ecclesiastical methods, and communal activities must be reconstituted as rapidly as experience allows, in order to function effectively in the modern world." Faupell's fellowship of religious humanists was thus a relatively modest, local embodiment of a more grandiose vision of advancing a new denominational order fully attuned to the ethos of secularity upon which modernity was ostensibly predicated.[5]

The fact that the Fellowship of Humanity imagined itself from the start as an organized religion soon proved legally significant. In 1952, Alameda County officials denied the society's claim for property tax exemption as a religious group. Paying the $330 in levies under protest, the society initiated a court case to recover its funds and to reclaim its religious status under the tax code—that its meeting hall was being used, as the state required, "solely and exclusively for religious worship." The fellowship had prevailed in the trial court, but county and city officials chose to appeal the decision, arguing that religious worship "necessarily requires reverence to, and adoration of, a Supreme Being" and that Oakland's nontheistic humanists failed that test. Finally, in 1957, the First District Court of Appeal, on a 2–1 vote, ruled in favor of the congregation's tax exemption. With a detailed and expansive opinion written by Judge Raymond Peters, *Fellowship of Humanity v. County of Alameda* would become a landmark case for widening the legal definition of religion to include nontheistic groups. When that decision was combined with a similar case decided a month later, *Washington Ethical Society v. District of Columbia*, it became apparent that a belief in God was coming undone as the criterion for determining what would and would not count as religion, at least under the tax code and soon enough in further instances as well. In other words, the courts had now weighed in on a question that had long vexed secularists, freethinkers, and post-Christian liberals themselves—whether their various versions of a religion of humanity should actually be categorized as a religion or its functional equivalent. In the 1950s, the Fellowship of Humanity and its defenders thought it only fair, and only useful, to be counted as a religion. They had taken their stand on "religious humanism" as it had been forged in the 1920s and 1930s, and they were intent on sticking with that religious identification.[6]

The First District Court of Appeal carefully examined the religious claim that the Fellowship of Humanity was making. Much in the findings made the group look a lot like any other church. The congregation met every Sunday morning; it sang tunes from its own hymnbook, *Fellowship Songs for the New Era*; it took a collection; it had readings, even "occasionally from the Bible"; and it had a sermon-like lecture "on a subject of interest to humanists." Admittedly, though, the congregation uttered "no audible prayers" and made "no expressions of adoration of a god or gods" at its meetings. That meant the fellowship's practices fell outside the "commonly accepted" definition of religious worship, which involved "reverence, homage and adoration paid to a deity," including "seeking out by prayer . . . the will of the deity for divine guidance." If the court maintained that "strict and limited" definition of religious worship, Judge Peters acknowledged, it would be in keeping with current rulings regarding conscientious objection to military service. The Selective Service Act of 1940 granted such exemptions only to those "conscientiously opposed to participation in war 'by reason of religious training and belief,'" and the courts had ruled that "sincere devotion to a high moralistic philosophy" fell outside accepted definitions of religion in such cases. Humanistic challenges to local draft boards had been routinely rebuffed as a matter of social, political, or personal conviction, not religious conscience. Indeed, Congress had been even more specific in the Universal Military Training and Service Act of 1948, making it legislatively plain that any exemption based on "religious training and belief" necessarily entailed "an individual's belief in relation to a Supreme Being." To rule for the Fellowship of

Humanity, Peters would have to work around these prevailing
limitations on religious conscience and worship—that commonplace public definitions of "religion" hinged on humanity's
reverential relationship to God. That wider cultural orthodoxy
had been clearly underlined in 1954 with the addition of the
phrase "under God" to the nation's Pledge of Allegiance.[7]

Peters suggested that religion was better understood in far
broader perspective—one that included nontheistic devotion
to cherished principles and ideals. Of course, that was exactly
the sort of definitional move that religious humanists themselves had been making to justify retaining the word *religion* to
describe their own passionate loyalties to certain humanitarian
values and virtues. Among his "authorities in the field" for the
study of religion, Peters relied especially on the humanist champion Charles Francis Potter, whose "inclusive definition" of
religion revolved around the need to recognize "both varieties
of religion, theistic and non-theistic." As Potter observed in *The
Story of Religion* (1929), "The idea of religion without God is
shocking to Christians, Jews, and Muhammadans, but Buddha
and Confucius long ago founded non-theistic religions, and
some modern Unitarian Humanists insist that the idea of God
is a positive hindrance to the progress of real religion." Peters
leaned on that passage and on Potter's expertise to explain the
turn in his legal reasoning, even though academic credentials
were actually not Potter's strong suit. A media-savvy booster,
Potter lacked the prominent intellectual perch that several of
his humanist colleagues occupied: Dewey at Columbia, Roy
Wood Sellars at the University of Michigan, and A. Eustace
Haydon at the University of Chicago. Still, Potter was as successful as any of them in promoting the notion that the scope
of religion required widening to include a nontheistic humanism. Two of Potter's other popular books, for example, carried

the titles *Humanism: A New Religion* (1930) and *Humanizing Religion* (1933). In the 1920s and 1930s, Potter and his colleagues insistently categorized humanism as a religion—a classificatory move that came to constitutional fruition in the 1950s and 1960s. The majority opinion that Peters wrote for *Fellowship of Humanity v. County of Alameda* was an important bellwether of those larger shifts. Faupell's small Church of Humanity had wound up playing an oversized role in that history, the organized exemplum of those bookish redefinitions of religion.[8]

That peculiar role continued when the Fellowship of Humanity got implicated in the origination of secular humanism, what many religious conservatives came to see by the 1970s and 1980s as "the most dangerous religion in America." In 1959, an atheist named Roy R. Torcaso had sought appointment as a notary public in Maryland, but the state's constitution required a sworn belief in God as a condition of holding any office of public trust. When asked to make that declaration, Torcaso refused, and his commission was thus denied. Torcaso had unsuccessfully challenged that theistic requirement in state courts, and the case ended up on final appeal before the US Supreme Court, which decided unanimously in his favor in June 1961. Justice Hugo Black, a judicial lion in the postwar jurisprudence on church-state separation, delivered the court's opinion with his characteristic historical sweep on how religious liberty had developed in the colonies and the new nation. He had already staked out the boundaries of religious establishment in *Everson v. Board of Education* (1947) and *McCollum v. Board of Education* (1948). In broad formulations, Black imagined a high wall of separation between religion and the state built on neutrality: that no laws could be passed that showed preference for one religion over another; that the government must treat believers and nonbelievers, churchgoers and nonchurchgoers, with

Supreme Court

impartiality. Black initially applied those principles to overruling a release-time program in Champaign, Illinois, in which religious education was being conducted in the public schools. With *Torcaso,* he extended his strict separationist logic to "the historically and constitutionally discredited policy of probing religious beliefs by test oaths or limiting public offices to persons who have, or perhaps more properly profess to have, a belief in some particular kind of religious concept." Invoking *Everson* and *McCollum,* Black reaffirmed the principle of neutrality: neither a state nor the federal government "can aid those religions based on a belief in the existence of God as against those religions founded on different beliefs." Maryland's religious test for public office violated Torcaso's constitutional rights to freedom of religion. Nontheists, as much as theists, were protected by the First Amendment.[9]

The *Torcaso* decision might have faded from view once the court extended Black's views on disestablishment to prayer and Bible reading in the public schools in 1962 and 1963. Those rulings ignited a firestorm—far more engulfing than the proposition that atheists were entitled to equal rights and liberties (though that claim in itself remained plenty controversial amid the Cold War). But tucked away in footnote 11 of his *Torcaso* opinion, Black had specified what other religions he had in mind when mentioning faiths that did not depend on a belief in God: "Among religions in this country which do not teach what would generally be considered a belief in the existence of God are Buddhism, Taoism, Ethical Culture, Secular Humanism and others." The blanket recruitment of Buddhists and Taoists to nontheistic ranks was highly problematic—and also entirely incidental in this context. What actual flesh-and-blood groups did Black have in mind? The cases he cited referred to the two tax-exemption cases of 1957—the one involving the

Ethical Society in Washington, DC, and the other the Fellowship of Humanity, now misidentified as an embodiment of Secular Humanism, a designation that Faupell and company had never used to describe themselves. Even Torcaso hardly identified with the capitalized descriptor of Secular Humanism. Although a self-described atheist, he insisted that he was a person of "deep religious conviction"—one who took his religion from the Golden Rule as well as "the beauties and marvels of nature," just not from belief in a Supreme Being. In other words, he was, like Faupell, a religious humanist. Black had picked up the misnomer from a brief filed in support of Torcaso's case by the American Jewish Committee, the Anti-Defamation League, and the Unitarian Fellowship for Social Justice, which included a list of nontheistic groups for the court to consider: "followers of the Ethical Culture Movement, Secular Humanists, Taoists, Buddhists and others." Again, the Fellowship of Humanity case stood in for the Secular Humanists. Black's use of that list made for a strangely consequential footnote. In 1961, secular humanism was a figment, a misattribution, a misnaming, but over the next quarter century it would permeate national debates over church-state relations and public school curricula—and much else besides.[10]

Once *Engel v. Vitale* (1962) and *Abington v. Schempp* (1963) were handed down—rendering state-mandated prayer and Bible reading unconstitutional practices in the public schools— many Christians became convinced that the Supreme Court had declared war on the country's basic religious mores. These decisions were not about enshrining neutrality but instead about licensing hostility toward the nation's majority faith. They effectively established the "religion of secularism" as the guiding educational norm and pared away valuable devotional habits that reflected America's abiding Christian heritage.

Writing in the wake of *Abington v. Schempp*, Bishop Richard S. Emrich of the Episcopal Church warned that it was now crystal clear that "two great religions confront each other in America"—namely, "the Judeo-Christian tradition and secularism":

> They disagree with each other fundamentally. The one honors God, the other ignores Him. The one says that man needs redemption, the other denies it. The one says that the meaning of life is to honor God, the other sees no need of God. The one says that man fulfills his life beyond this earth, the other says that this earth is enough. These two interpretations of life disagree on God, the nature of man, and the purpose and destiny of human life. Now, the Supreme Court has not been neutral; it has, rather, given over the schools lock, stock and barrel to this secular religion.

The United States was now on a path, Emrich concluded, not much different than Russia, Nazi Germany, and China in which the state was replacing God as the ultimate source of authority. That was a very bleak prognosis from a mainline Protestant leader, but that Manichean scenario only became grimmer as the culture wars deepened with the rise of the Moral Majority and the acceleration of right-wing religious activism in the 1970s and 1980s.[11]

Atheists and humanists had focused their legal causes especially on minority rights and equal liberties. Nobody at the Ethical Society in Washington, DC, or the Fellowship of Humanity in Oakland imagined in the 1950s that they were plotting a takeover of the religious establishment. Their claims to count as a religion for tax-exemption purposes were about gaining equal recognition for their minority forms of congregational assembly, that their arrangements of "religious worship"—however different in theology from mainstream Christianity—deserved impartial treatment before the law. Likewise, Roy Torcaso's case advanced the notion that even atheists as a much-dreaded minority were entitled to the protections of the First Amendment, that irreligion as much as religion was a matter of free exercise, that the state could not establish belief in a monotheistic God as a test for holding public office. Also, the run of cases involving humanistic conscientious objectors—at local, state, and federal levels—all aimed at expanding the individual rights of nontheistic claimants: those with ethical convictions not obviously grounded in a belief in a Supreme Being should nonetheless be recognized as capable of the same religious seriousness as those with more orthodox backgrounds. The ground shifted under the Faupells of the world after 1963. Religious humanists were no longer part of small fellowships subject to discrimination, but instead they represented a massive conspiracy to take over American public life and establish their religion of secular humanism as an unchecked hegemon, especially in education, but really everywhere. They were no longer religious outliers looking for recognition of their minority rights, much like other religious minorities of the period, including Jehovah's Witnesses and Seventh-day Adventists. They were the dangerous and powerful enemies of a Christian nation.[12]

The rhetoric became engulfing. The contrast between biblical Christianity and secular humanism emerged as the linchpin of evangelical polemics: Jerry Falwell, Tim LaHaye, Francis Schaeffer, Pat Robertson, James Dobson, and David Noebel— they all weighed in repeatedly on the poisonous effects of secular humanism's takeover of the nation's schools, thanks to a derelict Supreme Court. The attacks often invoked footnote 11 of the *Torcaso* decision to show that the court recognized that secular humanism was a religion and then, with flagrant contradiction, had gone on to establish that very religion as the nation's official religion, the only one that could be practiced and taught in the public schools. As Tim LaHaye observed in his book *The Battle for the Mind* in 1980, "Humanism has surreptitiously commandeered our once-great school system. It has ingeniously conceived a plan to introduce an inordinate number of humanists into government, where they continually advance laws that favor the advancement of humanism and chaos, at the expense of the biblical base for a moral society." Not to be outdone by her Protestant counterparts, the conservative Catholic activist Phyllis Schlafly editorialized in *USA Today* about the horrific impact this "secular religion" was having on American culture since the Supreme Court had "chased God and the Bible" out of the public schools. "Every time a teacher tells a child that he can decide for himself," Schlafly fulminated, "whether to steal, lie, cheat, throw people out of the lifeboat to drown, blaspheme, fornicate, covet, or commit abortion, suicide or euthanasia, that teacher is teaching the religion of humanism. Every time a teacher rejects or ridicules the notion that God created man and the earth, that teacher is teaching the religion of humanism." Anything and everything conservative Christians feared—feminism, homosexuality, sex education, evolutionism, Marxist communism, pornography, Planned Parenthood, the United Nations—was the fault of the demonic reign of the religion of secular humanism. It was, LaHaye concluded, "the world's greatest evil."[13]

Commentators were often mystified by how much moral panic was getting distilled into the religion of secular humanism, how the scale of this phantom dwarfed any groups of actual humanists, religious or secular. It was remarkably out of all proportion—how the mention of Secular Humanism in footnote 11 of the *Torcaso* opinion had metamorphosed from the Fellowship of Humanity into a vast conspiracy of apocalyptic consequence. During Faupell's salad days with his new Church of Humanity in the mid-1930s, somewhere between 70 and 125 people typically gathered from one Sunday morning to the next; by 1946, the numbers ran between 54 and 84. It was said to have 150 members in 1957, but weekly attendance was surely a lot less on average. At no point was the Fellowship of Humanity a serious threat to the Protestant establishment, the public schools, family values, or American free enterprise, even in Oakland, let alone in the country writ large. Likewise, when the Unitarian minister Edwin H. Wilson organized the Fellowship of Religious Humanists in 1963 as a cooperative hub for the heirs of Dietrich and Potter, he hoped to revive the spirit of the Free Religious Association of the late nineteenth century. It was intended as a loose-knit society for humanists who still cared about liberal churches, for those who wanted to be organized and counted as religious. In 1970, it had 594 members. The numbers had always been like this. By the standards of the religion of humanity, Felix Adler's Ethical Culture movement had been one of the big nineteenth-century successes with 1,064 members spread over four societies in 1890. More typical were the anemic totals that the positivist David Croly or the atheist W. H. Kerr managed for their distinct versions of the Church of Humanity. At the turn of the twentieth century, the most devoted Paineites, those who peopled the Thomas Paine National Historical Association, could be gathered in one hall in Manhattan. To be sure, these secularists and humanists shared a universalistic rhetoric about being the emissaries of the all-encompassing religion of the future, but then what sect is not possessed of an inflated sense of the singularity of the truth to which it witnesses? A millenarian fantasy is poor proof of realized power.[14]

The insidious sovereignty attributed to the religion of secular humanism was always far in excess of anything that actual proponents of religious humanism were managing. That gap was on display in the political fate of Walter Mondale in the presidential election of 1984 against Ronald Reagan, the chosen knight of religious conservatives. Jimmy Carter, a born-again Southern Baptist, had been a political disappointment to most evangelicals who rallied to Ronald Reagan's side in 1980 and then again in 1984 against Mondale, Carter's vice president, whom religious conservatives assailed as a card-carrying secular humanist. The son of a Methodist minister in small-town Minnesota, Mondale had married the daughter of a Presbyterian minister. He had grown up with a self-sacrificing, warm-hearted, populist Protestantism and kept that allegiance quietly intact in his public life, but then there was his older half-brother Lester, a Unitarian minister who had been (in a gift to religious conservatives) one of the thirty-four signatories of the Humanist Manifesto in 1933 and had served for almost a decade as the president of the tiny Fellowship of Religious Humanists.[15]

Lester Mondale had left the Bible classes, prayer meetings, and revivals of his youth to attend Hamline University in 1922, a church-related college in St. Paul, where his "strictly Methodist" upbringing began to fray. The turning point came when he discovered John Dietrich's First Unitarian Society, just across the river in Minneapolis, and became enthralled with his humanist sermons. (One of the first and most memorable sermons Mondale heard Dietrich deliver was, unsurprisingly, on Thomas Paine.) Dietrich saw potential in the young Methodist, recommended him for Harvard Divinity School, and urged him to switch allegiances to the Unitarian humanists—all of which combined to set Lester on his lasting vocational path. In the meantime, Lester's mother had died in 1923; his father remarried a couple of years later, and in 1928 Walter was born. Half-brothers, separated by almost a quarter century in age, Lester and Walter had not grown up together, but their fraternal kinship became strangely consequential decades later.[16]

By 1984, Lester Mondale had just turned eighty years old, had been retired for over a decade and a half, and was living in a self-built cabin in the Ozarks in southeastern Missouri. An admirer of the homesteaders Scott and Helen Nearing, he valued his back-to-nature privacy, his studied retreat from "our consumer-oriented society." He did not like the way his brother's national campaigns had been disrupting that seclusion, but his retirement had never been hermit-like. He had remained as committed as ever to his "humanistic gospel," "a celebration in every sense of the wonder and joy of living the good life of heart and mind and flesh." He had remained active in Unitarian circles, published a tract called *The New Man of Religious Humanism*, and had even signed the revised version of the Humanist Manifesto in 1973. Better still, as a longtime exponent of "the glories of the sensuous," he had been at work on a novel called "In Erosland: The Tempting of Pastor Goodfellow Hanson," which, he insisted, was not autobiographical but did represent "a distillation of 40 years of dealing with the erotic side of the ministry." In 1970, through Lester's connections, Walter had agreed to address a congress of the International Humanist and Ethical Union in Cambridge, Massachusetts, with "Critical Liberalism and Social Action," a speech on the nation's failed politics surrounding poverty and inequality. By way of introduction, the Minnesota senator and future vice president told the group that, while he had "never formally joined a humanist society," he considered the tradition an important part of his familial inheritance, particularly through the socially engaged ministries of his Methodist father and his Unitarian brother. It was meant, innocuously enough, to establish some rapport with his audience before proceeding with the business at

hand, but it almost sounded like a cue for a McCarthyite inter-
rogative. Are you now or have you ever been a member of the
communist party or, rather, a humanist society?[17]

Republicans, especially religious conservatives, leaned into
this story: Walter Mondale was clearly implicated in the humanist movement through his octogenarian brother, who embodied a liberal trifecta as a long-time Unitarian minister, a
leader of the Philadelphia Ethical Society, and the president of
the Fellowship of Religious Humanists. Prominent evangelical
spokesmen, including Tim LaHaye, had already honed in on
Walter Mondale's guilt by association by the late 1970s. His humanist connections were used as a sign of Carter's failure to
involve real Christians in his administration; they were proof of
secular humanism's reach into the highest levels of the federal
government; they needed to be exposed. By the fall of 1984, the
humanist charge was a standard part of the rhetoric being used
among religious conservatives to depict the presidential election as an Armageddon: Reagan, the protector of Christian
America; Mondale, the standard-bearer of secular humanism.
As one woman from Indiana put the choice in late October,
"President Reagan is a Christian, and many, many Christians
are sure he is God's man for our time. Mondale has asserted that
he is a Humanist and is proud of it." That belief system made
him "a serious threat to America"—an obvious danger to the
public schools and an ally (in her listing) of homosexuals, les-
bians, pro-abortionists, and sex activists. "This election," she
warned with apocalyptic clarity, "is one between the forces of
God and Satan!" Reagan won in a massive landslide the next
month—Mondale carried only his home state of Minnesota—
but at least one aspect of the religious right's worldview appeared to have gone down to defeat: namely, the theory that
secular humanists controlled the country. Lester Mondale's

Fellowship of Religious Humanists was clearly no match for Jerry Falwell's Moral Majority, Phyllis Schlafly's Eagle Forum, Pat Robertson's Christian Broadcasting Network, or Beverly LaHaye's Concerned Women for America.[18]

Of course, the myth about the hegemony of the religion of secular humanism did not die with Walter Mondale's humiliating defeat. That apocalyptic battle had proven far too useful to be dented by this cognitive dissonance. The rhetorical fog of secular humanism—with all its obscuring effects—would not lift, which meant that flesh-and-blood religious humanists like Lester Mondale were known, when they were known at all, mostly as caricatures: "a literary hillbilly" with a sexy novel to hawk, as the *Washington Post* depicted him in 1978; a radical humanist who had revealed his brother's true anti-Christian colors, as LaHaye and company insisted. It was no wonder that many secularists increasingly wanted to cut through that haze of distortion by denying that there was anything religious at all about their humanistic, scientific worldview. Freethinking purists had long suspected that the new humanists of the 1920s and 1930s had made a grave categorical error in so insistently casting themselves as the bearers of a new religion when religion inevitably savored of "supernaturalism" and "other-worldliness." Religion was "an archaic fossil," "a dubious relic," that had never been worth refurbishing in the first place. Now, given the high-voltage assault on the religion of secular humanism, it was all the more imperative to secularize secularism completely: there was, in point of fact, no such thing as a religion of secularism or a religion of humanism. Such constructs were category confusions that the philosopher Paul Kurtz especially wanted to clean up with the founding of the Council for Democratic and Secular Humanism in 1980 (its name was subsequently shortened to the Council for Secular Humanism). Whatever the new religious humanists had once said and whatever right-wing critics were now saying, secular humanism was a naturalistic, nonreligious worldview committed to the values of democracy, reason, and free inquiry. The future of humanism meant forswearing the church as a model of organization and ending the imaginative dalliance with religion. It was an old freethinking critique of the secularist misuse of religious language made newly relevant by the political landscape of the late 1970s and 1980s.[19]

The efforts on the part of Paul Kurtz and his colleagues at the Council for Secular Humanism to cleanse themselves of religious associations were perfectly understandable in the political context they confronted. Everywhere they turned there seemed to be another Establishment Clause challenge opening up: that the assignment of certain textbooks or novels represented the establishment of the religion of secular humanism; that instruction involving sex education, birth control, biological evolution, or women's equality presented similar violations of the First Amendment; that Christian schools deserved taxpayer support as much as public schools since the latter schools were receiving such funds to promote the religion of secular humanism. Moreover, these secular humanists genuinely disagreed with those religious humanists who held up Unitarian churches and Ethical Societies as model congregational ventures for organizing freethinking liberalism. They had no interest in maintaining the churchgoing habit or cultivating humanistic rites of passage; they were skeptics, rationalists, atheists, or materialists; any religious association, no matter how it was cast, was alien to their secular humanism. Among the many things the religious right accomplished, this was a relatively modest achievement, but nonetheless notable: their assault on the religion of secular humanism drove an old wedge deeper into liberal secularist ranks, marking out a divide between those who insisted on their unadulterated secularism and those who still saw their humanistic commitments as having religious and congregational significance. Secular humanists per se did not exist when Hugo Black mislabeled members of Faupell's Fellowship of Humanity that way in 1961; a generation later, the designation was being widely deployed, including by tough-minded secularists to distinguish themselves from their soft-headed religious counterparts.[20]

The rise of secular humanism—as political phantasm, as church-state affliction, as purist moniker—did a certain violence to the religious history of secularism. On the one hand, it accorded the religious humanists all too much imaginary power; it drowned them in a sea of apocalyptic abuse and moral panic. On the other hand, it encouraged their erasure from the history of secularism once subsequent secularists decided that their religious declarations had been all too costly in providing a cudgel for right-wing Christians. True secularists are pure secularists—end of story. Secularism has a complexly ambivalent religious history—stretching back through Ingersoll, Holyoake, Comte, and Paine; through Katie Kehm Smith, Nettie Olds, and Caroline Bartlett; through Moncure D. Conway and Thaddeus B. Wakeman; through Malcolm Quin and Octavius Frothingham. That mixed history need not be sacrificed to the stark oppositions upon which the culture wars have depended. To include religion in the history of twentieth-century secularism requires moving beyond the politically charged reign of secular humanism. That entails, in part at least, recovering the sectarian distinctiveness and minority standing of those humanistic projects that sought to give secularism religious significance of one kind or another.

The small Church of Humanity that A. D. Faupell built in Oakland, California, was one example of those projects. Another certainly was the Fellowship of Religious Humanists, which Lester Mondale presided over in the 1970s from his cabin in rural Missouri, and so was the Humanist Society of Friends, a group founded in Los Angeles in 1939. It was led by Lowell H. Coate, publisher of the *Humanist Friend*, who was intent on grafting the new religious humanism onto his birthright Quaker faith. Still another example was Dietrich's old church, the First Unitarian Society of Minneapolis, which embraced its historic role as a humanist pulpit and continued to cultivate that congregational identity. Likewise, the Ethical Societies in New York, St. Louis, Philadelphia, and Chicago retained active presences in their respective cities, evidence of a long institutional shadow cast from the late nineteenth century. The Ethical Society of Washington, DC, newly founded in 1944, became crucial, along with the Fellowship of Humanity, in establishing the equal standing of nontheistic congregations before the law. Its leader, Edward L. Ericson, was especially active in the ongoing struggle to legitimate humanistic claims for conscientious objection during the Vietnam War. Such exemptions, he argued, should not hinge on whether a draftee was able to make his ethical humanism appear "religious" enough to count as religion in the face of the Christian presuppositions of draft boards. "Conscience is conscience," Ericson insisted.[21]

Some of the twentieth-century projects took their inspiration more from Ingersoll's old freethinking iconoclasm than from the new religious humanism of the 1920s and 1930s. Through his magazine entitled the *Age of Reason* as well as his organization called the Freethinkers of America, the New Yorker Joseph Lewis kept up all of the timeworn battles against Bible stories, priestly impostures, and fetishistic superstitions. A legal gadfly for atheist causes—he had already filed a suit in 1956 against the recent addition of "under God" to the Pledge of Allegiance—Lewis was also an ardent Paineite, a mid-twentieth-century heir of Gilbert Vale and Moncure Conway. He led efforts to get monuments for his hero installed in Morristown, New Jersey, and Thetford, England; he staged annual banquets in honor of Paine's birthday; and, the summer before his own death in November 1968, he pledged to reenact an old infidel liturgy through quoting Paine on his deathbed. "There is more consolation in silent resignation than there is in the murmuring wish of a prayer," Lewis declared. At a ceremony in Philadelphia, held on Paine's birthday earlier that same year, he was excited to celebrate the belated success of another of his commemorative efforts, the issuing of a Paine-embossed postage stamp, a memorialization he had been championing for decades. Alarmed to find that an invocation and a benediction were to open and close the observance—the first by a representative of the Catholic archdiocese and the second by a Protestant minister—Lewis interrupted the civic proceedings at the outset to voice his opposition, sure that Paine "would oppose the injection of religion in his behalf," especially this clerical Christian version. "Never in the history of this country has so great a patriot been maligned, slandered and vilified by the clergy," Lewis continued in his impromptu protest that nonetheless sounded like a ritualized lament. "Religion has no place in this purely secular ceremony." Unsurprisingly, the observance continued as planned with Lewis stalking out before the offending prayers were uttered. Like one of the ruined secular funerals of the nineteenth century, Lewis's long-anticipated commemorative rite—he had hoped to be master of ceremonies—took a Christian turn that left the grizzled freethinker on the outside.[22]

As an atheistic purist, keen on confrontation, Lewis differed in tactics and tone from most religious humanists, but the devotion to Paine continued to be shared across that in-house divide. When Lester Mondale was serving as the leader of the Philadelphia Ethical Society in the 1950s, he became a sleuth hunting for a marble bust of Paine that had been unceremoniously removed from Independence Hall in 1931 (fig. E.2). The bust had not been installed until 1905, twenty-nine years after a group of freethinkers, led by Francis Ellingwood Abbot, had first offered it to the city as a centennial tribute, only to have their hero and their gift spurned because of Christian opposition to honoring a dissipated blasphemer. Mondale, together with his humanist colleague Edwin H. Wilson, found the bust gathering dust in a basement furnace room in 1953 and helped win approval the following year from the city's art commission for the renewed display of the Paine sculpture; Lewis gladly joined them in this campaign. A follow-up curatorial ruling from the National Park Service stymied their combined efforts, and the bust continued to languish in the cellar until some local freethinkers, members of the Friendship Liberal League, managed to get it moved to their modest meeting hall in 1957, dubbed the Thomas Paine Center, which still took Paine's hallowed motto as its shibboleth (fig. E.3). A leading architect of the new humanism, Wilson was nonetheless happy to cooperate with the more combative Lewis on a run of projects to commemorate Paine. In 1951, Wilson had written Lewis about the Third Unitarian Church in Chicago, which had dedicated the Thomas Paine Memorial Pulpit, supposedly made possible by funds originally raised from a lecture Ingersoll himself had given on Paine. The Church of St. Thomas Paine, at least with a little rummaging on the part of Wilson and Mondale, was still perceptible in the mid-twentieth century.[23]

Adopting a less acerbic stance than Lewis did with the Freethinkers of America, some twentieth-century builders of new

FIG. E.2. The most tangible project that the National Liberal League had undertaken at its founding in 1876 was the placement of a freshly commissioned marble bust of Thomas Paine in Independence Hall. Sculpted by Sidney H. Morse, the bust immediately became a lightning rod of controversy as evangelical opponents vehemently objected to its exhibition. Rejected multiple times despite the persistence of its freethinking champions, the bust was finally accepted for display in 1905. It is pictured here in Independence Hall in 1929. Removed two years later, it was consigned to subterranean obscurity until the 1950s when Paine's latter-day admirers, including the religious humanists Edwin Wilson and Lester Mondale, made an unsuccessful bid to restore it to a place of honor. Photograph from Richard Gimbel, comp., "Miscellaneous Material Concerning the Thomas Paine Bust by S[i]dney H. Morse," American Philosophical Society.

THOMAS PAINE

"The world is my country and to do good my religion."

FIG. E.3. Having been denied a triumphal return to Independence Hall, Sidney Morse's bust of Paine made its way to a local club of freethinkers known as the Friendship Liberal League, a surviving remnant of the National Liberal League from the late nineteenth century. That group had opened a new meeting hall called the Thomas Paine Center in 1956 and proudly put the sculpture on display there.

To its backers the bust was a heroic emblem of democratic revolution and cosmopolitan liberality to be cherished by all Americans (and the world), but it was left to serve instead as a totem of a local Paineite fellowship. Among the society's modest promotions of its new center was this postcard, emblazoned with Paine's portrait and still canonized motto. Postcard from Richard Gimbel, comp., "Miscellaneous Material Concerning the Thomas Paine Bust by S[i]dney H. Morse," American Philosophical Society.

organizations proved quite successful. Rabbi Sherwin T. Wine, founder of the Society for Humanistic Judaism, was especially effective. In 1963, Wine launched (along with a small group of supportive families) the Birmingham Temple, just outside Detroit, as an experiment in nontheistic Judaism. Depicted in the media as a Jewish representative of the Death of God theology newly infamous in liberal Protestant circles, Wine struck any mention of divinity from the community's rituals while encouraging an agnostic spirit of free inquiry. At the same time, he retained the Jewish calendar, reinterpreting the holy days in terms of particular humanistic values (such as compassion, courage, and responsibility). "Passover does not need to celebrate supernatural events," one of Wine's typical announcements suggested. Instead, it can celebrate "human freedom," "human ingenuity," or "the creative renewal of the Jewish spirit." Ever controversial, Wine nonetheless succeeded in making the Birmingham Temple a lasting congregational venture with more than four hundred families associated with it by the time of his death in 2007. The formation of "a secular humanistic Judaism" was Wine's lifework, and the Birmingham Temple had seeded a network of affiliated communities by the 1980s and 1990s. Having spent years reimagining traditional religious practices, Wine offered through the Society for Humanistic Judaism an alternative model of fellowship for expressly secular Jews. A mentor of Greg Epstein, the prominent chaplain of the Humanist Community at Harvard, Wine proved an influential figure in shaping a congregational humanism for the new millennium.[24]

Wine's Birmingham Temple and the Society for Humanistic Judaism were flourishing ventures, particularly by the modest numerical standards of twentieth-century religious humanism. Most enterprises were less substantial and enduring. Take, for example, the Society of Evangelical Agnostics, organized by William Henry Young near Auberry, California, on the edge of the Sierra Nevada National Forest, in 1975. Young had a complicated religious background. He had grown up in the 1930s and early 1940s as "a very active mainline Protestant" but then had a born-again experience in high school that turned him into a fervent evangelical. That lasted until the end of his freshman year in college, when he then converted to the Church of Jesus Christ of Latter-day Saints, but becoming a Mormon did not settle his mind either. His metaphysical questions just kept multiplying. Then, in 1947, still only in his early twenties, Young had his third and final "conversion experience":

> I was driving alone in the Colorado mountains—up a long stretch of road going east from Tabernash—when the realization struck me as a gentle theistic lightning bolt that if God wanted his creatures to have answers to the big questions about "Ultimate Reality," the purpose of the universe, the meaning of life and death for man, etc., He would have provided more definite and convincing information. This brought a deep realization of and resignation to the reality of not knowing. From that moment on, I was an Agnostic.

It took Young quite a while to anchor that agnostic insight, but eventually he had done enough reading in Thomas Huxley, Robert Ingersoll, and Bertrand Russell to see himself as part of a longer intellectual tradition among freethinkers. He was convinced of the importance of religious uncertainty, of living peaceably with a lot of unanswered questions, and was only half-jokingly ready to evangelize for that posture of suspended judgment. That is how he landed on the name for his loose-knit fellowship, the Society of Evangelical Agnostics, or SEA.[25]

Young's agnostic awakening was not a conversion to eye-rolling cynicism but a spur to join what he saw as a larger humanist quest. After graduating from Colorado State in 1949, he went to seminary, first in Chicago and then in Berkeley, to explore the Unitarian ministry as a vocational option. He did not follow through on that possibility, though his ties to the religious humanists, including the indefatigable go-between Edwin Wilson, were still evident three decades later in his work with SEA. The Unitarian Universalist Church of Fresno remained an important part of Young's local community network—an audience more than ready to hear him out on his favorite agnostics. He spent much time as well in silence with the Religious Society of Friends, a practice he found congenial to his nontheistic posture. That Quaker influence was evident in the reflective gatherings he pulled together in the 1970s and 1980s at his mountain property—what he called the Cedar Springs Retreat—which commonly included a communal "Silent Hour" as "an acknowledgment of agnosticism before 'the altar of the Unknown.'" In sum, Young was an eclectic of a certain kind: the freethinking writings of Huxley, Ingersoll, and Russell were staples, but strands of Unitarian religious humanism and Quaker practice were also evident. Young viewed SEA as a group for freethinkers, but one without the dogmatic air he considered characteristic of atheist provocateur Madalyn Murray O'Hair and her organization of strict church-state separationists. No doubt the nation's most infamous atheist from the mid-1960s through the 1980s, O'Hair despised conciliation; with her usual saltiness, she summarily dismissed Young's brand of charitable agnosticism as total "bullshit." Unlike O'Hair and her comrades-in-arms at the *American Atheist*, Young and those involved with SEA still had room for religion. Of course, like other humanistic liberals, Young defined the religion in play at Cedar Springs "quite broadly. It has to do with one's Ultimate Concerns, with what one does with one's solitariness, with one's approach to death and the meaning which one gives to life."[26]

As an exponent of *evangelical* agnosticism, Young necessarily wanted to extend the reach of his new society beyond the forested retreat center northeast of Auberry. In March 1975, he placed small advertisements for SEA in the *Humanist*, the *Unitarian Universalist World*, the *Saturday Review*, and the *Nation*. By the end of the year, he had started publishing a newsletter, the *SEA Journal*, for those who joined up. It was composed of week-to-week jottings about what was on his mind or what he was hearing from fellow associates, and it frequently included personal accounts from SEA participants about their journeys out of "organized religion" into an open-ended agnosticism. Growth was modest. Young had enrolled 315 members by the end of 1978, of which he counted 175 as active. One wry entry in the *SEA Journal* in July 1980 suggested that Young was taking his mediocre evangelistic advances in stride: "Seven persons joined SEA at a party in what must be viewed as a 'mass conversion.'" Not that he lacked grand ambitions for growing SEA's membership—he called his plan Operation Tidal Wave—but he had few resources for achieving that kind of surge. By 1987, with SEA's total membership over the twelve years of its existence standing at 1,151, Young decided that it was time to give up on recruitment and disband. One member wrote him a note of encouragement in his admitted defeat: "You may not have started a tidal wave (how seldom do we come near our goals!) but every ripple counts." Young himself struck a somber, but realistic note: "I guess that, as freethought groups come and go, we didn't do too badly."[27]

All was not lost. Over the twelve years of SEA's existence, Young saw plenty of reason for hope. Wanting to be a bridge builder, Young used his *SEA Journal* to curate the concurrent development of any number of other humanistic, rationalistic, and atheistic ventures. He was in close contact with the American Humanist Association (AHA), particularly through the group's long-time executive director Edwin Wilson, who had joined SEA. With roots in the religious humanism of the 1920s and 1930s, the AHA seemed to be punching above its weight, thanks in part to all the free publicity right-wing evangelicals were generating for it (the group had about thirty-five hundred members in 1983). Along the way, Young had joined its cadre of Humanist Counselors and had begun performing weddings and funerals under the AHA's auspices. He had also been keeping an appreciative eye on the Freedom from Religion Foundation (FFRF), which had been incorporated in 1978 under the leadership of Anne Nicol Gaylor; it was pushing secularist demands for total church-state separation with renewed urgency. As Young closed down his own operation in February 1987, he noted that the FFRF was hosting its tenth anniversary convention in St. Louis in October—another fine opportunity, he announced cheerfully, "for freethinkers of all kinds to get together." The unalloyed secularism of the Council for Democratic and Secular Humanism was not his favored approach, but he was nonetheless supportive of Paul Kurtz's vigilant skepticism. Kurtz had reciprocated by joining SEA; Young was always interested in presenting a united front. SEA had failed to take lasting hold, but surely the freethinking tradition, including its agnostic and humanistic strands, would continue—so Young made clear in his patient accumulation of journal entries. Among the last items in his record, two weeks before SEA disbanded, was a reassuring note of continuity:

29 January 1987 250th anniversary of the birth of Thomas Paine.

Young reminded his readers that he had a large collection of books by and about Paine ready for guests to read at the Cedar Springs Retreat.[28]

back to
un serious
Rel.
Ry

Young's failed hopes for SEA played out against the backdrop of the resurgent political force of evangelical Protestantism and its television preachers. Bill Bright's Campus Crusade for Christ, Jerry Falwell's "electronic church," and Ronald Reagan's rise to power through his courtship of religious conservatives were never far from Young's mind. From his outpost south of Yosemite Valley, he watched with incredulity as "fundamentalists" built "the boogie-man of 'secular humanism'" into an object of relentless attack. Its horrifying dimensions bore little resemblance to those folks who wrote Young about their frequently isolated religious journeys; as often as not, his newsletter sounded like a lonely hearts club of freethinkers beleaguered by Christian family members or by neighbors who were "jingoists of the Religious Right." As the political world kept disappointing Young and his small band of devoted agnostics, he reached back to Ingersoll's humanistic, this-worldly affirmations for sustenance: "We can fill our lives with generous deeds, with loving words, with art and song, and all the ecstasies of love. We can flood our years with sunshine—with the divine climate of kindness, and we can drain to the last drop the golden cup of joy." That Ingersoll's religion of humanity—and its various twentieth-century successors—remained a minority practice in the United States was all too apparent as Young's Society of Evangelical Agnostics expired in 1987. Religious humanism was a mountain redoubt fifty miles northeast of Fresno, not a secularist hegemon controlling the courts, the public schools, and the federal government. Young knew that marginality from intimate experience as did Lester Mondale in his hideaway in the Missouri Ozarks. Both the history and ethnographic grain of secularism look significantly different after the centering of its religious peripheries. The stories shift: from the religion of secularism as a reigning establishment to a minority sect; from the pure secularity of secularism itself to its persistently confounding religious hybridity.[29]

Those storylines have continued their relevance into the twenty-first century. "When all you know and all you see in the world is dichotomy," the humanist chaplain Chris Stedman lamented in his youthful memoir in 2012, "there's no way to be anything other than religious or antireligious." Becoming a freethinker during a decade in which the bare-knuckle bravado of the "New Atheists" was ascendant, Stedman looked for a different "brand of secularism"—one that resisted the polarizing of "the religious and the secular into opposing camps." He found a middle space in a humanism that was open to religious engagement, that sought church-like forms of community, and that concentrated on humanitarian commitments rather than metaphysical dismissals. Amid the fiery polemics separating rancorous atheists and doomsday evangelicals, Stedman's bridge-building designs sounded like a novel turn among religion-deserting millennials, but his humanist chaplaincy occupied a recognizable secularist niche. It ran through the new humanism of the twentieth century back to the ethical creed that Robert Ingersoll, George Jacob Holyoake, and Felix Adler, among others, had imagined. It still echoed with the ecumenism and philanthropy of Paine's motto: "The world is my country, and to do good is my religion." Clearly, Stedman was not going to build his university-tied chaplaincy into a megachurch; there would be no institutional giant to compare with the bornagain evangelicalism that he had left behind in becoming a humanist. As an interfaith atheist, Stedman was offering another minority report—in a long series of them—on the religious shadows that secularism continues to cast.[30]

NOTES

Preface

1. "'Milk and Cider Liberalists' Religion?" *Torch of Reason*, Nov. 12, 1903, 8; Robert G. Ingersoll, "Religious Prejudice," in *The Works of Robert G. Ingersoll*, 12 vols. (New York: Ingersoll League, 1929), 8: 226–27; Robert G. Ingersoll, "Secularism," in *Works*, 11: 405–6; Robert G. Ingersoll, "The Gods," in *Works*, 1: 89.

2. O. B. Frothingham, *Religion, and a Religion* (New York: D. G. Francis, 1873), 24.

3. "'Milk and Cider Liberalists,'" 8; "The Liberal Club and Paine Celebration," *Truth Seeker*, Feb. 6, 1886, 85.

Introduction: The Religion of Secularism

1. Henry Shipley to the editor, *Truth Seeker*, Feb. 20, 1892, 123. The *Truth Seeker* had the orthographic quirk of sometimes leaving the *e* off the end of words. It did this inconsistently. I have silently corrected such spellings here and elsewhere: in this case, "hav" appears as "have" and so forth. The particular wording of Paine's motto that Shipley used was a mid-nineteenth-century invention of his most devoted followers who reworked a single line from Paine's *Rights of Man* and turned it into his shibboleth. The process by which Paine's original observation was elevated to motto status is discussed in more detail in Chapter 1.

2. C. Severance, "The Worst of All Religions," *Truth Seeker*, Aug. 21, 1897, 534–35.

3. George Jacob Holyoake, *Secularism a Religion Which Gives Heaven No Trouble* (London: Watts, [1881]), 6; George Jacob Holyoake, *The Origin and Nature of Secularism; Showing That Where Freethought Commonly Ends Secularism Begins* (London: Watts, 1896), 45; George Jacob Holyoake, *The Principles of Secularism Illustrated* (London: Austin, 1871), 8–10, 12; John Sholto Douglas, *The Religion of Secularism and the Perfectibility of Man* (London: Watts, [1881]); "A New Religion," *Truth Seeker*, June 23, 1888, 392. Holyoake's coinage of *nontheist* was similar in function to his more commonly used label of secularist; he employed it to characterize an ostensibly

neutral, irenic ground between theism and atheism and to sidestep the opprobrium associated with the atheist and infidel labels. See Brewin Grant and George Jacob Holyoake, *Christianity and Secularism: Report of a Public Discussion between the Rev. Brewin Grant, B.A., Editor of "The Bible and the People," and George Jacob Holyoake, Esq., Editor of "The Reasoner"* (London: Ward, 1853), 7–8, 10. For a lively discussion of the various secularist versions of religion in the air by the beginning of the twentieth century, see "At the Manhattan Liberal Club," *Truth Seeker*, Feb. 21, 1903, 120. The debate had been occasioned by the post-Christian socialist George D. Herron's speech "The Religion of Life." One member, the free-speech activist Edward Chamberlain, argued for getting rid of the "religion" category altogether. The anarchist Emma Goldman weighed in as well about banishing the very idea of authority, but another member thought the "devil of despotism" should not have "all the good words," so secularists were right to claim "religion" for themselves on their own terms.

4. Robert G. Ingersoll, "Secularism," in *The Works of Robert G. Ingersoll*, 12 vols. (New York: Ingersoll League, 1929), 8: 390–96; Robert G. Ingersoll, "Secularism," in *Works*, 11: 405–6; Moncure D. Conway, *What Is the Religion of Humanity? A Discourse at South Place Chapel, May 16th, 1880* (London; South Place, [1880]), 3–4, 16; Holyoake, *Secularism a Religion*, 7. For the broader usage of the idea of "the religion of humanity" among religious liberals and post-Christian universalists, including the sense that they were in no way beholden to Comte, see Octavius B. Frothingham, *The Religion of Humanity* (New York: Francis, 1873), esp. 32–36. For a good overview, see Lawrence W. Snyder, Jr., "The Religion of Humanity in Victorian America," in Peter W. Williams, ed., *Perspectives on American Religion and Culture* (Malden, MA: Blackwell, 1999), 378–89.

5. Thomas Paine, *The Age of Reason* (Amherst, NY: Prometheus Books, 1984), 8; Ingersoll, "Secularism," 8: 393; Ingersoll, "Secularism," 11: 405–6; "G. L. Henderson's Article," *Truth Seeker*, Dec. 15, 1874, 9. For another example of defining the religion of humanity by what it is not—no hellfire, no devil, no demons, no superstition— see M. Babcock, *The Religion of Humanity Better Than Eternal Punishment* (New York: Truth Seeker, [1890]).

6. J. D. Shaw, "Liberalism Stated and Defended," *Truth Seeker*, Nov. 21, 1885, 738; G. W. Foote, "Gems of Thought," *Truth Seeker*, Feb. 16. 1901, 110; G. W. Foote, "Mr. John Davidson's Position," *Freethinker*, Sept. 22, 1907, 594; George Chainey, *The Infidel Pulpit: Lectures* (Boston: Ellis, n.d.), 129.

7. *Connecticut Common School Journal*, March 1, 1839, 100; Francis E. Abbot, *A Study of Religion: The Nature and the Thing* (Toledo: Index Association, 1873), 6–14.

8. John Prescott Guild, "The Secular Saint Thomas," *Torch of Reason*, Jan. 31, 1901, 1. For one important prompt to consider secularism in terms of its embodied

sensibilities alongside its politics for defining religion's relationship to the state, see Charles Hirschkind, "Is There a Secular Body?" *Cultural Anthropology* 26 (2011): 633–47.

9. Holyoake, *Origin and Nature*, 121.

10. *Abington School District v. Schempp*, 374 U.S. 203 (1963). Stewart was not the first to use the phrase *a religion of secularism* in this critical way in defense of a broadly Protestant cultural consensus, but his judicial utterance carried the most weight, especially over the ensuing decades. The idea had come up earlier in wider critiques of secularism's corrosive effects on the nation's Christian mores, especially in education. See, for example, Harold Cooke Phillips, *In the Light of the Cross* (New York: Abingdon-Cokesbury, 1948), 113–24; Committee on Educational Institutions, to the Synod of North Carolina, Presbyterian Church, *The Church and Higher Education* (Raleigh, NC: Synod, 1955), 11–12. For a prior analysis that anticipated elements of both Clark's majority opinion and Stewart's critique, see J. Paul Williams, *The New Education and Religion: A Challenge to Secularism in Education* (New York: Association Press, 1945), 118–21. For a robust defense of "the religion of Secularism" as the "common faith" of a cultural pluralist, see Horace M. Kallen, *Secularism Is the Will of God: An Essay in the Social Philosophy of Democracy and Religion* (New York: Twayne, [1954]), 11–17, 39–41. For an indictment of the ways in which American Christians, including ecumenical Protestants, were increasingly using secularism as a catchall for a host of social threats and existential anxieties, see Edwin Ewart Aubrey, *Secularism a Myth: An Examination of the Current Attack on Secularism* (New York: Harper, 1954). Debates over religion and secularism became especially fraught with the rise of totalitarianism and the onset of the Cold War. Seeing democracy's very survival at stake, many anchored the American political order in religion, specifically in a Judeo-Christian inheritance—a view usually built on a sharp rejection of secularism as a dangerous antagonist at home and abroad. For an incisive examination of that intellectual and religious landscape, see K. Healan Gaston, *Imagining Judeo-Christian America: Religion, Secularism, and the Redefinition of Democracy* (Chicago: University of Chicago Press, 2019), esp. 153–207.

11. Ronald Reagan, "Radio Address to the Nation on Prayer in Schools," Feb. 25, 1984, in *Public Papers of the Presidents of the United States: Ronald Reagan 1984* (Washington, DC: U. S. Government Printing Office, 1986), 261–62; Michael Luo, "Romney, Eye on Evangelicals, Defends His Faith," *New York Times*, Dec. 7, 2007, A1, A28.

12. "The Liberal Club and Paine Celebration," *Truth Seeker*, Feb. 6, 1886, 85. The study of secularism has been a growth industry across the humanities during the last two decades. Much of that work has concerned itself with secularism as a disciplinary discourse, a political grammar for the regulation of religion that had imperial reach. A key starting point in that discussion is Talal Asad, *Formations of the Secular:*

Christianity, Islam, Modernity (Stanford, CA: Stanford University Press, 2003), but this literature is now enormous and represents a significant series of interventions. For indications of that critical reorientation's generativity among Americanists, see John Lardas Modern, *Secularism in Antebellum America* (Chicago: University of Chicago Press, 2011); Tisa Wenger, *Religious Freedom: The Contested History of an American Ideal* (Chapel Hill: University of North Carolina Press, 2017); Emily Ogden, *Credulity: A Cultural History of US Mesmerism* (Chicago: University of Chicago Press, 2018); Peter Coviello, *Make Yourselves Gods: Mormons and the Unfinished Business of American Secularism* (Chicago: University of Chicago Press, 2019). A significant portion of this contemporary scholarly reevaluation has flowed from French secularism's mobilizing of social and legal prescriptions—marked as emancipatory—that are designed to coerce Muslim women to conform to liberal secular norms of dress and bodily comportment. For benchmark works in that wider scholarship, see Joan Wallach Scott, *Sex and Secularism* (Princeton, NJ: Princeton University Press, 2017); and Linell E. Cady and Tracy Fessenden, eds., *Religion, the Secular, and the Politics of Sexual Difference* (New York: Columbia University Press, 2013). A second major strand of scholarship has continued to be preoccupied with secularization as an unfolding process of Weberian disenchantment, particularly the erosion of Christianity's cohesion in the face of scientific naturalism, this-worldly humanism, and pluralizing fragmentation. It posits that secularity has become the dominant ethos of modernity and seeks to explain that epochal transformation. A relatively recent landmark in that long-running mode of inquiry is Charles Taylor, *A Secular Age* (Cambridge, MA: Harvard University Press, 2007). What secularization entails— the privatization of religion, the differentiation of secular statecraft, the demystification of the universe through the natural sciences, the decline of religious adherence, the triumph of instrumental rationality, among other indicators—and to what extent secularization as a process actually characterizes the history of the modern world are matters of endless debate. Not surprisingly, secularization narratives themselves have been subjected to critical, demythologizing scrutiny—twinned fables of triumphant progress and tragic loss that obscure religion's undiminished presence in the contemporary world. See, for example, Jason Ā. Josephson-Storm, *The Myth of Disenchantment: Magic, Modernity, and the Birth of the Human Sciences* (Chicago: University of Chicago Press, 2017). While Asad's proposed "anthropology of secularism" emphasized the study of secularism as an abstracted discourse (more "conceptual analysis" than "intensive fieldwork"), it was also a call for the study of the "practice of secularism" (e.g., attitudes toward the body or the education of the senses), which meant that history and ethnography remained indispensable (pp. 16–17, 25). Still, there has been somewhat less interest shown in taking "secular studies" in these historical and ethnographic directions—that is, in fostering engagement with lived, material, and embodied forms of deism, secularism, humanism, freethought, agnosticism, and atheism. That literature, though, is now also growing apace. See, for example, Christopher Grasso, *Skepticism and American Faith: From the Revolution to the Civil War* (New York: Oxford University Press, 2018), 4; Eric R. Schlereth, *An Age of Infidels: The Politics of Religious Controversy in the Early United States* (Philadelphia: University of Pennsylvania Press, 2013), 8–9, 244; Leigh Eric Schmidt, *Village Atheists: How America's Unbelievers Made Their Way in a Godly Nation* (Princeton, NJ: Princeton University Press, 2016), 17–18; Gillis J. Harp, *Positivist Republic: Auguste Comte and the Reconstruction of American Liberalism, 1865–1920* (University Park: Pennsylvania State University Press, 1995), 23–48; Matthew Engelke, "The Coffin Question: Death and Materiality in Humanist Funerals," *Material Religion* 11 (2015): 26–48; Joseph Blankholm, "Secularism and Secular People," *Public Culture* 30 (2018): 245–68; Johannes Quack, *Disenchanting India: Organized Rationalism and Criticism of Religion in India* (New York: Oxford University Press, 2012), 221–44; Alec Ryrie, *Unbelievers: An Emotional History of Doubt* (Cambridge, MA: Belknap Press of Harvard University Press, 2019); Anna Bigelow, "Lived Secularism: Studies in India and Turkey," *Journal of the American Academy of Religion* 87 (2019): 725–64.

13. Ingersoll, "Secularism," 8: 392. For an especially strong case on how political secularism, under the guise of neutrality, serves as a way for the state to manage and regulate religion, particularly minority traditions, see Saba Mahmood, *Religious Difference in a Secular Age: A Minority Report* (Princeton, NJ: Princeton University Press, 2016).

14. *Equal Rights in Religion: Report on the Centennial Congress of Liberals, and Organization of the National Liberal League, at Philadelphia, on the Fourth of July, 1876* (Boston: National Liberal League, 1876), 14–15.

15. "Signs of the Times," *Christian Witness*, Jan. 13, 1837, 2.

16. Douglas, *Religion of Secularism*, 3–5. From the minority rights of infidels, Douglas turned to a still more controversial topic: the need for open discussion of birth control and sexual reproduction. Broaching that tabooed subject had created legal problems for freethinkers for decades, from Charles Knowlton and Abner Kneeland to Annie Besant, Charles Bradlaugh, Moses Harman, Elmina Slenker, and Ida Craddock. Whether to make such issues part of the secularist movement created recurring clashes inside the ranks. Many, including Ingersoll and Abbot, resisted that alliance, seeing the embrace of sex reform as abetting those who linked infidels to immorality, licentiousness, and obscenity. There were, however, other reasons to question that partnership, including the ways in which many advocates of the free discussion of birth control, including Douglas, privileged the fit over the unfit for the improvement of the race. I have elsewhere explored the conflicts that sex reform generated among freethinking liberals. See Schmidt, *Village Atheists*, 210–48; and

Leigh Eric Schmidt, *Heaven's Bride: The Unprintable Life of Ida C. Craddock, American Mystic, Scholar, Sexologist, Martyr, and Madwoman* (New York: Basic Books, 2010). As in Christian circles, there was no singular political alignment on matters of gender, race, civilization, and empire in freethought circles. Secularists, especially Paineites, had a radical democratic inheritance, but that was no guarantee against scientific racism, gender essentialism, or civilizational hierarchy. For good entry points into these complexities, see Nathan Alexander, *Race in a Godless World: Atheism, Race, and Civilization, 1850–1914* (Manchester: Manchester University Press, 2019); Christopher Cameron, *Black Freethinkers: A History of African American Secularism* (Evanston, IL: Northwestern University Press, 2019); Evelyn A. Kirkley, *Rational Mothers and Infidel Gentlemen: Gender and American Atheism, 1865–1915* (Syracuse: Syracuse University Press, 2000); and Laura Schwartz, *Infidel Feminism: Secularism, Religion, and Women's Emancipation, England 1830–1914* (Manchester: Manchester University Press, 2013).

17. "The Agnostic's Religion," *Northern Christian Advocate*, Aug. 2, 1888, 4; Shubael Carver to the editor, *Twentieth Century*, May 4, 1889, 156.

18. The University of California copy of Abbot's report *Equal Rights in Religion* has been digitized and is accessible through the HathiTrust Digital Library. The librarian's notation is in the front of the volume.

Chapter 1: Relics of the Secular Saint Thomas

1. Samuel P. Putnam, "News and Notes from the Field," *Truth Seeker*, Feb. 7, 1885, 85; Robert G. Ingersoll, "Which Way?" *Truth Seeker*, Jan. 17, 1885, 38; Robert G. Ingersoll, *Superstition: A Lecture* (New York: Farrell, 1898), 9–10.

2. Watson Heston, "A Few of the Fraudulent Relics Exhibited to the Faithful," *Truth Seeker*, June 7, 1890, 353; Watson Heston, *Part II. of the Freethinkers' Pictorial Text-Book* (New York: Truth Seeker, 1898), 24; Watson Heston, "A Worshiper of Moldy Relics—Why the Christian Cannot See the Truth," *Truth Seeker*, Nov. 10, 1894, 705; Watson Heston, "Some Old Relics," *Truth Seeker*, Feb. 11, 1899, 81. See also the bag of "fetiches" that Heston attached to the back of a Protestant minister in "A Hopeless Case—Why the Christian Can't Get on a Higher Plane," *Truth Seeker*, Jan. 14, 1893, 17. On Heston's leading role in creating a visual repertory for freethinkers and secularists, see Leigh Eric Schmidt, *Village Atheists: How America's Unbelievers Made Their Way in a Godly Nation* (Princeton, NJ: Princeton University Press, 2016), 73–170.

3. "Resurrection Man," *Cobbett's Weekly Register* 40 (1821): 546–47; [Jabez Hunns], *Thomas Paine's Bones and Their Owners* (Norwich: Burgess, 1908), 3–4. *Resurrection man* was a label used to describe those engaged in the illicit practice of robbing graves to sell corpses to anatomists and physicians for study. The

commitment of nineteenth-century freethinkers to Paine has been widely noted in the historiography, though not the materiality of that devotion: Albert Post, *Popular Freethought in America, 1825–1850* (New York: Columbia University Press, 1943), 155–59; Sidney Warren, *American Freethought, 1860–1914* (New York: Columbia University Press, 1943), 110–16; Susan Jacoby, *Freethinkers: A History of American Secularism* (New York: Henry Holt, 2004), 64–65; Susan Jacoby, *The Great Agnostic: Robert Ingersoll and American Freethought* (New Haven, CT: Yale University Press, 2013), 18–20, 142–48; Eric R. Schlereth, *An Age of Infidels: The Politics of Religious Controversy in the Early United States* (Philadelphia: University of Pennsylvania Press, 2013), 190–200; Harvey J. Kaye, *Thomas Paine and the Promise of America* (New York: Hill and Wang, 2005), 127–32, 164–68, 182; Schmidt, *Village Atheists*, 85–90. On Cobbett's exploits with Paine's bones, see Leo A. Bressler, "Peter Porcupine and the Bones of Thomas Paine," *Pennsylvania Magazine of History and Biography* 82 (1958): 176–85; Paul A. Pickering, "A 'Grand Ossification': William Cobbett and the Commemoration of Tom Paine," in Paul A. Pickering and Alex Tyrrell, eds., *Contested Sites: Commemoration, Memorial and Popular Politics in Nineteenth-Century Britain* (London: Routledge, 2004), 57–80. See also Paul Collins, *The Trouble with Tom: The Strange Afterlife and Times of Thomas Paine* (London: Bloomsbury, 2005), 31–82. Collins's book is a work of popular nonfiction—a combination of historical musings, literary digressions, and contemporary travels. It is interesting as a piece of historical research, but it is still more instructive as a creative contribution to the storytelling that has gone on around Paine's bones since Cobbett's day. How Collins's work fits within the larger secularist mythology surrounding Paine's remains is discussed below. More broadly, Cobbett's investment in Paine's bones had several counterparts in the era—projects of bodily reclamation and sepulchral memorialization that served a variety of nationalistic, revolutionary, counterrevolutionary, and filiopietistic projects on both sides of the Atlantic. See Michael Meranze, "Major André's Exhumation," and Matthew Dennis, "Patriotic Remains: Bones of Contention in the Early Republic," in Nancy Isenberg and Andrew Burstein, eds., *Mortal Remains: Death in Early America* (Philadelphia: University of Pennsylvania Press, 2003), 123–48; Michael Kammen, *Digging Up the Dead: A History of Notable American Reburials* (Chicago: University of Chicago Press, 2010); Thomas W. Laqueur, *The Work of the Dead: A Cultural History of Mortal Remains* (Princeton, NJ: Princeton University Press, 2015). Meranze, Kammen, and Laqueur all make at least brief mention of the saga of Paine's bones. Among the most suggestive religious parallels of the period is the devotion that developed around the evangelist George Whitefield's tomb and his mortal remains in Newburyport, Massachusetts. It is especially evocative because the standard Protestant resistance to relics broke apart over Whitefield's bones in ways analogous to how the usual secularist rhetoric cracked in the face of Paine's bones. At one point in 1829, a British admirer stole Whitefield's right arm bone; when it was finally reclaimed in 1849, the bone was ceremonially returned to the vault in Newburyport, attended by a procession of two thousand people. See Robert E. Cray, Jr., "Memorialization and Enshrinement: George Whitefield and Popular Religious Culture," *Journal of the Early Republic* 10 (1990): 339–61; Kammen, *Digging Up the Dead*, 167–73. Patriotic, nationalistic, and religious projects were far from the only uses to which such sepulchral pursuits were put. The collecting of bones and skulls by American naturalists—whether from battlefields, robbed graves, or anthropological field sites—became, over the course of the nineteenth century, deeply implicated in the formation of a science of racial difference and superiority. See Ann Fabian, *The Skull Collectors: Race, Science, and America's Unburied Dead* (Chicago: University of Chicago Press, 2010); and Samuel J. Redman, *Bone Rooms: From Scientific Racism to Human Prehistory in Museums* (Cambridge, MA: Harvard University Press, 2016).

4. John Sholto Douglas, *The Religion of Secularism and the Perfectibility of Man* (London: Watts, [1881]), 3–5. "Paineites," or "Painites," was a designation that Moncure Conway and other Paine disciples used to describe themselves. See Moncure Daniel Conway, *The Life of Thomas Paine*, 2 vols. (New York: Putnam's, 1892), 1: xv; Moncure D. Conway, "Where Are Paine's Bones? Strange Adventures of the Freethinker's Remains," *Truth Seeker*, June 21, 1902, 390; James B. Elliott, "Wilson MacDonald, Sculptor," *Humanitarian Review* 3 (1905): 343; James B. Elliott, "The Paine Museum," *Humanitarian Review* 9 (1910): 435; "The Paine Memorial Debt," *Boston Investigator*, Nov. 8, 1882, 6. Since Paine's name had become something of a Protestant curse word, opponents had often used the tag as a term of reproach to label degraded infidels, deists, and radicals, but like Methodists and Quakers, the Paineites had embraced the derogatory as a positive marker. As for the literature on religious materiality and modernity, it is extensive. For two especially wide-ranging collections, see Dirk Houtman and Birgit Meyer, eds., *Things: Religion and the Question of Materiality* (New York: Fordham University Press, 2012); and Sally M. Promey, ed., *Sensational Religion: Sensory Cultures in Material Practice* (New Haven, CT: Yale University Press, 2014). For the complex, paradoxical Christian frameworks behind post-Reformation and post-Enlightenment debates about religious materiality, see especially Caroline Walker Bynum, *Christian Materiality: An Essay on Religion in Late Medieval Europe* (New York: Zone Books, 2011).

5. Thomas Paine, *The Age of Reason* (Amherst, NY: Prometheus Books, 1984), 8; Robert G. Ingersoll, "Thomas Paine," in *The Works of Robert G. Ingersoll*, 12 vols. (New York: Ingersoll League, 1929), 1: 135. The attacks on Paine for his irreligion were nested within fears of his radical politics and the desire to tame his unruly revolutionary vision. Federalist antagonists especially used his blasphemous reputation for partisan

leverage; by the first decade of the nineteenth century, Jeffersonians often found association with Paine a political liability. See Alfred F. Young, *Liberty Tree: Ordinary People and the American Revolution* (New York: New York University Press, 2006), 265–95; and Seth Cotlar, *Tom Paine's America: The Rise and Fall of Transatlantic Radicalism in the Early Republic* (Charlottesville: University of Virginia Press, 2011).

6. Paine, *Age of Reason*, 7; "Thomas Paine: Celebrations in Honor of the Author-Hero's Birthday," *Truth Seeker*, Feb. 15, 1880, 99; Conway, *Life of Paine*, 2: 254–56, 426–27. On the small groups of organized deists in the early republic, including Theophilanthropists, see Christopher Grasso, *Skepticism and American Faith: From the Revolution to the Civil War* (New York: Oxford University Press, 2018), 114–15. For one nineteenth-century defender of Paine who struck all the religious notes, see L. K. Washburn, *America's Debt to Thomas Paine* (Boston: Coburn, 1878), 12–14.

7. Thomas Paine, *Rights of Man: Part the Second, Combining Principle and Practice* (Boston: Fleet, 1792), 64; Kate DePeatt, "A Memorial Tribute to the Late Katie Kehm Smith and Mrs. Warren Carsner," *Free Thought Magazine* 16 (1898): 494; Ingersoll, "Paine," in *Works*, 1: 131, 165; "Thomas Paine: Celebrations," 99. For an early and influential instance of the altered phrasing of Paine's line from *Rights of Man*, see Gilbert Vale, *The Life of Thomas Paine* (New York: Vale, 1841), 162. For the motto's use with Paine's portrait and on a banner, see "The Paine Celebration," *New York Observer*, Feb. 7, 1846, 2; and "A Paine Anecdote," *Beacon*, Feb. 10, 1844, 103. The dictum was used as a watchword for several early freethought journals, including the *Age of Reason*, the *Independent Beacon*, and the *Citizen of the World*, all between 1845 and 1850, which meant that two of the most influential early Paineites, Gilbert Vale and Peter Eckler, were both promoting the revised motto as an epitome of Paine's deistic cosmopolitanism. The motto appeared on the title page of all three volumes of Paine's collected *Works* in an edition published in Philadelphia in 1854. It also appeared as "Paine's Motto" on the title page of Joseph N. Moreau, ed., *Testimonials to the Merits of Thomas Paine* (Burlington, NJ: Taylor, 1861). The motto still leapt to mind for Hubert Harrison in the early twentieth century as an embodiment of Paine's ethical, deistic legacy. See Hubert Harrison, "Paine's Place in the Deistical Movement," *Truth Seeker*, Feb. 11, 1911, 87–88. Harrison gave this as an address at a Paine celebration the previous month under the auspices of the Thomas Paine National Historical Association.

8. Ingersoll, "Paine," in *Works*, 1: 135. For three versions of this ubiquitous funeral story as told by Christian detractors, see "Paine," *True Wesleyan*, March 9, 1844, 38; "Tom Paine," *Morning Star* (Limerick, ME), April 24, 1850, 8; "The End of Tom Paine," *Christian Expositor*, May 11, 1876, 1.

9. *Cobbett's Political Register* 35 (1820): 332–34, 635–36, 783–84; Lewis Melville, *The Life and Letters of William Cobbett in England and America*, 2 vols. (London: Lane,

1913), 2: 116. For the ways in which Cobbett's particular investment in locks of Paine's hair resonated with wider nineteenth-century memorializing patterns involving hair keepsakes and hair-containing jewelry, see Teresa Barnett, *Sacred Relics: Pieces of the Past in Nineteenth-Century America* (Chicago: University of Chicago Press, 2013); and Deborah Lutz, *Relics of Death in Victorian Literature and Culture* (Cambridge: Cambridge University Press, 2015). For one scrapbook compilation, assembled by the poet Leigh Hunt, a contemporary of Cobbett's, see "Collection of Hair," Harry Ransom Center, University of Texas at Austin.

10. "A Radical Reformer," Dec. 1819, British Museum, Prints and Drawings, no. 1862.1217.527; "Sonnet to the Bone-Juggler," *Morning Post*, Jan. 11, 1820; "The Political Champion Turned Resurrection Man," Dec. 1819, British Museum, Prints and Drawings, no. 1868.0808.8476; *Cobbett's Political Register* 35 (1820): 777; "Paine's Corpse," *Royal Cornwall Gazette*, Nov. 27, 1819.

11. "Radical Reformer"; "The Botley Showman," 1820, British Museum, Prints and Drawings, no. 1865.1111.857; T. C. Hansard, ed., *The Parliamentary Debates from the Year 1803 to the Present Time*, 41 vols. (London: Hansard, 1820), 41: 1265.

12. Robert Huish, *Memoirs of the Late William Cobbett*, 2 vols. (London: Saunders, 1836), 2: 266, 296–97; Charles Hastings Collette, *A Reply to Cobbett's "History of the Protestant Reformation in England and Ireland"* (London: Partridge, 1869), 4–5, 7–8, 291.

13. *Cobbett's Political Register* 35 (1820): 777.

14. [James Watson], *A Brief History of the Remains of the Late Thomas Paine, from the Time of Their Disinterment in 1819 by the Late William Cobbett, M.P. Down to the Year 1846* (London: J. Watson, 1847), 5–8; "Selected Summary," *National Philanthropist*, June 15, 1827; "Tom Paine's Bones," *Notes and Queries*, Jan. 25, 1868, 77; [Hunns], *Thomas Paine's Bones*, 17–20.

15. Benjamin Offen, "Origin of the Paine Celebration in New-York," *Beacon*, Aug. 10, 1844, 309; "To the Memory of Paine—(Peter Bussey's Saviour)," *New-York Beacon*, Jan. 24, 1846, 33; William M. Allen, "An Oration," *Age of Reason*, Feb. 4, 1849, 38.

16. "Paine's Anniversary," in *The Truth Seeker Collection of Forms, Hymns, and Recitations* (New York: Bennett, 1877), 244; John Prescott Guild, "The New Atheism," *Free Thought Magazine* 20 (1902): 651–52; John Prescott Guild, "The Secular Saint Thomas," *Torch of Reason*, Jan. 31, 1901, 1; *Thomas Paine Bicentennial Celebrations, 1737–1937* (New Rochelle, NY: Thomas Paine National Historical Association, 1937), 11.

17. Vale, *Life of Paine*, 190–91; Gilbert Vale, "Visit to the Paine Monument," *Beacon*, Dec. 7, 1839, 22–23; "The New Rochelle Monument," *Truth Seeker*, June 3, 1899, 337, 344–45, 348; "The Celebration of the 4th on the Paine Farm," *Citizen of the World, or Sunday Beacon*, July 20, 1851, 289–92; "The Paine Celebration at Camptown, N.J.," *Beacon*, Feb. 10, 1844, 102–3; Joseph N. Moreau, "Thomas Paine's Monument at New Rochelle," *Boston Investigator*, Oct. 10, 1860, 195. For other pilgrimage accounts, see

J. W. Jones, "The Paine Monument," *Boston Investigator*, Sept. 10, 1851, n.p.; Joseph Carpenter, "Thomas Paine and His Monument," *National Standard*, July 15, 1871, 2; Asa K. Butts, "A Pilgrimage to the Grave of Paine," *Boston Investigator*, Nov. 25, 1874, 2; "Rededication of Paine's Monument," *Truth Seeker*, June 4, 1881, 356–57; "The Paine Monument," *Truth Seeker*, April 28, 1894, 265; "In Memory of Paine: Impressive Decoration Day Services at New Rochelle," *Truth Seeker*, June 9, 1894, 356–61; "By the Grave of Thomas Paine," *Truth Seeker*, June 8, 1895, 357, 360–61; "The Paine Bust Dedicated," *Truth Seeker*, June 10, 1899, 359–61. For context on Vale's subscribers and the sculptor John Frazee, whom he enlisted, see Frederick Voss, "Honoring a Scorned Hero: America's Monument to Thomas Paine," *New York History* 68 (1987): 138–47.

18. "The Citizen of the World, and Sunday Beacon and Its Objects," *Citizen of the World, or Sunday Beacon*, March 9, 1851, 129–31; "The Paine Farm," *Citizen of the World, or Sunday Beacon*, Feb. 22, 1851, 114–15; Gilbert Vale, "Monument to the Memory of Thomas Paine," *Beacon*, July 22, 1837, 345–46; Gilbert Vale, "Thomas Paine's Monument," *Beacon*, Aug. 19, 1837, 372; Gilbert Vale, "The Paine Monument," *Beacon*, March 2, 1839, 127; [Hunns], *Thomas Paine's Bones*, 17; Gilbert Vale, "Thomas Paine's Bones," *New-York Beacon*, Dec. 27, 1845, 7; Gilbert Vale, "Paine and Cobbett," *New-York Beacon*, Aug. 29, 1846, 283–84; Gilbert Vale, "A Brief History of the Remains of the Late Thomas Paine," *Monthly Beacon* 1 (June 1847): 32; "Remains of Thomas Paine," *Monthly Beacon* 2 (July 1847): 33–41; "Remains of Thomas Paine," *Boston Investigator*, July 28, 1847, n.p.; John Morey to the editor, *Boston Investigator*, Oct. 27, 1847, n.p.

19. Jones, "Paine Monument," n.p.; John Morey, "Thomas Paine's Bones," *Boston Investigator*, Dec. 12, 1860, 266; Morey to the editor. For evidence of Morey's long devotion to Paine, see "Celebration of Thomas Paine's Birth-Day," *Boston Investigator*, Feb. 4, 1846, n.p. and Feb. 3, 1847, n.p.; John Morey, "The Celebration," *Boston Investigator*, Jan. 25, 1854, n.p.; "Paine Celebration at Saratoga," *Boston Investigator*, March 26, 1856, n.p. As late as 1874, Morey wrote of his excitement over memorializing Paine with a statue and a hall: "I am one of the most enthusiastic admirers of the memory of Paine that lives." See John Morey, "Statue to Thomas Paine," *Boston Investigator*, Feb. 25, 1874, 6.

20. William Henry Burr, "Thomas Paine's Bones," *Boston Investigator*, Nov. 20, 1872, 4; "Paine's Bones," *Boston Investigator*, Dec. 11, 1872, 5; "The 'Bones' Question," *Boston Investigator*, Dec. 25, 1872, 5; W. H. Burr, "Thomas Paine's Bones," *Boston Investigator*, Nov. 1, 1876, 2; W. H. Burr, "Jefferson Not the Author of the Declaration of Independence," *Truth Seeker*, Oct. 2, 1886, 630. See also "Thomas Paine's Bones," *Boston Investigator*, March 17, 1875, 5; "Thomas Paine's Bones, &c.," *Boston Investigator*, Nov. 15, 1876, 4. Paine Memorial Hall was dedicated on the 138th anniversary of Paine's birth, January 29, 1875, with considerable fanfare but obviously without the

relics Burr had wanted. See "Dedication of the Paine Memorial Building," *Boston Investigator*, Feb. 3, 10, and 17, 1875, for the full proceedings. The comparison to contemporaneous Roman Catholic practices involving relics was telling. Nineteenth-century American Catholics were in the midst of an extensive translation of European religious relics to the United States. That meant Catholic devotions surrounding relics were a proximate source of Protestant and secularist concern and not practices and objects easily consigned to a distant medieval past. See Michael S. Carter, "Glowing with the Radiance of Heaven: Roman Martyrs, American Saints, and the Devotional World of Nineteenth-Century American Catholicism," *U.S. Catholic Historian* 36 (Winter 2018): 1–26. One chapel in Pittsburgh, with a particularly industrious priest, boasted a collection of relics (about five thousand) so large that it was claimed to be second only to the Vatican's holdings by the end of the nineteenth century. See Kathleen N. Bishop, "Saint Anthony's Chapel: A Hidden Treasure of Saints, Passion, and Faith," *Western Pennsylvania History* 93 (Fall 1910): 42–48.

21. "The Tom Paine Memorial—A Suggestion," *Christian at Work*, Nov. 2, 1876, 862; "Glimpses," *Index*, July 20, 1876, 337. After the National Liberal League's failure to secure placement of Paine's bust in Independence Hall in 1876, local freethinkers kept the sculpture in town, periodically raising anew the issue of public display. Finally, in 1905, city officials decided to accept it for exhibition in Independence Hall—a belated reversal that attracted front-page notice in the *New York Times*. See "Place for Paine's Bust," *New York Times*, Sept. 12, 1905, 1. See also James B. Elliott, "The Rejected Bust," *Humanitarian Review* 3 (May 1905): 182–83; [Singleton W. Davis], "The Accepted Bust," *Humanitarian Review* 4 (Jan. 1906): 11–14. For the bust's tortuous history after 1905, see the epilogue.

22. "Liberal Opinions Freely Expressed: A Conversation with George J. Holyoake," *New York Tribune*, Nov. 10, 1879, 2; H. L. Green, "Liberal News Items," *Boston Investigator*, Nov. 19, 1879, 2; "The Liberal Club," *Truth Seeker*, Jan. 19, 1884, 36; Conway, "Where Are Paine's Bones?," 390. For an early iteration of the button story, see "Thomas Paine's 'Bones,'" *Boston Investigator*, March 1, 1854, n.p. D. M. Bennett retold the ground-to-powder story in which the bones were then mixed with fine clay to make "articles of ornament" for "friends and admirers of Paine." Bennett concluded with a sentence that could apply to most of the speculations after 1850: "How much truth there is in this statement is not known." See D. M. Bennett, *The World's Sages, Thinkers and Reformers* (New York: Bennett, 1885), 550. The 1884 notice about the formation of the TPNHA called it a society, not an association; it was for twenty-plus years essentially a subset of the Manhattan Liberal Club. It was usually referred to simply as the Paine Historical Society. See "Paine's Birthday at the Liberal Club," *Truth Seeker*, Feb. 7, 1885, 84. It was formally incorporated in 1906 as the TPNHA with Moncure Conway as president. See "What Paine Wanted and What We Have,"

Truth Seeker, Feb. 10, 1906, 82–83, 86; "The Paine Historical Society Incorporated," *Truth Seeker*, Sept. 22, 1906, 600. The records of the TPNHA are now housed at Iona College, New Rochelle, New York. They were moved there from the headquarters of the TPNHA in 2011 and have been only partially processed and catalogued.

23. Moncure Daniel Conway, *Autobiography: Memories and Experiences*, 2 vols. (Boston: Houghton, Mifflin, 1904), 1: 260–61, 275, 304–305; Edwin C. Walker, *A Sketch and Appreciation of Moncure Daniel Conway, Freethinker and Humanitarian* (New York: Walker, 1908), 21, 26–27; Moncure D. Conway, *Thomas Paine: A Celebration* (Cincinnati: Dial, 1860).

24. Moncure D. Conway, "London Letter," *Cincinnati Commercial*, May 16, 1874, 1; Burr, "Jefferson Not the Author," 630; Burr, "Thomas Paine's Bones," 2; Moncure D. Conway, "London Letter," *Cincinnati Commercial*, Jan. 8, 1875, 4; Conway, "Where Are Paine's Bones?," 390; "Manhattan Liberal Club's Celebration of Paine Birthday," *Truth Seeker*, Feb. 22, 1902, 114; Conway, *Life of Paine*, 2: 427. Conway also alluded to Paine's skeleton, "which infidels are said to be keeping somewhere," in *The Earthward Pilgrimage* (London: Hotten, 1870), 375, and he already had access to James Watson, a member of his congregation and a publisher devoted to disseminating Paine's works, who was one of the central players in the British intrigue surrounding the whereabouts of the bones. See Conway, *Autobiography*, 2: 40. Watson thought Ainslie never had any of the remains and was guilty of a tall tale, hence his silence once pressed. See Edward Truelove to Conway, May 1896, Box 21, Moncure Daniel Conway Papers, Rare Book and Manuscript Library, Columbia University. Conway's essay on his quest for Paine's bones first appeared in the *New York Sun* on May 25, 1902, and then in two parts in the *Truth Seeker* the next month (June 14 and June 21). The TPNHA also published the essay under Conway's original title "The Adventures of Thomas Paine's Bones," in *Thomas Paine: Journal of the Thomas Paine National Historical Association* no. 3 (March 2002): 2–12. This was reproduced from an autograph copy in the TPNHA's collection (a facsimile of the first page was printed with the transcription). The autograph manuscript has not yet been located among the partially catalogued records of the TPNHA at Iona College. At this point scholars have to rely on the published transcription of Conway's manuscript—a version that is more detailed in places than the versions in the *New York World* and the *Truth Seeker*.

25. "In Memory of Paine: Impressive Decoration Day Services at New Rochelle," *Truth Seeker*, June 9, 1894, 359. The relic-collecting habits of Conway and his colleagues in the TPNHA were congruent with wider museum practices of the nineteenth century in which associative objects—a splinter of wood from Lincoln's cabin, a chair belonging to the Penn family, a sprig from Connecticut's Charter Oak, a fragment of Plymouth Rock—were crucial to historical representations and exhibitions. See Barnett, *Sacred Relics*, esp. 22–28.

26. *Thomas Paine Exhibition at South Place Institute, Finsbury* (London: Bradlaugh Bonner, [1895]), entries 8, 66, 87, 93, 94, 218, 274, 276, 297, 369, 485. The line about the brain's size comes from Conway, "Where Are Paine's Bones?," 390; the line about its impressiveness appears in the TPNHA's published manuscript version of Conway's essay, "Adventures of Thomas Paine's Bones," 12. Some manuscript evidence survives in the TPNHA files at Iona College documenting Conway's interest in the brain and hair relics. See George Reynolds to Moncure D. Conway, August 1900; George Reynolds to William M. van der Weyde, April 14, 1909, Records of the TPNHA. Additional evidence of Conway's efforts at collecting bodily relics for the London exhibition survives in the small collection of Conway's correspondence at the Library of Congress. See Conway to [Edward Smith], Sept. 24, 1895; Sept. 29, 1895, Oct. 7, 1895; Nov. 13, 1895, Moncure Daniel Conway Correspondence, 1889–1895, MSS5134, Library of Congress Manuscript Division, Washington, DC. Some relevant correspondence on Conway's relic-hunting is also contained in the far larger Conway collection at Columbia University. See Edward Smith to Conway, Nov. 22 [no year], Box 20; Edward Truelove to Conway, May 1896; Harriet Truelove to Conway, April 16, 1900, Box 21, Conway Papers. The pertinent correspondence suggests how persistently Conway courted a network of collectors, antiquarians, and Paine devotees to garner materials for his exhibition and for the TPNHA. A significant portion of Conway's South Place exhibition migrated the next month to the Bradlaugh Club and Institute, a small federation of London freethinkers, who timed a secondary display to the celebration of Paine's birthday. See the separate catalogue *Thomas Paine Exhibition, 1896* (London: George Standring, 1896). That showing included one lock of hair but not the portion of Paine's brain.

27. "Manhattan Liberal Club's Celebration," 114–15; Conway, "Where Are Paine's Bones?," 390; Moncure Daniel Conway, ed., *The Writings of Thomas Paine*, 4 vols. (New York: Putnam's, 1894–1896), 4: xx; Conway, "Adventures of Thomas Paine's Bones," 11.

28. George E. Macdonald, *Fifty Years of Freethought*, 2 vols. (New York: Truth Seeker, 1929), 2: 266; "Paine Bust Dedicated," 359; James B. Elliott, ed., *Rededication of the Paine Monument and Assignment of Its Custody to the City of New Rochelle* (Philadelphia: Paine Memorial Association, 1909), 8–14, 23–25; Moncure D. Conway, "A Letter from Paris," *Truth Seeker*, Oct. 21, 1905, 663; "Guns Boom for Thomas Paine," *Truth Seeker*, Oct. 21, 1905, 664–65; "The Paine Monument at Last Finds a Home," *New York Times*, Oct. 15, 1905, 10.

29. *Memorial Celebration of the One Hundredth Anniversary of the Death of Thomas Paine* (New York: Paine Historical Association, [1909]); "Souvenir Programme: Thomas Paine Centennial Celebration New Rochelle June 5, 1909," Thomas Paine Archive, Bishopsgate Institute, London; "Thomas Paine Honored after 100 years,"

New York Times, May 8, 1910, Magazine Section, 10; William M. van der Weyde, "Paine's Long Lost Remains Home by Parcel Post," *New York Times*, May 31, 1914, Magazine Section, 2. Before becoming president of the TPNHA, van der Weyde had served for years as the group's corresponding secretary and was the organization's linchpin for a quarter century. The TPNHA records show him to have been very diligent in making Conway's relic-hunting quest his own. See Moncure D. Conway to William M. van der Weyde, Aug. 14, 1906; George Reynolds to William M. van der Weyde, April 14, 1909, and May 7, 1914; William M. van der Weyde to Clair J. Grece, June 26, 1910; William M. van der Weyde to Thaddeus B. Wakeman, March 11, 1912, Records of the TPNHA.

30. William M. van der Weyde, "Memo. Regarding Paine's Remains," June 1, 1914, Records of the TPNHA. The secret was more of a modest misdirection than anything else since the leading British inquirers after the remains had not played along with this conceit. See [Hunns], *Thomas Paine's Bones*, 16; [Watson], *Brief History*, 5–6; Reynolds to van der Weyde, April 14, 1909.

31. Conway, *Life of Paine*, 2: 428; "Guns Boom," 664; Conway, "Adventures of Thomas Paine's Bones," 12. Paine's motto was added to the face of the monument sometime after its initial dedication in 1839, but by 1860. See Moreau, "Thomas Paine's Monument," 195.

32. "Paine Bust Dedicated," 359; Conway, *Autobiography*, 1: 447. Contra Foote's point, Thaddeus B. Wakeman's address at the same event in 1899 invoked the "desecrated" sepulcher with the old reverential longing for the restoration of Paine's remains: "The time may come when they will be found and returned to the land he freed and loved." See T. B. Wakeman, "The Father of Republics," *Truth Seeker*, June 24, 1899, 391. Conway's observation about no longer living in a period in which saints could be real was itself rife with ambiguity; he made it in the course of describing a meeting with John Henry Newman, who, haloed in candlelight, seems to Conway (momentarily at least) very much like a living successor to medieval saints. For another suggestive passage in which Conway viewed his ability to play imaginatively with myths about the saints as part of his emancipated stance toward such lore, see Conway, *Autobiography*, 2: 132. Parsing the "religion" involved with "secular relics" has proven a complicated task in other cases as well. For example, in her study of the materiality of Victorian memorialization practices, Deborah Lutz draws a distinction between religious and secular relics, situating Victorian mementoes within a larger story of secularization in which the nineteenth-century enchantment with relics is primarily "lyrical" or poetic rather than religious. See Lutz, *Relics of Death*, 4–5, 9–10, 12. In his study of the short-lived "cult" built around José Antonio López de Santa Ana and the relics of a heroic Mexican nationalism in the second quarter of the nineteenth century, Alan Knight concluded that such religious borrowings were

212 NOTES TO CHAPTER 1

merely "a series of metaphors," largely inapt and ineffectual. This attempt at "secular religion" was not "real religion," which requires "a supernatural or transcendental quality." See Alan Knight, "The Several Legs of Santa Ana: A Saga of Secular Relics," *Past and Present* 206 (2010): 227–55. Perhaps that is the case with Santa Ana's leg relic in nineteenth-century Mexico—that such "devotion" did not rise to "genuine secular/religious hybridization"—but that conclusion hinges on Knight's prior definition of "real religion" as involving "a supernatural or miraculous cult." Hence his more sweeping conclusion that all "talk of secular saints, cults, and relics is, at best, metaphorical, and, at worst, seriously misleading" is an overreach (250–55). The definition of religion was up for grabs in the nineteenth century, just as it is in twenty-first-century scholarship; the religious dimensions of secularism were (and are) similarly under negotiation, all of which makes such classificatory judgments about what is and is not "real religion" or "genuine" hybridity highly problematic. A similarly sharp distinction between the religious relics of saints and the historical relics of nineteenth-century collectors, again based on an efficacious "transcendent power" in the former that is lacking in the latter, is evident in Barnett, *Sacred Relics*, 36–37, 50–51. But as Barnett also argues, the two types of relics were deeply entangled in nineteenth-century sentimental discourses of memory, sacredness, family, and loss (53–64). Likewise, my emphasis is on studying the negotiations and entanglements: in this case, not only how Paineites variously navigated the materiality of charged objects but also, more broadly, how avowed secularists permitted or refused "religion" in their lives—metaphoric, material, ethical, or otherwise. It is the contortions involved in both the embrace and denial of "religion" (and its associated terms) that warrant scrutiny. A historical judgment of religious authenticity is beside the point.

33. T. B. Wakeman, "A Positivist's View of Thomas Paine," *Truth Seeker*, March 6, 1880, 159; T. B. Wakeman, "Thomas Paine as a Winged Angel," *Torch of Reason*, Jan. 31, 1901, 6; "Tributes to Thomas Paine," *Truth Seeker*, Feb. 9, 1901, 87–88; "At the Liberal Club," *Truth Seeker*, Feb. 9. 1901, 88. For the ways in which the saint and angel tropes were simultaneously treated as mere "fancies" yet embraced as revealing the "solid reality" of Paine's "disembodied influence" and his surpassing excellence as a modern saint, see "Paine as a Saint or Angel?" *Torch of Reason*, Jan. 31, 1901, 8. Still, any use of religious words in freethinking contexts could draw criticism, including the use of the word *saint*. See "Religion and Saints," *Boston Investigator*, April 8, 1885, 4.

34. T. B. Wakeman, *Evolution or Creation? An Address* (New York: New York Liberal Publishing, [1883]), 53, 56–58; M. M. Mangasarian, *A New Catechism*, 5th ed. (Chicago: Independent Religious Society, 1906), 121–22. On the contradictions within modern anti-fetishism, see Bruno Latour, *On the Modern Cult of Factish Gods* (Durham, NC: Duke University Press, 2010), 7–11, 18–19. Also see J. Lorand Matory, *The Fetish Revisited: Marx, Freud, and the Gods Black People Make* (Durham, NC:

Duke University Press, 2018), which effectively analyzes fetishism within both European and African history. Matory thus exposes the "asymmetrical privilege" that the enlightened assumed in applying the term "to other people's highly cathected things," while presupposing "their own invulnerability to the accusation of fetishism" (27). The racialization of fetishes and relics to subordinate the unenlightened was given graphic visual expression in Heston's cartoon, "Some Old Relics," 81. "St. Sambo the Coon" is pictured providing warrant to Roman Catholic relics such as a bone from the arm of St. Anthony of Padua. Wakeman's version of these racial hierarchies, built on the primal fetishizing of objects, was more erudite than Heston's visual repertory but no less engrained.

35. Thaddeus B. Wakeman, "Address," in Elliott, *Rededication*, 23–25; Thomas Paine, "The Crisis, No. VII," *Pennsylvania Packet*, Nov. 12, 1778, 1; Conway, *Writings of Thomas Paine*, 273–74; Conway, *Life of Paine*, 2: 206–10, 215, 218–19, 256. For Paine as the originator of "the Religion of Humanity," with the phrase usually capitalized for sacred emphasis, see also Thaddeus B. Wakeman, *The Emancipation of Education* (Silverton, OR: Torch of Reason, [1899]), 7; James B. Elliott, "What Thomas Paine Accomplished," *Humanitarian Review* 1 (1903): 97–98; Wakeman, "Father of Republics," 406; John E. Remsburg, *Thomas Paine, the Apostle of Liberty* (New York: Truth Seeker, 1917), 146–47, 179, 211; F. J. Gould, *Thomas Paine* (London: Parsons, 1925), 54–55. With the help of digitization it is now a simple matter to see that Wakeman's claim for Paine being the first to use the phrase *the religion of humanity* is inaccurate. There are a couple of prior and contemporaneous instances, though none clearly with the staying power of Paine's. Of course, that staying power was largely a product of late nineteenth-century Paineites underlining that passage from *The Crisis* and conferring singular importance upon it. For two prior instances in keeping with Paine's own enlightened religious sensibility, see *Literary Register: Or, Weekly Miscellany* 1 (1769): 254; Jonathan Richardson, *Richardsoniana: Or, Occasional Reflections on the Moral Nature of Man* (London: Dodsley, 1776), 22. For an American example nearly contemporaneous with Paine's usage, see B. Waterhouse, *On the Principle of Vitality* (Boston: Fleet, 1790), 24. The larger point is that the phrase was of little consequence in the eighteenth century; its currency was almost entirely a nineteenth-century creation in the hands of Comteans, Paineites, secularists, and religious liberals.

36. [T. B. Wakeman], "Secularism—Our Religion—Why Not?" *Torch of Reason*, Jan. 8, 1903, 4. See also [T. B. Wakeman], "Secularism—How Can It Replace 'Religion'?" *Torch of Reason*, Jan. 1, 1903, 5; T. B. Wakeman, "Saint Ingersoll," *Free Thought Magazine* 19 (1901): 93–94. For Wakeman's intellectual trajectory as well as an appended biographical sketch, see Thaddeus Burr Wakeman, *Free Thought: Past, Present and Future* (Chicago: H. L. Green, 1899), 22–23.

37. "Tributes to Thomas Paine," 86; Susan H. Wixon, "Address," *Proceedings at the Ninth Annual Meeting of the Free Religious Association* (Boston: Free Religious Association, 1876), 47. Conway's reminiscences are borne out by the religious qualities of one well-documented Paine celebration in Cincinnati from this period. One speaker invoked the "crosses" and "crowns" of the "world's saviors" in connection to Paine's sacrifices; another orator compared the "*true religion*" expressed in Paine's motto with the "hatred, bigotry, and passion" of those Cincinnatians who still took delight in lambasting Paine and his devoted followers. See *The Paine Festival: Celebration of the 119th Anniversary of the Birth-Day of Thomas Paine, at Cincinnati* (Cincinnati: Nicholson, 1856), 9, 31.

38. John Emerson Roberts, "Thomas Paine's Labor for the Liberties of Man," *Liberal Review* 2 (1905): 483, 494; "Thomas Paine: Celebrations," 99, 102.

39. James Feron, "Paine Tombstone Uncovered Upstate Revives Mystery about Pamphleteer," *New York Times*, July 19, 1976, 42; "Paine's Gravestone Reported Discovered," *Hartford Courant*, July 20, 1976, 7; James Feron, "Thomas Paine Mystery at Tivoli, N.Y., Solved," *New York Times*, July 20, 1976, 35.

40. Hazel Burgess, "An Extended History of the Remains of Thomas Paine," *Journal of Radical History* 8 (2007): 1–29, with mention of the exhibit at p. 15.

41. Collins, *Trouble with Tom*, 233. The repetition of Conway's globalizing gesture could be hard to resist even for the most exacting historians. As Sean Wilentz observed in a review essay in 1995, Paine's lost bones "were never recovered. So Paine rests nowhere. Or better, he is everywhere." See Sean Wilentz, "The Air around Tom Paine," *New Republic*, April 23, 1995, 41.

42. The prophet motif was developed at particular length by David Muzzey, a leader of the Ethical Culture Society, in his address at the centennial celebration of Paine's death in 1909. See *Memorial Celebration*, 10–12. Also see John S. Crosby's address, "Thomas Paine as a Political Prophet," in *Truth Seeker*, Feb. 9, 1901, 89; Wakeman, "Father of Republics," 407.

Chapter 2: Positivist Rites and Secular Funerals

1. Courtlandt Palmer, "A Positivist Funeral and Its Lesson," *Truth Seeker*, March 26, 1881, 199. For Palmer's views more broadly, see Courtlandt Palmer, *The Cause of Humanity; or, The Waning and the Rising Faith* (New York: Society of Humanity, 1879).

2. "Mournful," *Truth Seeker*, June 15, 1875, 5; "Obituary," *Truth Seeker*, Aug. 1, 1875, 5; "Funeral Service," *Truth Seeker*, June 8, 1878, 363; Hugh Byron Brown, "Remarks on Marriage, etc.," in *The Truth Seeker Collection of Forms, Hymns, and Recitations* (New York: Bennett, 1877), 48–50; Palmer, "Positivist Funeral," 199. "The choir

invisible" passage was quoted from George Eliot, who had been strongly influenced by Comte's religion of humanity.

3. "Courtlandt Palmer's Funeral," *Truth Seeker*, Aug. 4, 1888, 484; "How an Agnostic Died," *Cleveland Plain Dealer*, July 27, 1888, 1; J. H. Beadle, "A Sign of the Times? The Funeral of the Late Courtlandt Palmer," *Aberdeen Daily News* (Aberdeen, SD), Aug. 10, 1888, 2. The coverage of Palmer's death and funeral was very extensive, especially in the New York papers, but accounts were also widely reprinted across the country. In what was by then a very long tradition, Palmer's story became another prominent example in debates about infidel deathbeds, involving Hume, Voltaire, and Paine, among others. See "Agnostic Deathbeds," *Truth Seeker*, Aug. 11, 1888, 503; "The Fellows That Solomon Meant," *Truth Seeker*, Aug. 18, 1888, 520; G. W. Foote, *Infidel Death-Beds* (New York: Truth Seeker, 1892), 76–79. For a broad-ranging consideration of the genre, see Bradley Kime, "Infidel Deathbeds: Irreligious Dying and Sincere Disbelief in Nineteenth-Century America," *Church History* 86 (2017): 427–57.

4. "Courtlandt Palmer's Funeral," 484.

5. "Courtlandt Palmer's Funeral," 485; "Two Views," *Truth Seeker*, Aug. 18, 1888, 520–21; "Courtlandt Palmer's Funeral," *Truth Seeker*, Aug. 25, 1888, 532–33.

6. George Jacob Holyoake, *The Origin and Nature of Secularism; Showing That Where Freethought Commonly Ends Secularism Begins* (London: Watts, 1896), 121–32; "Courtlandt Palmer's Funeral," 532.

7. Herbert Croly, "The Breach in Civilization," 6–7, 11, Felix Frankfurter Papers, Box 215, Manuscript Division, Library of Congress. A portion of this manuscript has been published in Charles Hirschfield, ed., "The Memoirs of Herbert Croly: An Unpublished Document," *New York History* 58 (1977): 313–29. For two outlines of the sacramental structure of Comte's positivism, including the sacrament of presentation, see Auguste Comte, *The Catechism of Positive Religion*, trans. Richard Congreve (London: Chapman, 1858), 128–39; and Richard Congreve, *The Sacraments of the Religion of Humanity as Administered at the Church of Humanity* (London: Kenny, 1893). For an especially helpful historical account of organized positivism on the American side, see Gillis J. Harp, "'The Church of Humanity': New York's Worshipping Positivists," *Church History* 60 (1991): 508–23. That piece forms the basis of the second chapter in Harp's *Positivist Republic: Auguste Comte and the Reconstruction of American Liberalism, 1865–1920* (University Park: Pennsylvania State University Press, 1995), 23–48. For the British side, see especially John Edwin McGee, *A Crusade for Humanity: The History of Organized Positivism in England* (London: Watts, 1931); and T. R. Wright, *The Religion of Humanity: The Impact of Comtean Positivism on Victorian Britain* (Cambridge: Cambridge University Press, 1986), 73–124. Comte had initially built his philosophy around an evolutionary schema that mapped the advancement of knowledge out of theological and metaphysical stages into its

positivist phase in which the natural sciences—mathematics, astronomy, physics, chemistry, and biology—reigned supreme. Religion with its long history (fetishism to polytheism to monotheism) was doomed to fade away with the ascendancy of the sciences, including Comte's new science of society, sociology. Comte's stance toward religion shifted in his *Système de politique positive* (1851–1854) and his *Catéchisme positiviste* (1852). He offered the new positivist religion—alternately labeled "the universal religion" or "the religion of humanity"—as a way forward out of the upheavals roiling nineteenth-century society. Religion would no longer be displaced but instead find evolutionary fulfillment in the full-fledged religion of humanity. This second stage of Comte's work alienated many of his earlier admirers, who frequently dismissed it as a deranged or enfeebled turn in his intellectual labors. But for religious positivists, this shift constituted the heart of his work.

8. David Goodman Croly, *A Positivist Primer: Being a Series of Familiar Conversations on the Religion of Humanity* (New York: David Wesley, 1871), 14–15, 18.

9. Jennie June Croly, "Love-Life of Auguste Comte," *Modern Thinker*, July 1, 1870, 185–91; Croly, *Positivist Primer*, 22–25, 27. An advertisement for the portraits appears in the back of Croly's *Primer*. Comte conflated his Clotilde with her patron saint of the same name, whose feast day was June 3. See Albert Crompton, ed., *Confession and Testament of Auguste Comte: And His Correspondence with Clotilde de Vaux* (Liverpool: Henry Young and Sons, 1910), xi, 304, 343. For a summary of Clotilde de Vaux's impact on Comte's religious turn, see Wright, *Religion of Humanity*, 13–17, 35–36. For a full exposition of how prayer worked in these circles not as a petitionary practice but as a practice of moral discipline and effusive aspiration, see Joseph Lonchampt, *Positivist Prayer*, trans. John G. Mills (Goshen, NY: Independent Republican, 1877).

10. Henry Edger, *The Positivist Calendar: Or, Transitional System of Public Commemoration Instituted by Auguste Comte, Founder of the Positive Religion of Humanity* (Long Island, NY: Modern Times, 1856), 21, 31–32.

11. Frederic Harrison, *Autobiographic Memoirs*, 2 vols. (London: Macmillan, 1911). 2: 279–81. For Edger's chapel or oratorio addition, see Harp, "Church of Humanity," 510; and Robert Edward Schneider, *Positivism in the United States: The Apostleship of Henry Edger* (Rosario, Argentina: n.p., 1946), 77–78, 83.

12. "The Festival of Humanity," *Modern Thinker*, Jan. 1, 1873, 159–60. For a reading of Comtean positivism that emphasizes how American feminists reworked it for their own reform purposes, see William Leach, *True Love and Perfect Union: The Feminist Reform of Sex and Society* (New York: Basic Books, 1980), 133–57. Those appropriations centered on Comte's critique of self-centered individualism, his stress on social altruism, and his idealization of women's moral example, but they required ignoring Comte's insistent domestication of women, his sharply gendered division of the public and the private, and his perpetuation of a patriarchal priesthood.

13. Croly, "Breach in Civilization," 11–12; *Memories of Jane Cunningham Croly "Jenny June"* (New York: G. P. Putnam's Sons, 1904), 55, 64–65, 75–76. The First Congregation of the Society of the Church of Humanity had fallen into "innocuous desuetude" by 1883 according to one report but was briefly revived for a course of lectures in 1886 after receiving a bequest. See "The Society of Humanity," *Truth Seeker*, Nov. 13, 1886, 729. There were some ongoing efforts to organize positivist reading groups or Sunday meetings after that, but they were thin at best. See "Can Freethinkers Organize?" *Truth Seeker*, Feb. 20, 1892, 115.

14. For the quip about how small these churches were, see Malcolm Quin, *Memoirs of a Positivist* (London: George Allen and Unwin, 1924), 130–31. On the decorative designs and worship practices in these Church of Humanity congregations in England, see McGee, *Crusade for Humanity*, 114–19, 130–47; and Wright, *Religion of Humanity*, 82–86, 249–60. For an examination of the use of hymnody among religious positivists, see Paul Watt, "The Function of Hymns in the Liturgical Life of Malcolm Quin's Positivist Church, 1878–1905," *Yale Journal of Music and Religion* 5 (2019): 55–70. On the movement's architectural ambitions for new churches and halls, see Matthew Wilson, "On the Material and Immaterial Architecture of Organised Positivism in Britain," *Architectural Histories* 3 (2015): 1–21.

15. Quin, *Memoirs*, 22, 28–29, 41–42.

16. Quin, *Memoirs*, 41, 50–52, 58.

17. Quin, *Memoirs*, 87, 109, 120–21, 129–30, 145.

18. Quin, *Memoirs*, 151–58, 168. One sacrament Quin never performed was marriage, and this was in fair measure because he could not wrap his mind (or body) around Comte's "severe conditions" governing that rite. Receiving this positivist sacrament, on Comte's terms, would have perpetually forbidden any remarriage, even in the case of being widowed; it also entailed a three-month waiting period for sexual relations after its celebration—a "preamble" of chastity within marriage. Quin, though, was still attracted to the Virgin-Mother imagery and the sexless utopia to which it pointed in the remote future. See Quin, *Memoirs*, 157, 193–94. Henry Edger was similarly pained over Comte's strenuous rules regarding marriage, chastity, and remarriage; he spent a good portion of his life as a positivist apostle trying to evade those rules in a tangle of sexual relationships that markedly deviated from Comte's sacramental norms, which had been heavily informed by his hyper-idealization of Clotilde de Vaux. On Edger's travails, see Schneider, *Positivism*, 107–23, 176–90.

19. Quin, *Memoirs*, 185–86, 196–98, 200–204.

20. Quin, *Memoirs*, 164–65, 203–6, 222–23.

21. Thaddeus B. Wakeman, "The Positivist Episode," in *Memories of Jane Cunningham Croly*, 51–56. For Wakeman's sharp dissociation of the religion of humanity from Comte's Catholic and papal tendencies, see Thaddeus B. Wakeman, *The Religion*

of Humanity (New York: New York Liberal Publishing, 1878), 29; T. B. Wakeman, "The Father of Republics," *Truth Seeker*, July 1, 1899, 406.

22. Congreve, *Sacraments*, 54–55. Brown's intent to publish a manual of "rational ceremonies" for "Liberal Societies and Churches of Humanity" was mentioned in a short excerpt of his in *Truth Seeker Collection*, 49–50. On the later careers of Brown and Henderson, see "The Death and Funeral of Hugh Byron Brown," *Truth Seeker*, Aug. 6, 1898, 504. The "atheistical parody" criticism comes from a contemporaneous review of Edger's program of positivist worship. See Schneider, *Positivism*, 86. The notion of the "Church of Humanity," like the construct "the Religion of Humanity," passed out of specific positivist contexts into wider circulation. An ecumenical body known as the Liberal Congress of Religion made the development of churches of humanity part of its platform in the 1890s, and twentieth-century humanist fellowships sometimes embraced the phrasing as well. There was also an atheist Church of Humanity in Great Bend, Kansas, in the first two decades of the twentieth century, which is discussed in Chapter 3. In a couple of other instances, New Thought metaphysicians had adopted the label as well. See *All Souls Church* (Chicago: n.p., 1899), 96; J. Arthur Ragsdale, ed., *The Story of a Humanist Church* (Oakland, CA: n.p., 1972), 4; W. H. Kerr, "The 'Church of Humanity' Defended," *Humanitarian Review* 2 (July 1904): 556–59; Singleton W. Davis, "The Church of Humanity," *Humanitarian Review* 6 (Jan. 1908): 6–10.

23. "Romanus Emerson—His Funeral Address," *Boston Investigator*, Oct. 20, 1852, n.p. Emerson's years of infidel activism are traceable in the pages of the *Boston Investigator*. See, for example, "Social Reform Convention," *Boston Investigator*, June 12, 1844, n.p.; "Infidel Relief Society," *Boston Investigator*, March 24, 1847, n.p.; "The Ninth Anniversary of the Liberation of Abner Kneeland from Boston Jail," *Boston Investigator*, Aug. 25, 1847, n.p.; "Celebration of Thomas Paine's Birth-Day," *Boston Investigator*, Feb. 2, 1848, n.p.; Samuel Barnes, "Death of Romanus Emerson," *Boston Investigator*, Nov. 10, 1852, n.p.

24. "Romanus Emerson," n.p. For Emerson's memorialization at the next Paine festival, see "Celebration of Thomas Paine's Birth-Day," *Boston Investigator*, Feb. 2, 1853, n.p. His memory was invoked in Boston's freethought circles at least into the 1880s. See "Reform Is Infidel," *Boston Investigator*, Aug. 26, 1885, 6.

25. Foote, *Infidel Death-Beds*, 6–7; George L. Pratt, "Be Buried as Befits Sensible Men," *Truth Seeker*, March 5, 1892, 154; "The International Freethought Congress at Madrid," *Truth Seeker*, Jan. 14, 1893, 25. For the monitoring of the transnational spread of "secular funerals," see "Items of Foreign Freethought News," *Truth Seeker*, Nov. 22, 1890, 741; "Items of Foreign Freethought News," *Truth Seeker*, June 13, 1891, 373; "Items of Foreign News Interesting to Freethinkers," *Truth Seeker*, April 30, 1892, 279. For local examples of "secular funerals" within the United States, see illustrative

obituary notices in *Truth Seeker*, Aug. 2, 1890, 491; *Truth Seeker*, Feb. 11, 1893, 90; *Truth Seeker*, May 13, 1893, 295; *Truth Seeker*, Feb. 3, 1894, 72; *Truth Seeker*, Jan. 12, 1895, 26; *Truth Seeker*, July 18, 1896, 459; *Truth Seeker*, March 4, 1899, 139. On the relative success of freethinkers in countering Christian tales about infidel deathbeds by the end of the nineteenth century, see Kime, "Infidel Deathbeds," 431–32, 451–54.

26. Austin Holyoake, "Secular Ceremonies," *National Reformer*, Nov. 15, 1868, 313–14; Austin Holyoake and Charles Watts, eds., *The Secularist's Manual of Songs and Ceremonies* (London: Austin, [1871]), 4, 126–28. For an advertisement for the fourth edition, see *Secular Review and Secularist*, Aug. 4, 1877, 144. For subsequent entrants, see [Charles Watts], *A Secular Burial Service* (London: Watts, n.d.); George N. Hill, "A Secular Burial Service," *Boston Investigator*, June 9, 1886, 2. For one that combined Holyoake's burial service with an Ingersoll elegy, see J. Weston, "Obituary," *Secular Review*, Feb. 13, 1886, 110. For another that relied on one of Ingersoll's funeral orations, see "Form 10" in *Truth Seeker Collection*, 95–96.

27. C. B. Reynolds, "Obituary," *Truth Seeker*, Feb. 9, 1889, 94; Austin Holyoake, *Secular Ceremonies: A Burial Service* (London: Austin, [1869]), 3–5; Foote, *Infidel Death-Beds*, 53–54.

28. Holyoake, *Burial Service*, 3; Holyoake and Watts, *Secularist's Manual*, 4; Goblet d'Alviella, *The Contemporary Evolution of Religious Thought in England, America, and India*, trans. J. Moden (London: Williams and Norgate, 1885), 150–52; *Truth Seeker Collection*, 74–75; Holyoake, *Origin and Nature*, 129. Bennett's *Truth Seeker Collection* had the added wrinkle that he wanted to keep freethinking liberals and liberal-minded spiritualists in alliance with one another, so he mixed "materialist" and "spiritualist" ceremonies together. He thought their shared anticlericalism was enough to keep them working in common, but the sustainability of that kind of coalition was a repeated flashpoint in secularist ranks. It frequently blew apart. See the fate of the Society of Moralists, which is discussed below.

29. d'Alviella, *Contemporary Evolution*, 150–52; A. R. Ayres, "The Society of Moralists," *Truth Seeker*, May 1, 1886, 279; "A New Society," *Truth Seeker*, June 11, 1881, 378. Membership numbers were reported in Ayres, "Society of Moralists," 279; "Brotherhood of Moralists," *Truth Seeker*, April 12, 1890, 231; "Brotherhood of Moralists," *Truth Seeker*, Nov. 22, 1890, 739.

30. D. C. Hall, "Nature's Work Finished," *Truth Seeker*, Aug. 26, 1882, 539; F. F. Rau, "Secular Funerals," *Boston Investigator*, Nov. 24, 1886, 1. For favorable notices and short reviews, see "Book Notices," *Truth Seeker*, May 22, 1886, 334; "A Very Useful Book," *Boston Investigator*, May 26, 1886, 6; "Book Notices," *Index*, May 27, 1886, 574. Ayres's handbook was first advertised in the *Truth Seeker* in April 1886 and frequently thereafter. There was a second edition with a modified title, *A Secular Marriage and Funeral Ritual and Collection of Secular Hymns*, which began to be advertised in

December 1893. The pamphlets themselves were undated. The only extant copy I have been able to locate is a copy of the first edition at the New York Public Library. A copy of the second edition, with pictured title page and preface, sold on eBay a few years ago, but its whereabouts are unknown.

31. A. R. Ayres, ed., *A Secular Funeral and Marriage Hand-Book* (Hannibal, MO: Standard, [1886]), 5, 7, 15, 29; "Book Notices," *Index*, 586.

32. Elmina D. Slenker, "Children's Department," *Boston Investigator*, July 14, 1886, 8; "Letters from Friends," *Truth Seeker*, Jan. 26, 1889, 58; "Letters from Friends," *Truth Seeker*, Aug. 16, 1890, 522; "Letters from Friends," *Truth Seeker*, March 30, 1889, 202; "Letters from Friends," *Truth Seeker*, June 14, 1890, 378; "Letters from Friends," *Truth Seeker*, May 10, 1890, 298; "Letters from Friends," *Truth Seeker*, April 16, 1887, 251. For examples of how Ayres's book was used from place to place, see "Letters from Friends," *Truth Seeker*, Aug. 14, 1886, 522; "Obituary," *Truth Seeker*, March 19, 1887, 190; George L. Pratt, "An Organization to Conduct Freethinkers' Burial Services," *Truth Seeker*, July 23, 1892, 475; "Said He," *Boston Investigator*, March 2, 1887, 3; "Obituary," *Boston Investigator*, April 20, 1892, 6; "Letters of Friends," *Truth Seeker*, Sept. 28, 1895, 618; George L. Pratt, "A 'Confession of Faith,'" *Truth Seeker*, May 23, 1896, 331; Maurice Pechin, "Captain George W. Watson—Funeral Address," *Free Thought Magazine* 15 (1897): 433–36.

33. Ayres, "Society of Moralists," 279; Ayres, *Secular Funeral*, 37; A. R. Ayres, "Can Liberals Organize?," *Truth Seeker*, April 16, 1892, 247.

34. Frank O'Mahony, "Banding Together," *Truth Seeker*, Jan. 27, 1883, 53; Frank O'Mahony, "An Old Editor Talks," *Truth Seeker*, May 12, 1883, 301; J. R. Perry to the editor, *Truth Seeker*, Dec. 15, 1888, 795; A. R. Ayres, "The Term 'Agnostic,'" *Boston Investigator*, Dec. 5, 1888, 2; A. R. Ayres to the editor, *Truth Seeker*, Dec. 6, 1890. 778. On the critique of the American Secular Union as being too ecumenical, see A. R. Ayres to the editor, *Truth Seeker*, Oct. 11, 1890, 650; F. H. Rau, "Wants Only True Liberals," *Truth Seeker*, Nov. 29, 1890, 757. On the schism or separation, see "Lectures and Meetings," *Truth Seeker*, June 25, 1887, 405; "Letters from Friends," *Truth Seeker*, Aug. 6, 1887, 506; "Letters from Friends," *Truth Seeker*, Jan. 21, 1888, 42.

35. Pratt, "Organization to Conduct," 475; Pratt, "'Confession of Faith,'" 331; George L. Pratt, "Don't Let the Priest Get You at Death," *Truth Seeker*, March 23, 1895, 187.

36. Warren Allen Smith, "Sinclair Lewis Died a Humanist," *Humanist* 11 (Jan. 1951): 103–4. For another example of the shaping influence of Ingersoll's era on a mid-century freethinker's self-designed funeral, see Charles Alvah Robinson, *A Secular Funeral Service* (East Orange, NJ: n.p., 1952). For subsequent guides that filled the role that the works of Austin Holyoake, D. M. Bennett, and A. R. Ayres formerly performed, see F. J. Gould, *Funeral Services without Theology* (London: Watts, 1923); and Corliss Lamont, *A Humanist Funeral Service* (Boston: Beacon Press, 1947). For

analysis of contemporary funeral practices among British humanists, see Matthew Engelke, "The Coffin Question: Death and Materiality in Humanist Funerals," *Material Religion* 11 (2015): 26–48.

37. Edwin H. Wilson, "Humanist Manifesto Book: Chapter XVI Liturgical Agnosticism," Box 191, f. (folder) 3, Edwin H. Wilson Papers of the American Humanist Association, 1913–1989, Special Collections Research Center, Southern Illinois University, Carbondale, Illinois. Wilson kept files on several humanistic leaders who were attempting to create liturgies and rituals congruent with their religious sensibility, including Charles Francis Potter, Kenneth Patton, Alfred Cole, Vincent Silliman, and Sherwin Wine. Charles Francis Potter called his experiments with rites of passage "applied humanism"; he developed a variety of christening, wedding, and funeral services for the First Humanist Society of New York, which he founded in 1929. See Charles Francis Potter, *The Preacher and I: An Autobiography* (New York: Crown, 1951), 378–92. For the fruition of Patton's long-running liturgical projects, see Kenneth L. Patton, *A Religion for One World: Art and Symbols for a Universal Religion* (Boston: Beacon Press, 1964).

38. C. H. Roman, "C. H. Roman's Agnostic Monument," *Progressive World* 3 (Sept. 1949): 419.

39. C. H. Roman to Curtis W. Reese, June 9, 1949, Box 96, f. 23, Wilson Papers; Photographs of C. H. Roman's Monument, Box 96, f. 23, Wilson Papers. There are also photographs, along with a clippings file on Roman, available through the Shelby County Historical Society, Sidney, Ohio.

40. "Rev. Meister Denounces Roman Monument," and "Lipstick Mars C. H. Roman's Agnostic Monument," *Sidney Daily News*, clippings file, Shelby County Historical Society. On Wilson's "grave doubts" about the wisdom of a public dedication, see Edwin H. Wilson to C. H. Roman, May 9, 1950, Box 96, f. 23, Wilson Papers. He thought the staging of a public event would be taken as another "frontal attack on your neighbors there."

41. "Last Rites for Christian Henry Roman," Box 96, f. 23, Wilson Papers.

42. The brief manuscript for the dedication ceremony is untitled, but it is in the same file with Wilson's manuscript for the "Last Rites," Box. 96, f. 23, Wilson Papers. For Wilson's role in memorializing Roman, see also "In Memoriam: Christian Henry Roman (1881–1951)," *Progressive World* 5 (May 1951): 131.

Chapter 3 Churches of Humanity

1. "Col. Robert G. Ingersoll, Rev. Caroline J. Bartlett and the Independent Church," *Free Thought Magazine* 14 (1896): 101–6; "George Jacob Holyoake on the People's Church of Kalamazoo, Michigan," *Free Thought Magazine* 14 (1896): 311;

"Letter from Rev. Caroline J. Bartlett to George Jacob Holyoake," *Free Thought Magazine* 14 (1896): 530–31. For Bartlett's full account in a subsequent sermon of why she would welcome Ingersoll as a member, see Caroline J. Bartlett, *Why the People's Church of Kalamazoo Would Fellowship Col. Ingersoll* (Kalamazoo, MI: People's Church, 1896).

2. A compendium of the debate over Ingersoll's "conversion," including selections from the *Wesleyan Christian Advocate* and letters of explanation from Ingersoll, can be found in E. M. Macdonald, *Col. Robert G. Ingersoll as He Is: A Complete Refutation of his Clerical Enemies' Malicious Slanders* (New York: Truth Seeker, [1896]), 101–10.

3. "A Promising Myth," *Truth Seeker*, Jan. 25, 1896, 51; "That Kalamazoo 'Conversion' of Colonel Ingersoll," *Truth Seeker*, Feb. 1, 1896, 68; "Holyoake on the People's Church," 311; "Letter from Rev. Caroline J. Bartlett," 530; Macdonald, *Col. Robert G. Ingersoll*, 108.

4. "A Town without a Church," *Boston Investigator*, Aug. 29, 1883, 4; "The Godless Town of Liberal, (MO.)," *Boston Investigator*, Nov. 26, 1884, 2. For an overview of Liberal's convoluted religious history in the 1880s and 1890s, see H. Roger Grant, "Freethinkers and Spiritualists: A Missouri Case Study," *Bulletin of the Missouri Historical Society* 27 (1971): 259–71.

5. Ralph Waldo Emerson, *The Conduct of Life* (Boston: Ticknor and Fields, 1860), 210; Walter L. Sheldon, *The Meaning of the Ethical Movement* (St. Louis: Commercial Publishing, 1891), 40–41.

6. Emerson, *Conduct of Life*, 177, 180–81, 186; Ralph Waldo Emerson, "Essential Principles of Religion" (1862), in David Robinson, ed., *The Spiritual Emerson* (Boston: Beacon, 2003), 240.

7. Emerson, "Self-Reliance" (1841), in Robinson, *Spiritual Emerson*, 99; Octavius Brooks Frothingham, *Recollections and Impressions, 1822–1890* (New York: G. P. Putnam's Sons, 1891), 116, 120; Ralph Waldo Emerson, "Remarks at the Meeting for Organizing the Free Religious Association" (1867), in *The Complete Works of Ralph Waldo Emerson*, 12 vols. (Boston: Houghton, Mifflin, 1903–1904), 11: 478, 480. On the history of the Free Religious Association, see Stow Persons, *Free Religion: An American Faith* (New Haven, CT: Yale University Press, 1947).

8. Edmund C. Stedman, *Octavius Brooks Frothingham and the New Faith* (New York: G. P. Putnam's Sons, 1876), 11–13, 47–48; Frothingham, *Recollections*, 118–20, 126–32; Moncure Daniel Conway, ed., *The Sacred Anthology: A Book of Ethnical Scriptures* (New York: Henry Holt, 1874), xii. For a biographical study, see J. Wade Caruthers, *Octavius Brooks Frothingham, Gentle Radical* (Tuscaloosa, AL: University of Alabama Press, 1977), esp. 70–97 on his New York ministry.

9. O. B. Frothingham, *Why Go to Church?* (New York: Francis, 1874), 5, 13–14, 19–21; O. B. Frothingham, "Secular Religion," *Index*, Jan. 8, 1870, 5–6; *Proceedings at a Reception in Honor of the Rev. O. B. Frothingham Given by the Independent Liberal*

Church (New York: G. P. Putnam's Sons, 1879), 85; Stedman, *Octavius Brooks Frothingham*, 47.

10. Frothingham, "Secular Religion," 5–6; Stedman, *Octavius Brooks Frothingham*, 19–20, 36–38. Frothingham's favorable view of Parker was a given, but his inclusion of Paine and Ingersoll in the pantheon of his religion of humanity was also evident. See Frothingham, *Recollections*, 248–54. On the express inclusion of atheists in the FRA, see *Proceedings at the Fifth Annual Meeting of the Free Religious Association* (Boston: Cochrane, 1872), 6–7; *Proceedings at the Seventh Annual Meeting of the Free Religious Association* (Boston: Cochrane, 1874), 51.

11. Felix Adler, *How Far Does the Ethical Society Take the Place of a Church?* (Philadelphia: S. Burns Weston, 1897), 44; Frothingham, *Recollections*, 270. Frothingham's considerable influence on the Ethical Society, particularly through the example of his Independent Liberal Church, can be clearly seen in the memorial addresses given by Adler and others in honor of Frothingham in 1895. See "Octavius Brooks Frothingham Memorial Exercises," in *Ethical Addresses: Second Series* (Philadelphia: S. Burns Weston, 1896), 169–94.

12. Felix Adler, "Practical Needs of Free Religion," *Proceedings at the Twelfth Annual Meeting of the Free Religious Association* (Boston: Free Religious Association, 1879), 44. For an examination of Adler's fraught relationship with Judaism as he moved away from it to create the Ethical Society, see Benny Kraut, *From Reform Judaism to Ethical Culture: The Religious Evolution of Felix Adler* (Cincinnati: Hebrew Union College Press, 1979).

13. Adler, *How Far*, 41–44; Felix Adler, *The Religion of Duty* (New York: McClure, Phillips, 1905), 199. For an ample selection of Adler's Easter services, see "Easter Addresses," Felix Adler Papers, Boxes 79–80, f. 1–37, Rare Book and Manuscript Library, Columbia University. As time went on, leaders of Ethical Culture paid more sustained attention to the question of ceremony and ritual in their societies. Stanton Coit in London was especially productive, but it was never Adler's strong suit. For some of the efforts, mostly after 1900, see "Ethical Ceremonies," Felix Adler Papers, Box 34, f. 1.

14. Adler, *How Far*, 44–47, 50, 55; "The Ethical Society," *Truth Seeker*, May 22, 1886, 325. *Creed and Deed* (1877) was also the title of an early collection of Adler's lectures in which he hammered home the point that the Ethical Society was organized around right living, not right beliefs.

15. Adler, *How Far*, 52; Felix Adler, *Atheism: A Lecture* (New York: Co-operative Printers' Association, 1879), 17–19. On the various social welfare programs that Adler launched through the Ethical Society, see Howard B. Radest, *Toward Common Ground: The Story of the Ethical Societies in the United States* (New York: Ungar, 1969), 36–44.

16. Felix Adler, "Have We Still a Religion?" Adler Papers, Box 59, f. 5; Adler, "Practical Needs," 51, 55; Felix Adler, "The Religion of Humanity in Its Relation to Judaism and Christianity," Box 59, f. 1; Felix Adler, "The Religion of Humanity: Its Dawn in Palestine," Box 60, f. 26. Adler gave multiple lectures on the religion of humanity between 1877 and 1881; like Frothingham, he expressly distanced himself from Comte's version. See Felix Adler, "Auguste Comte's 'Religion of Humanity,'" Adler Papers, Box 59, f. 17.

17. S. B. Weston, *Ethical Culture: Four Lectures Delivered at Institute Hall* (Philadelphia: Edward Stern, 1885), 10–11, 16; Felix Adler, *Our Part in This World*, ed. Horace L. Friess (New York: King's Crown Press, 1946), 66–68, 71.

18. O. B. Frothingham and Felix Adler, *The Radical Pulpit* (New York: D. M. Bennett, n.d.); "The Radical Pulpit," *Truth Seeker*, Dec. 10, 1881, 793; "O. B. Frothingham," *Boston Investigator*, April 19, 1882, 4; "O. B. Frothingham," *Boston Investigator*, March 28, 1883, 4; Adler, "Religion of Humanity: Its Dawn in Palestine." On Adler's relationship with his father, see Kraut, *From Reform Judaism*, 85–86, 160–61.

19. "Frothingham and Beecher," *Boston Investigator*, March 11, 1874, 4; "Free Religion—Faith," *Boston Investigator*, Nov. 24, 1875, 4; "Free Religion—Once More," *Boston Investigator*, Dec. 15, 1875, 4; "Rev. O. B. Frothingham," *Boston Investigator*, Dec. 22, 1875, 4; "A Letter from Mr. Frothingham," *Boston Investigator*, Dec. 29, 1875, 6; "Free Thought—Religion," *Boston Investigator*, June 21, 1882, 4.

20. M. M. Mangasarian, *The Story of My Mind: Or, How I Became a Rationalist* (Chicago: Independent Religious Society, 1909), 20, 23–29, 31–32, 35.

21. "Frothingham Memorial Exercises," 193; Mangasarian, *Story of My Mind*, 48–51.

22. Mangasarian, *Story of My Mind*, 10, 49, 52, 55, 64, 70; M. M. Mangasarian, *Persecution! Or, The Attempt to Suppress Freedom of Speech in Chicago* (Chicago: Independent Religious Society, n.d.), 19–20. A run of Sunday programs for the Independent Religious Society (Rationalist) for the years 1907–1912 can be found at the Research Center, Chicago History Museum. Mangasarian's lectures on Paine were featured in the programs for Feb. 16 and 23, 1908. For his defense of Paine from Roosevelt's defamation, see the program for Feb. 14, 1909. His "Human Prayer" set against the Lord's Prayer appears in the program for Feb. 13, 1910.

23. M. M. Mangasarian, "The Religion of Ethical Culture," in *Ethical Addresses: First Series* (Philadelphia: S. Burns Weston, 1895), 69–90; "What Is the Independent Religious Society?" *Liberal Review* 2 (Dec. 1905): 185; Mangasarian, *Story of My Mind*, 8. The citation of Emerson's prediction of a new church based on moral science can be found in the programs for Nov. 17, 1907; Dec. 1, 1907; Jan. 12, 1908; Jan. 19, 1908; Oct. 4, 1908; Oct. 3, 1909. Mangasarian usually garbled the Emerson quotation—or had picked it up in garbled form from elsewhere—but the prophecy was

recognizable. He used it repeatedly as a motto to indicate the "spirit" of his religious society. See M. M. Mangasarian, *How the Bible Was Invented* (Chicago: Independent Religious Society, n.d.), 26. The idea that the society was dedicated to promoting "the religion of truth, righteousness, joy and freedom" regularly appeared in the weekly programs as the last line of the "Creed of the Independent Religious Society." See, for example, the program for Oct. 18, 1908, but it was recurrent. For his lecture on Comte's religion of humanity, see the program for Jan. 30, 1910.

24. Robert G. Ingersoll, "The Foundations of Faith," in *The Works of Robert G. Ingersoll*, 12 vols. (New York: Ingersoll League, 1933), 4: 290–91. The question about the religiousness of Mangasarian's society was addressed in the Sunday programs for Jan. 29, 1911, and May 16, 1909. The Holyoake endorsement appeared in "A Model Liberal Association: Independent Religious Society of Chicago," *Humanitarian Review* 11 (1903): 254. Mangasarian's citation of Ingersoll's "creed" was in keeping with wider usage of it in these circles. Pulled from Ingersoll's lecture "The Foundations of Faith," first delivered in 1895, the passage was frequently invoked as an epitome of Ingersoll's religion; it was intoned, for example, at Ingersoll's own funeral in July 1899, at the memorial service of his mother-in law, and at a commemoration of Ingersoll's birthday in Los Angeles in 1904. See "At the Bier of Ingersoll," *Truth Seeker*, Aug. 5, 1899, 487; "Death of a Notable Woman," *Truth Seeker*, Aug. 15, 1903, 519; "Ingersoll Birthday Celebration," *Humanitarian Review* 2 (1904): 648–49.

25. Curtis W. Reese, "Large Society in Chicago Joins Western Conference," *Christian Register*, March 23, 1922, 280; M. M. Mangasarian, *Humanism: A Religion for Americans* (Chicago: Independent Religious Society, [1922]), 3–7. The move from Orchestra Hall to the Studebaker Theatre was fraught with controversy. Mangasarian claimed his society had been evicted through a pressure campaign from Protestant groups concerned about upholding the ideal of Christian citizenship and appalled by Mangasarian's freethinking provocations. See Mangasarian, *Persecution!*, 3–9, 22–23.

26. Reese, "Large Society," 280; Mangasarian, *Humanism*, 10–11; Mangasarian, *Story of My Mind*, 49–50. On the rise of a clearly defined humanist movement within Unitarianism after World War I, see Mason Olds, *American Religious Humanism*, rev. ed. (Minneapolis, MN: Fellowship of Religious Humanists, 1996; repr., Hamden, CT: HUUmanists Association, 2006), 33–46.

27. Katie Kehm Smith, "What Shall Liberals Do to Be Saved?" *Truth Seeker*, March 19, 1892, 182–83. For a good overview of secular organizing in Oregon, see Patricia Brandt, "Organized Free Thought in Oregon: The Oregon State Secular Union," *Oregon Historical Quarterly* 87 (1986): 167–204.

28. Smith, "What Shall Liberals Do?," 182–83; Katie Kehm Smith, "The Necessity for Aggressiveness on the Part of Liberals," *Boston Investigator*, Jan. 3, 1894, 1; Katie Kehm Smith, "The Cause in Oregon," *Truth Seeker*, Dec. 30, 1893, 824. On the

church's founding on Paine's birthday, see "Some Good Sermons," *Morning Oregonian*, Jan. 30, 1893, 6; "Join the Secular Church," *Truth Seeker*, April 1, 1893, 202; Katie Kehm Smith, "The Cause in Oregon," *Truth Seeker*, July 8, 1893, 424.

29. For a sampling of Smith's Sunday lecture topics, see "Some Good Sermons," *Morning Oregonian*, Feb. 6, 1893, 8; "He Talked of Judas," *Morning Oregonian*, April 10, 1893, 8; "Pulpits and Pews," *Morning Oregonian*, June 25, 1893, 15; "City News in Brief," *Morning Oregonian*, Nov. 26, 1893, 5; "Some Work in Washington," *Truth Seeker*, Oct. 6, 1894, 635. On the Secular Sunday school, see "First Secular Church of Portland, Oregon," and "Freethinkers of the Pacific Coast, Attention!" *Truth Seeker*, Dec. 9, 1893, 778–79; Katie Kehm Smith, "Secular Sunday-Schools," *Truth Seeker*, Nov. 10, 1894, 711; Katie Kehm Smith, "Secular Sunday-Schools," *Truth Seeker Annual and Freethinkers' Almanac, 1895* (New York: Truth Seeker, 1895), 104–9; Katie Kehm Smith, "Paine Celebration at the First Secular Church of Portland, Or.," *Boston Investigator*, March 21, 1894, 2.

30. Katie Kehm Smith, "Christmas Celebration at Portland, Ore.," *Boston Investigator*, Feb. 14, 1894, 2; "Two Reports from Oregon," *Truth Seeker*, Feb. 3, 1894, 75.

31. Smith, "Christmas Celebration," 2; "Two Reports," 75; "First Secular Church," 778.

32. On Oregon Secular Park, see Katie Kehm Smith, "The Cause in Oregon," *Boston Investigator*, Aug. 11, 1894, 3. For the financial controversy involving it, see Charles Hagner, "Shake Hands and Settle It, Friends," *Truth Seeker*, Feb. 23, 1895, 123; and Charles Hagner, "An Explanation," *Truth Seeker*, Nov. 24, 1894, 746. Smith mentions her resignation without giving a reason in "The Cause in Oregon," *Boston Investigator*, Jan. 19, 1895, 2.

33. On the ten-day "Secular revival," see "Some Work in Washington," 635. Her shift to the leadership of the Silverton Secular Church is mentioned in Katie Kehm Smith, "The Cause in Oregon," *Truth Seeker*, June 29, 1895, 410, and in Katie Kehm Smith, "Right Living," *Truth Seeker*, July 6, 1895, 428. The remaining traces of Smith's churches and Sunday schools can be followed in Silverton's freethought newspaper, the *Torch of Reason*, which began appearing in November 1896. See *Torch of Reason*, Nov. 5, 1896; Nov. 26, 1896; Dec. 3, 1896; Jan. 14, 1897; Jan. 21, 1897; May 6, 1897; July 8, 1897; July 29, 1897; Oct. 7, 1897. The paper was unpaginated in its first year (Nov. 1896– Oct. 1897). The Secular Sunday schools remained in evidence longer than did the regular lecture meetings; there was little news at all about church activities in Portland, McMinnville, or Silverton. By the end of 1897, local secularists in Silverton were hosting lectures and entertainments in Liberal Hall without referring to Silverton Secular Church. See *Torch of Reason*, Dec. 16, 1897, 8.

34. "Katie Kehm Smith," *Truth Seeker*, Nov. 16, 1895, 730–31; "Death-Bed 'Conversions,'" *Truth Seeker*, Nov. 9, 1895, 715; "In Eastern Oregon—Katie Kehm Smith's Work and Death," *Truth Seeker*, Oct. 19, 1895, 667; "Pearl Geer Abroad," *Truth Seeker*,

Sept. 26, 1896, 618–19; Kate DePeatt, "The Cause in Oregon," *Truth Seeker*, July 30, 1898, 490; Pearl W. Geer, "Tenth Annual Convention," *Torch of Reason*, July 28, 1898, 5–6; Smith, "Paine Celebration," 2.

35. Kate DePeatt, "A Memorial Tribute to the Late Katie Kehm Smith and Mrs. Warren Carsner," *Free Thought Magazine* 16 (1898): 491; "The Secular Church," *Torch of Reason*, March 11, 1897, n.p. That the Silverton group, led by Hosmer and Geer, still supported Smith's church plan—in the abstract, at least—can also be seen in their reprinting of her original paper, "What Shall Liberals Do to Be Saved?" in *Torch of Reason*, Dec. 16, 1897, 1, 5. But in practice, the *Torch of Reason* and Liberal University had replaced the Silverton Secular Church. For a postmortem, see "Secular Churches and Sunday Schools," *Torch of Reason*, Jan. 25, 1900, 4.

36. For a sense of the divisions that plagued Oregon secularists, see "A Review," *Torch of Reason*, Oct. 28, 1897, n.p. Hosmer and Geer arrayed themselves against spiritualists, free lovers, and anarchists, insisting on secularist purity, which caused various grievances and fractured local alliances. Such divisions were common among freethinkers, but the ones over marriage and sexuality were at a particularly high boil after the scandal-ridden death of the secularist leader Samuel Putnam in December 1896, whom some in the movement denounced posthumously as a free lover. See Leigh Eric Schmidt, *Village Atheists: How America's Unbelievers Made Their Way in a Godly Nation* (Princeton, NJ: Princeton University Press, 2016), 60–65. Wakeman, for all his stature in these circles, could not put these conflicts to rest. See T. B. Wakeman, "President J. E. Hosmer," *Torch of Reason*, Oct. 12, 1899, 2.

37. W. H. Kerr, "The New Church of Humanity," *Torch of Reason*, April 30, 1903, 2; "The Greatest Discovery of Modern Times: God Is Not a Real Being, But a Myth," *Christian Educator and God's Defender* 1 (Dec. 1903): 1. Notice of Kerr's Church of Humanity also appeared in "News and Notes," *Torch of Reason*, April 2, 1903, 8; Aug. 13, 1903, 8; Aug. 27, 1903, 8.

38. W. H. Kerr, *Jesus Analyzed: The Good-will Missionary to All the World* (Great Bend, KS: n.p., [1928]), 31–32; W. H. Kerr, *Kerr's Discoveries: The Truth about God, Soul and Immortality* (Great Bend, KS: n.p., [1926]), 9. For basic biographical details on Kerr, see *Biographical History of Barton County, Kansas* (Great Bend, KS: Tribune Publishing, 1912), 70–71.

39. Kerr published a memorial issue for Albert ten years after his death, which recounted the whole episode in unsparing detail. See *Truth about God and Life* 5 (June 1910): 1–3. He reprinted his letter to the editor in that issue, but also see *Barton County Democrat* (Great Bend, KS), Jan. 18, 1901, 1.

40. Kerr, *Jesus Analyzed*, 39. For one of Kerr's initial organizational pleas, see W. H. Kerr, "Organization," *Truth Seeker*, May 16, 1903, 313. For remarks on the oddity of Kerr's journal title, see "A New Paper," *Barton County Democrat* (Great Bend, KS),

Dec. 4, 1903, 1. For local meetings and lectures, see "Missionary Work by the Church of Humanity," *Truth about God and Life* 5 (May 1910): 2; "Church Notices," *Great Bend Tribune* (Great Bend, KS), March 10, 1917, 2.

41. "The Building of the Church of Humanity," *Truth about God* 1 (July 1906): 1–2; "The Church of Humanity: Formal Organization and Incorporation," *Truth about God and Life* 2 (July 1908): 1–2. Kerr changed the journal title from the *Truth about God* to the *Truth about God and Life* in April 1908. He kept meticulous membership records, recording names in what he called his own atheist Book of Life. For the numbers used here, see "Second Semi-Annual Report of the Church of Humanity," *Christian Educator and God's Defender* 1 (Nov. 1904): 1; "The Church of Humanity," *Truth about God* 1 (Dec. 1905): 1; "The Building of the Church of Humanity," *Truth about God* 1 (Dec. 1906): 1. He published a full, detailed roll of his first one hundred members in *Truth about God* 1 (May 1906): 3. The most famous freethinker to join was the cartoonist Watson Heston, another grassroots atheist from the Midwest, whose combative images matched Kerr's own belligerence. Of Kerr's 252 members in 1908, he counted 209 men and 43 women. That kind of dramatic disproportion was often in evidence among the most uncompromising atheists, who were usually the most intent on defining themselves against what they saw as Christian effeminacy. For the gendered performance of freethought as well as the massively disproportionate number of men in the American Association for the Advancement of Atheism, an especially bellicose atheist group in the 1920s and 1930s, see Schmidt, *Village Atheists*, 127–37, 210–48, 253.

42. "The Founding of the Church of Humanity: Limitation of Membership a Necessity," *Truth about God* 2 (Dec. 1907): 1. For Kerr's catechism, which he frequently reprinted, see, for example, "A Catechism of the True Knowledge of God," *Truth about God* 1 (Dec. 1905): 4; "The Church of Humanity Catechism: Commit It to Memory," *Truth about God and Life* 7 (Nov. 1913): 2.

43. "Unite! Unite!!" *Christian Educator and God's Defender* 1 (March 1904): 3; W. F. Jamieson, "Are Religious Questions Settled?" *Humanitarian Review* 2 (May 1904): 474–76; W. F. Jamieson, "Should Freethinkers Join a Church?" *Humanitarian Review* 2 (Oct. 1904): 671–73; W. H. Kerr, "The 'Church of Humanity' Defended," *Humanitarian Review* 2 (July 1904): 557; Kerr, *Jesus Analyzed*, 29; Singleton W. Davis, "'The Church of Humanity,'" *Humanitarian Review* 6 (Jan. 1908): 7. One instance of support for Kerr from more urbane freethinkers came when it looked like meddlesome postal authorities were harassing him for publishing an infidel newspaper. For an expression of solidarity at that point, see "A Circular to the Editors of the Freethought Press," *Truth Seeker*, July 15, 1905, 441.

44. "Ingersoll Goes to Church and Finds a Philosopher in the Pulpit," *Truth Seeker*, Feb. 11, 1899, 86. For a helpful biography of Roberts, see Ellen Roberts Young,

John Emerson Roberts, Kansas City's "Up-to-Date" Freethought Preacher (Bloomington, IN: Xlibris, 2011). The *Truth Seeker* closely followed Roberts's freethinking, secularist church from its founding in the fall of 1897, often reprinting his lectures/sermons (or selections therefrom) over the next two decades. For two early examples, see "Man the Savior of Man," *Truth Seeker*, Oct. 2, 1897, 632; and "John Roberts on Secular Demands," *Truth Seeker*, Dec. 18, 1897, 809. Ingersoll and Roberts had formed a mutual admiration for one another when Roberts was still a Unitarian minister at All Souls Church in Kansas City. See Young, *John Emerson Roberts*, 88–92.

45. Thaddeus B. Wakeman, "Dr. Roberts and Religious Evolution," *Torch of Reason*, May 7, 1903, 6.

46. "Sermon on Church of This World," *St. Joseph Gazette*, Jan. 5, 1903, 6; "Note and Comment," *Truth Seeker*, Feb. 15, 1902, 97: "Dr. Roberts to the Front," *Torch of Reason*, Feb. 13, 1902, 5; "J. E. Roberts Honored," *Truth Seeker*, Feb. 22, 1902, 117; Young, *John Emerson Roberts*, 92–93, 122–23, 172–75.

47. "To the Unknown God," *St. Louis Globe-Democrat*, Nov. 6, 1888, 6. For a sample of such church notices, see *Waco Daily Examiner*, Sept. 6, 1885, 3; Nov. 15, 1885, 3; Nov. 29, 1885, 4. Shaw's Liberal Hall was pictured in two engravings in the *Truth Seeker Annual and Freethinkers' Almanac, 1886* (New York: Truth Seeker, 1886). It was called Freethought Hall there, but Shaw used the designation Liberal Hall. It opened in 1884 and seated about four hundred. It burned down in 1889, after which Shaw's Religious and Benevolent Association dissolved as a congregation. Shaw continued his freethought activities, primarily as editor of the *Independent Pulpit* and later the *Searchlight*. His career is covered well in Blake W. Barrow, "Freethought in Texas: J. D. Shaw and *The Independent Pulpit*" (M.A. thesis, Baylor University, 1983).

Epilogue: Beyond Secular Humanism

1. J. Arthur Ragsdale, ed., *The Story of a Humanist Church: A Short History of the Fellowship of Humanity* (Oakland, CA: n.p., 1972), 4–5, 27–28, 30; "Glenview to Have a Big Day," *Oakland Tribune*, Jan. 17, 1940, 10; Edwin H. Wilson, *The Genesis of a Humanist Manifesto*, ed. Teresa Machiocha (Amherst, NY: Humanist Press, 1995), 11. Ragsdale gathered the recollections of early members of the society, several of whom had memories going back to the founding, including one from Karen Johnson, who recalled Faupell's stories about Ingersoll's influence on him. In addition to Ragsdale's history, I have reconstructed the details about Faupell's Unitarian activities and the early fellowship from coverage in the *Oakland Tribune*. His chief involvement was with the First Unitarian Church, but Faupell was active in a number of different discussion groups and political organizations; one called the Progressive Forum took shape in late 1934 under Faupell's direction, and it was likely the catalyst for creating

230 NOTES TO EPILOGUE

the Church of Humanity. See "New Fellowship Is Inaugurated," *Oakland Tribune*, Dec. 1, 1934, 6.

2. "'New Religion' to be Faupell Topic," *Oakland Tribune*, Jan. 5, 1935, 6; "Discussion on Famous Book," *Oakland Tribune*, July 13, 1935, 6; "Faupell Speaks on Ingersoll," *Oakland Tribune*, July 20, 1935, 6; "Fellowship of Humanity," *Oakland Tribune*, Aug. 12, 1944, 6; "Faupell Will Continue Talk," *Oakland Tribune*, Feb. 1, 1936, 6. Faupell also spoke for the Thomas Paine Fellowship Forum in 1939. See "Democracy Topic of Speaker Tonight," *Oakland Tribune*, Feb. 14, 1939, 10. See also the announced lecture on Paine by a guest speaker in "Fellowship of Humanity," *Oakland Tribune*, Oct. 13, 1945, 6. The inheritance from Ingersoll and Paine was quite evident in John H. Dietrich's work as well. See his pair of sermons on Ingersoll and Paine in John H. Dietrich, *The Humanist Pulpit: A Third Volume of Addresses* (Minneapolis: First Unitarian Society, 1931), 81–112.

3. Upton Sinclair, *The Profits of Religion: An Essay in Economic Interpretation* (Pasadena, CA: n.p., [1917]), 301–2, 304; "'New Religion' to be Faupell Topic," 6; "Upton Sinclair to Be Subject of A. D. Faupell," *Oakland Tribune*, Feb. 16, 1935, 7; "Famous Poem Inspires Talk," *Oakland Tribune*, Aug. 10, 1935, 6; "Faupell Continues Study in Contrasts," *Oakland Tribune*, Feb. 15, 1936, 21 .

4. John Dewey, *A Common Faith* (New Haven, CT: Yale University Press, 1934), 6–7. For Faupell's lectures on Dewey, see "Dewey Volume Basis of Talk," *Oakland Tribune*, Feb. 23, 1935, 7; and "Dewey, Sunday Sermon Theme," *Oakland Tribune*, Feb. 22, 1936, 7. For the Humanist Manifesto as originally published in the *New Humanist*, see Wilson, *Genesis*, 96–99. Faupell's first lecture on Dewey was called "The Religious and Social Views of John Dewey, America's Leading Philosopher and Humanist"; it was based directly on *A Common Faith*. But the question posed—"Is Humanism the answer to the religious quest of the ages?"—showed the influence of another leading humanist work of the period, A. Eustace Haydon's *The Quest of the Ages* (New York: Harper, 1929). Haydon was a professor of comparative religion at the University of Chicago and, by turns, a Unitarian minister and a leader of the Chicago Ethical Society. For good historical accounts of the rise of religious humanism as a movement, see Mason Olds, *American Religious Humanism*, rev. ed. (Minneapolis, MN: Fellowship of Religious Humanists, 1996; repr., Hamden, CT: HUUmanists Association, 2006); Donald H. Meyer, "Secular Transcendence: The American Religious Humanists," *American Quarterly* 34 (1982): 524–42; William F. Schulz, *Making the Manifesto: The Birth of Religious Humanism* (Boston: Skinner House Books, 2002). For a perceptive overview of how twentieth-century humanism as a term and as a movement related to nineteenth-century forms of secularism and free religion, see Joseph Blankholm, "Secularism, Humanism, and Secular Humanism: Terms and Institutions," in Phil Zuckerman and John R. Shook, eds., *The Oxford Handbook of Secularism* (New York: Oxford University Press, 2017), 689–705.

5. Wilson, *Genesis*, 98. In the late 1920s and early 1930s, Dietrich collected his sermons annually into a volume called the *Humanist Pulpit*. Those volumes provide an excellent window on the prevailing humanist themes of the period. Abell had launched his own journal called the *Humanist* in 1927 when still a Unitarian minister, two years before establishing his independent Hollywood Humanist Society. Reese published a number of books crucial to the development of religious humanism as a movement, including *Humanism* (1926) and *Humanist Religion* (1931).

6. *Fellowship of Humanity v. County of Alameda*, 153 CA2d 673 (1957); Ragsdale, *Story of a Humanist Church*, 9–10, 61–67; *Washington Ethical Society v. District of Columbia*, 249 F. 2d 127 (1957). Like Alameda County, the District of Columbia taxing authority took the position that the Ethical Society did not warrant a tax exemption since "belief in and teaching of the existence of a Divinity" was an essential stipulation.

7. *Fellowship of Humanity v. County of Alameda*, 153 CA2d 673 (1957).

8. *Fellowship of Humanity v. County of Alameda*, 153 CA2d 673 (1957); Charles Francis Potter, *The Story of Religion: As Told in the Lives of Its Leaders* (New York: Grosset and Dunlap, 1929), xvii–xviii. For a particularly clear example of these humanistic moves to save "religion" as a category, see Roy Wood Sellars, *The Next Step in Religion* (New York: Macmillan, 1918), 211–25.

9. Homer Duncan, *Secular Humanism: The Most Dangerous Religion in America* (Lubbock, TX: Missionary Crusader, 1979); *Torcaso v. Watkins*, 367 U.S. 488 (1961).

10. *Torcaso v. Watkins*, 367 U.S. 488 (1961); Roy R. Torcaso, "The Religion of an Atheist," *Progressive World* 18 (Nov. 1964): 9; "Brief of American Jewish Committee, Anti-Defamation League of B'nai B'rith, and Unitarian Fellowship for Social Justice," in the Supreme Court of the United States, October Term, 1960, No. 373, 12. There was some later debate among those involved in writing briefs for Torcaso's case about who deserved credit—or blame—for Black inadvertently giving legal currency to the notion of secular humanism as a religion. See "Who First Used the Words 'Secular Humanism'?," *New York Times*, June 19, 1985, A22; Leo Pfeffer, "The 'Religion' of Secular Humanism," *Journal of Church and State* 29 (1987): 495–98. The phrase "secular humanism" had been used in a variety of contexts well before 1960, but its use in and around the Torcaso case to name secular humanists as a religious group marked a departure and a misnaming when joined to the Fellowship of Humanity. For the wider legal terrain for atheists and nonbelievers in this era, see Leigh Eric Schmidt, *Village Atheists: How America's Unbelievers Made Their Way in a Godly Nation* (Princeton, NJ: Princeton University Press, 2016), 266–83; Leigh E. Schmidt, "'Baptism of Ire': Atheist Plaintiffs and Irreligious Freedom in Postwar America," in Heather Sharkey and Jeffrey Green, eds., *The Changing Terrain of Religious Freedom* (Philadelphia: University of Pennsylvania Press, 2021), 114–32, 242–46.

11. Richard S. Emrich, "Supreme Court Aids Secularism," *Detroit News*, July 7, 1963, clipping in "Secularism," Box 161, f. 6, Edwin H. Wilson Papers of the American Humanist Association, 1913–1989, Special Collections Research Center, Southern Illinois University, Carbondale, Illinois. Emrich's analysis was a reflection of a much larger discourse on how the nation's Judeo-Christian inheritance was under siege from secularism as a competing worldview. On that broader intellectual landscape, see especially K. Healan Gaston, *Imagining Judeo-Christian America: Religion, Secularism, and the Redefinition of Democracy* (Chicago: University of Chicago Press, 2019), 153–207.

12. For the culminating cases in the long-running debate over humanistic claims for conscientious objection, see *United States v. Seeger*, 380 U.S. 163 (1965); and *Welsh v. United States*, 398 U.S. 333 (1970). In the opinion for *Seeger*, Justice Tom Clark borrowed a broadened definition of God as ground of being or ultimate concern from the Protestant theologian Paul Tillich and cited as well the prominent Ethical Society leader David Muzzey's definition of religion as "the devotion of man to the highest ideal that he can conceive." Muzzey claimed that the vision of perfected moral purpose that sustained the Ethical Society was the equivalent to a belief in God. By invoking Tillich and Muzzey, Clark gave some theistic cover to ethical humanists while avoiding the question of whether a full-blown atheist could ever qualify as a conscientious objector. The issue remained vexed, though, and was highly dependent on how sympathetic local draft boards were to particular religious, humanistic, and ethical claims. See the various cases and documents collected in "Conscientious Objectors," Box 153, f. 1–4, Wilson Papers.

13. Tim LaHaye, *The Battle for the Mind* (Old Tappan, NJ: Fleming H. Revell, 1980), 46, 57, 128–29; Phyllis Schlafly, "Secular Humanism a Real Threat to USA," *USA Today*, April 7, 1986, 8A. See also the compiled clippings in "Moral Majority," Box 158, f. 9; and "Secular Humanism," Box 161, f. 5, Wilson Papers. For the continuation of the attack, see Tim LaHaye and David Noebel, *Mind Siege: The Battle for Truth in the New Millennium* (Nashville: Word Publishing, 2000). The citation of footnote 11 from *Torcaso* became a reflex in this polemical literature. Of like importance was Potter Stewart's dissent in *Abington v. Schempp*, which was discussed in the introduction, particularly his warning against the establishment of a "religion of secularism." For an important reference point for the legal argument on the right against the establishment of the religion of secular humanism, see John W. Whitehead and John Conlan, "The Establishment of the Religion of Secular Humanism and Its First Amendment Implications," *Texas Tech Law Review* 10 (Winter 1978): 1–66, with the notorious footnote invoked at p. 13.

14. For the statistics on membership and attendance at the Fellowship of Humanity, see Ragsdale, *Story of a Humanist Church*, 20; "Hugh. R. Orr," Box 86, f. 7, Wilson

Papers; "'Religious Liberals' Win Tax Exemption," *San Francisco Examiner*, Sept. 12, 1957, 9. On the numbers for the Fellowship of Religious Humanists, see "Fellowship of Religious Humanists: 'Religious Humanism' Circulation Data, etc.," Box 203, f. 10, Wilson Papers.

15. For an indication of how Walter Mondale's early life as a preacher's kid played in mainstream media portrayals of his political career, see William Barry Furlong, "Walter Mondale: Some Insights from a Minnesota Boyhood," *Washington Post*, Jan. 20, 1977, 11, 26.

16. Lester Mondale, "For Humanist Historical Records," 2–5, in Box 80, f. 29, Wilson Papers. This document is a twelve-page autobiographical typescript that Lester Mondale composed in August 1983 describing his family history and his religious career. Mondale's memory of Dietrich's sermon on Paine comes from an interview William F. Schulz conducted with him in 1974. See Schulz, *Making the Manifesto*, 98.

17. Lester Mondale, "The Humanist Life at Copperhead Cliff," *Humanist* 43 (May–June 1983): 35; Mondale, "For Humanist Historical Records," 10; Lester Mondale, "Religious Humanism: A Testimonial," (1970), pamphlet of the Fellowship of Religious Humanists, Box 80, f. 29, Wilson Papers; Marsha May, "Vice President's Half Brother Writes an Erotic Novel about a Minister," newspapers clippings, Box 80, f. 29, Wilson Papers; Cable Neuhaus, "First Came Billy Beer, Now It's Lester's Leer as Mondale's Brother Writes a Sexy Novel," *People*, June 5, 1978, at https://people .com/archive/first-came-billy-beer-now-its-lesters-leer-as-mondales-brother-writes -a-sexy-novel-vol-9-no-22/; Corliss Lamont, "Memo on Walter Mondale and the Humanist Movement." Sept. 12, 1984, Box 80, f. 29, Wilson Papers; Walter Mondale, "Critical Liberalism and Social Action," in Howard B. Radest, ed., *To Seek a Humane World: Proceedings of the Fifth Congress of the International Humanist and Ethical Union* (London: Pemberton Books, 1971), 69–78.

18. LaHaye, *Battle for the Mind*, 139–40; LaHaye and Noebel, *Mind Siege*, 170–72; Whitehead and Conlan, "Establishment of the Religion," 33; Duncan, *Secular Humanism*, 13–14; "Reagan God's Man Now, But Mondale a Humanist," *Republic* (Columbus, IN), Oct. 30, 1984, 4. For another important early text linking Vice President Mondale to a malign humanist cabal of feminists, sex educators, and pro-choice activists, see Claire Chambers, *The SIECUS Circle: A Humanist Revolution* (Belmont, MA: Western Islands Press, 1977), 273, 346, 352.

19. Rudy Maxa, "The VP's Half-Brother Is a Literary Hillbilly," *Washington Post*, June 4, 1978, SM4; Harry Elmer Barnes and Herbert T. Rosenfeld, "Is Humanism a New Religion?" *Humanist* 22, no. 4 (1962): 127–29; Paul Kurtz, "The Future of Humanism," *Free Inquiry* 3 (Fall 1983): 8–13. See also Joseph Fletcher, "Secular Humanism: It's the Adjective That Counts," *Free Inquiry* 3 (Fall 1983): 17–18; "Symposium: Is Secular Humanism a Religion?" *Free Inquiry* 6 (Winter 1985/1986): 12–22.

20. For indications of how "secular humanist" versus "religious humanist" has become entrenched as a basic sorting device within the subculture, see Nicholas J. Little, Ronald A. Lindsay, and Tom Flynn, "Secular Humanism: *Not* a Religion," *Free Inquiry* 35 (Feb.–March 2015): 4–8; Fred Edwords, "What Is Humanism?" at https://americanhumanist.org/what-is-humanism/edwords-what-is-humanism/. Ironically, Paul Kurtz himself, long the presiding figure over the Council for Secular Humanism and the Center for Inquiry, got caught on the other side of this divide at the very end of his career, arguing that the organization's new leadership had become too harshly atheistic and had lost the old humanistic openness to cooperation. He lost that battle and resigned from the board. See Mark Oppenheimer, "Closer Look at Rift Between Humanists Reveals Deeper Divisions," *New York Times*, Oct. 2, 2010, A12. For an attempt to bridge the divide between religious and secular humanism through practical organizing, see Greg Epstein and James Croft, "The Godless Congregation: An Idea Whose Time Has Come," *Free Inquiry* 33 (Oct.–Nov. 2013): 23–28. The divide has also played itself out in the literature surrounding best-selling atheist apologists such as Richard Dawkins and Christopher Hitchens with renewed calls for practical mediations of the theism/atheism divide. For humanistic defenses of a "religious atheism" in the face of such across-the-board attacks on religion's poisons and delusions, see Ronald Dworkin, *Religion without God* (Cambridge, MA: Harvard University Press, 2013); Alain de Botton, *Religion for Atheists: A Non-believer's Guide to the Uses of Religion* (New York: Pantheon Books, 2012); Chris Stedman, *Faitheist: How an Atheist Found Common Ground with the Religious* (Boston: Beacon, 2012).

21. Edward L. Ericson, "Humanist Conscientious Objection," *Humanist* 29 (May–June 1969): unpaginated center section. There are files on all of these groups and their leaders in the Wilson Papers. For Lowell H. Coate and the Humanist Society of Friends, see Box 23, f. 12; Box 136, f. 22 and 23; for Ericson and the Washington Ethical Society, see Box 35, f. 11; Box 134, f. 21.

22. For the deathbed pledge, see Al Burt, "The Godless World of Joseph Lewis," *Age of Reason* 37 (July–August 1968): 1–2. On Lewis's memorialization projects, see William J. Fielding, "Thomas Paine Banquet," *Age of Reason* 17 (April 1953): 1–4; "The Amazing Story of the Thomas Paine Postage Stamp," *Age of Reason* 37 (March–April 1968): 8–11; "Objects to Prayer at Paine Stamp Ceremony," *Age of Reason* 37 (May–June 1968): 3; Dorine Clark-Moore, "The Thomas Paine Banquet," *Age of Reason* 37 (May–June 1968): 6–7.

23. On the various efforts of Lewis, Mondale, and Wilson to refurbish Paine's memory, including retrieval of the bust, see the files on the Paine Foundation and Thomas Paine in Box 88, f. 4 and 5, Wilson Papers, as well as Edwin H. Wilson to Richard Gimbel, Jan. 19, 1954, in Richard Gimbel, comp., "Miscellaneous Material Concerning the Thomas Paine Bust by S[i]dney H. Morse," American Philosophical

Society, Philadelphia. Gimbel was a prominent collector of Paine materials and a crucial player in the renewed bust campaign. Like Wilson, he emphasized the religious seriousness of Paine's deism rather than his anticlerical, Bible-bashing critiques (favored by Lewis), but all of them rallied together in this latest Paineite cause of rescuing a bust first promoted during the nation's centennial. After a decade on loan to the Thomas Paine Center, the bust was moved to the American Philosophical Society, where it still resides (though not on public display). See Whitfield J. Bell, Jr., *The Bust of Thomas Paine* (Philadelphia: Friends of the Library American Philosophical Society, 1974). On the newly created Paine Center in 1956, see "Thomas Paine Center," *Liberal: A Rationalist and Freethought Journal* 10 (Oct. 1956): 1–3. The affinities of religious liberals with Paine continued after the salvage operation of Mondale and Wilson. That was evident, for example, in the renaming in 1978 of the Greater Norristown Unitarian Fellowship as the Thomas Paine Unitarian Universalist Fellowship, located in Collegeville, Pennsylvania, outside Philadelphia.

24. "A Humanistic Alternative for Secular Jews Who Want to Celebrate Passover with Integrity," in Society for Humanistic Judaism, Box 146, f. 10, Wilson Papers. See also Sherwin Wine, Box 124, f. 11, Wilson Papers. Wine's career and the Birmingham Temple are very well documented in print form as well as in manuscript collections. For Wine's reworking of traditional services, ceremonies, and holy days, see Boxes 7–11, Sherwin T. Wine Papers, Bentley Historical Library, University of Michigan. For clippings on the ways in which he was linked to the widely covered Death of God theology, see Box 2, 1966–1969, Wine Papers. For a full delineation of his project of reinterpretation, see Sherwin T. Wine, *Judaism beyond God: A Radical New Way to Be Jewish* (Farmington Hills, MI: Society for Humanistic Judaism, 1985).

25. For Young's multipart conversion story, see "Agnostic Origins," Aug. 1979, 4–5, Society of Evangelical Agnostics, Box 146, f. 18, Wilson Papers. For an account of the historical sources Young employed to piece his agnostic gospel together, see William Henry Young, "Evangelical Agnosticism," *Free Inquiry* 5 (Summer 1985): 34–36. The debt he owed to Huxley, Ingersoll, and Russell is also evident in the run of his newsletter, the *SEA Journal*, 1975–1987, Society of Evangelical Agnostics, Box 146, f. 18 and 19, Wilson Papers. Besides the issues of that journal collected in the Wilson Papers, there is also a very good run in the pamphlet collection at the Wisconsin Historical Society.

26. For Young's connection to the Unitarian Universalist Church of Fresno, see *SEA Journal*, June 8, 1975 and Dec. 19, 1976, both in Society of Evangelical Agnostics, Box 146, f. 18, Wilson Papers. The correspondence file with Edwin Wilson shows his ties to religious humanism. See Bill Young, Box 125, f. 7, Wilson Papers. On the Quaker influences, see "Cedar Springs Retreat: Silent Hour," June 1975; and "Cedar Springs Retreat Newsletter," Winter 1975 and Winter 1976, both in Cedar Springs

Library, Box 131, f. 13, Wilson Papers. Young borrowed the phrase "the altar of the Unknown" from Thomas Huxley. For the definition of religion, see "Cedar Springs Retreat Newsletter," Winter 1976, Cedar Springs Library, Box 131, f. 13, Wilson Papers. For his rejection of O'Hair's brand of atheism, see *SEA Journal*, Dec. 1975, Society of Evangelical Agnostics, Box 146, f. 18, Wilson Papers. The rejection was necessarily undogmatic. Young allowed that the *American Atheist* often ran good material on religion and politics, and even when O'Hair sent him a letter saying that the agnostic posture he presented in the *SEA Journal* was "bullshit," he suggested that they should still aim for "mutually respectful association." Needless to say, his olive branch was not reciprocated. See *SEA Journal*, Oct. 19, 1976, and Jan. 28, 1977, Box 146, f. 18, Wilson Papers. For a full biographical examination of O'Hair, see Bryan F. Le Beau, *The Atheist: Madalyn Murray O'Hair* (New York: New York University Press, 2003).

27. "Financial Status Report," Dec. 31, 1978, Box 146, f. 18, Wilson Papers; *SEA Journal*, July 5, 1980, Box 146, f. 19, Wilson Papers; "Greetings to Former SEA Members," Jan. 24, 1988, Cedar Springs Library, Box 131, f. 13, Wilson Papers.

28. *SEA Journal*, Oct. 30, 1984; Nov. 9–10, 1984; Jan. 29, 1987; Feb. 6, 1987; Feb. 15, 1987, pamphlet collection, Wisconsin Historical Society. Young's application to become a Humanist Counselor, a role he compared to that of being a liberal Protestant minister, is in Bill Young, Box 125, f. 7, Wilson Papers. He mentions his ritual activities in his *SEA Journal*, Feb. 15, 1987, noted above. For the lackluster membership numbers for the AHA as of 1983, see Kurtz, "Future of Humanism," 13.

29. For Young's concern over the growing involvement of evangelicals in right-wing politics, see *SEA Journal*, Jan. 3, 1977; July–Sept. 1980; June 27, 1981; June 22, 1982; Jan. 1, 1984; Jan. 17, 1984; Feb. 4, 1984; Feb. 16, 1984; July 5, 1984; Aug. 24, 1984; Sept. 10, 1984; Oct. 26, 1984; Dec. 25, 1984; Dec. 6, 1985; Sept. 26, 1986, Box 146, f. 18 and 19, Wilson Papers, and pamphlet collection, Wisconsin Historical Society. The passage that Young lifted from Ingersoll came from his lecture, "Why I Am an Agnostic" (1896). See Robert G. Ingersoll, "Why I Am an Agnostic," in *The Works of Robert G. Ingersoll*, 12 vols. (New York: Ingersoll League, 1929), 4: 67; *SEA Journal*, Supplement, December 1975; and undated leaflet, Society of Evangelical Agnostics, Box 146, f. 18, Wilson Papers. The notes of isolation—being "surrounded by Born Agains," being "lonely down here in the Bible Belt," and being eager for some humanist company—were often part of the membership directories that Young put together and circulated from one year to the next. See SEA Directory, Jan. 1980, Jan. 1981, Feb. 1987, Society of Evangelical Agnostics, Box 146, f. 19, Wilson Papers.

30. Stedman, *Faitheist*, 13, 102. Stedman has carried on his humanist chaplaincy work at Harvard, Yale, and Augsburg College.

INDEX

Note: Page numbers in *italic* type indicate illustrations.

A NOTE ON THE TYPE

This book has been composed in Arno, an Old-style serif typeface in the classic Venetian tradition, designed by Robert Slimbach at Adobe.

Hard to take seriously -
a real secularist agnostic HLM would have longer

Marden + red
for atheist
funeral service

Rel. Right worry about
secular humanism is like
Journalists worried about QAnon

funny

Masons

unbelief agnostic religious   Unitarian   lib. Prot —   /13-/1?
                    secular   191 |28
                                                         |134
                                                         |15?
Is this the counter to religions |62
naturalism 60, 69, 53   168
    the politics of liberalism free from Jesus
    71, 108, 113, 115, 127, 164-65, 179
    deed over creed 128 — lib Protestants

tax status 169
    184 — say must — Rel. Right
    178 ff — the payoff — they take Rel. Hu
        funny that
        seriously?

        Timing — Paine vs
                    secular humanism
        Stewart Howard the
              essad — 196